AN ALLIANCE OF
WOMEN

Immigration and the Politics of Race

AN ALLIANCE OF
WOMEN

Heather Merrill

University of Minnesota Press
Minneapolis || London

Photographs in the book were taken by the author.

Published by the University of Minnesota Press
111 Third Avenue South, Suite 290
Minneapolis, MN 55401-2520
http://www.upress.umn.edu

Library of Congress Cataloging-in-Publication Data

Merrill, Heather.
    An alliance of women : immigration and the politics of race /
Heather Merrill.
        p.   cm.
    Includes bibliographical references and index.
    ISBN 10: 0-8166-4157-9 (hc : alk. paper) — ISBN 10: 0-8166-4158-7 (pb :
alk. paper)
    ISBN 13: 978-0-8166-4157-4 (hc) — ISBN 13: 978-0-8166-4158-1 (pb)
    1. Feminism—Italy.   2. Women, Black—Italy—Social conditions.
3. Women immigrants—Italy—Turin.   4. Feminism—International
cooperation.   I. Title.
    HQ1642.M47 2006
    305.420945—dc22

                                                                            2005031557

Printed in the United States of America on acid-free paper

The University of Minnesota is an equal-opportunity educator and employer.

12 11 10 09 08 07 06   10 9 8 7 6 5 4 3 2 1

For Donald, Nicolas, and Eliana,
whose wisdom and joy made this work possible

Contents

ACKNOWLEDGMENTS

Aspired my research, but the book is also the result of encouragement and astute comments from many individuals. It's hard to mention all the people who have made a difference, but I would like to extend special and boundless gratitude to particular individuals who have played pivotal roles in the development and execution of this project.

To Donald Carter, whose unerring support, guidance, and profound insight were vital to all phases of this project. To Allan Pred, with whom I worked as a graduate student and who allowed me just the right balance of creative and critical input and intellectual freedom. To the memory of the exceptional William Shack, who provided a role model and mentored me through some difficult hours. To Ruth Wilson Gilmore, whose personal generosity and broad intellectual knowledge and insight were invaluable. To David Harvey, whose friendship, intellectual depth, and dedication to issues of social justice encouraged me to complete this project. To the wonderful Helga Leitner, who has been an invaluable mentor and friend. To the many migrants in Turin who shared their concerns, feelings, and experiences. To the women of Alma Mater, who gave generously of their time and their hearts, particularly Giovanna Zaldini, Maria Viarengo, Vanessa Maher, Saida Ahmed, Marite Calloni, MaryAnn Akinyi, Maria Afonso, Laura Scagliotti, and Sonia Aimiumu. To the women of the Casa delle Donne, especially Rina Constantino, Elisabetta Donini, Patricia Celotto, and Jessica Ferrero. To Francesco Ciafaloni, Jean Marie Tschotsha, Vanessa Maher and her family, and Maria Viarengo and her family, who provided rich and deeply critical insights into the workings of Italian culture and politics. To Giuseppe Dematteis for facilitating my visit in 1996 and for introducing me to scholars in the faculty of political science at the University of Turin. To a number of Italian scholars, civil servants, and trade union representatives who gave generously of their time, particularly Arnaldo Bagnasco, Toni Negri, Enrico Alasino, Egidio Dansero, Terese Angela Migliasso, Anna Belpiede, Gianpiero Carpo, and

Vana Lorenzo. To the University of California, Berkeley, for mediating my access to a number of fellowships from the Center for German and European Studies, the Society for Women Geographers, a Humanities Graduate Research Grant, and a Humanities and Social Science Research Grant. To Dickinson College, for providing me with the funding necessary to complete the research in 2000 and granting me several course releases to work on the manuscript. To the dynamic University of Minnesota Press team, without whose faith in this project I would not have acknowledgments to write, especially Carrie Mullen and Jason Weidemann.

Last, to the many survivors young and old struggling to overcome painful obstacles. And to the present and future generations of African migrants, may your journeys be greeted with the dignity and respect you so greatly deserve.

Immigration and the Spatial Politics of Scale

> In the world through which I travel,
> I am endlessly creating myself.
> —*Frantz Fanon,* Black Skin, White Masks

> Everything that can be spoken is on the ground of the
> enormous voices that have not, or cannot be heard.
> —*Stuart Hall, "Old and New Identities, Old and New Ethnicities"*

> Sisterhood is powerful but difficult. . . . Feminism itself, the
> most original of what we can call "our own cultural creations,"
> is not a secure or stable ground but a highly permeable terrain
> infiltrated by subterranean waterways that cause it to shift
> under our feet and sometimes to turn into a swamp.
> —*Teresa de Lauretis,* Feminist Studies, Critical Studies

WHILE IN CAMEROON AS A U.S. PEACE CORPS VOLUNTEER in the early 1980s, I began to realize how little I knew about the world outside my birth country, especially Africa. Before I lived in Africa, my understanding was gained for the most part from popular ideologies and images about the place and its peoples, namely, jungles, wild animals, and primitive "tribes." Although I suspected that there was greater complexity to the continent than I had been taught, I was more surprised by the similarities than by the differences between the people I came to care about in Cameroon and my North American friends. Not only were African societies highly advanced in their own ways, but also people seemed to share some of the same values I had acquired growing up in the United States. The Cameroonian Beti, Bulu, Bamileke, and even Maka, among whom I lived and worked and who usually spoke French fluently and much better than I, were trained in or culturally influenced by modern European humanist philosophies of freedom, self-determination, social justice, and independence. Why hadn't anybody taught me about how much contact African societies had with Europe and about European colonialism all over the continent? Why was I led to believe that by traveling to West Africa, I would be going backward in space and time? For the next twenty years I would try to make sense of the contradiction between the preconceived ideas I held about Africa and Africans and my experiences among Cameroonians—a contradiction played out today and that I observed in Turin, Italy, and other parts of Europe in the 1990s while the migration of Africans and migrants from other parts of the economically peripheral world began to shake up taken-for-granted ideas about national, ethnic, "racial," and class identity. How do we understand the societies and cultures of "Africans" and other international migrants in Italy? How might we understand Turin-dwelling "Italians" in a context of international migration, European unification, and global time-space compression (Harvey 1989; Massey 1993)?

The presumed distance between Western European countries and the third world has steadily diminished over the past couple of decades because, as Chandra Mohanty points out, third world peoples are no longer residing only in the south but in London, Paris, Brussels, Rome, Florence, and Turin (1991). As ever-greater numbers of people from the many "southern" (a euphemism for poor countries also in the Eastern Hemisphere), economically struggling parts of the world migrate to advanced capitalist countries, Europeans are confronted with once-hidden histories and cultures systematically woven together over the course of at least a century. Whether they like it or not, Italians are now faced daily with their country's transformation from one of emigration until the 1980s to immigration and the presence of migrants from all over Africa, parts of South and Central America, the Middle East, Asia, and Eastern Europe. As the official map of a unified Europe is deliberately redrawn, an unofficial cartography of daily life in cities and neighborhoods is unfolding in ways that no urban planner could completely anticipate.

This study takes place over a decade, between 1990 and 2001, when in Italy international migration became a major theme in national politics and a topic of heated discussion all over the country. Along with Turinese Italians, the primary subjects of this story are migrants from various parts of Africa—especially Nigeria, Senegal, Somalia, Morocco, Cameroon, Ethiopia, Kenya, the Ivory Coast, and other parts of the continent—as well as Latin America and the Philippines. These migrants arrive from the specific historical context of decolonization, born into a political climate of newly independent states that recently underwent a search for "authentic" national identity. These are migrants who tend to have a good sense of their own African past, yet find themselves in a Europe in which they must create themselves anew, in some sense, at least in part to resist exclusion. In Italy in particular, migrants who arrive from many different countries find themselves face to face with Italians with peculiar local and regional concepts of themselves, along with a host of other migrants from all over the globe. This complexity explains, in part, why in the early 1990s in Turin many migrants claimed, for political purposes, a common political identity as *immigrati*. There were, of course, early signs of ethnic, religious, educational, and other status differences among migrants. Yet migrants initially seized the term *immigrati* for themselves to claim space in Europe, which many felt they had been part of for as long as they could remember. This did not last long, however, and by the middle of the 1990s the term *immigrati,* and especially *immigrazione,* had been appropriated by all sorts of Italian interest groups seeking to represent immigrants. The meaning of this term, and of the other Italian word for immigrants, *straniere* or *stranieri,* is a topic of ongoing negotiation as migrants and Italians struggle over cultural and political identities.

Global economic restructuring and peculiar constellations of ongoing historical geographies have triggered forms of discontent and struggle that often assume the form of diffuse social movements. In Turin, an industrial city with an ongoing history of grassroots political activism, many have taken up the cause of promoting migrant rights, and postcolonial migrants struggle to stretch the spatial boundaries that seem to confine them as outsiders or undeserving strangers. Contemporary political actors include female migrants who have not often been viewed as political participants in the public sphere (Simon and Brettell 1986). Social and political ideas are expressed in daily practices in a number of dispersed sites, including, but not limited to, the streets, markets, schools, offices, cultural institutions, and civic or voluntary organizations. Partially in response to the growing recognition of racism, a grassroots politics of difference has emerged that combines traditional, New Left, and contemporary forms of social activism. Turin feminists, female migrants, and the historical-political geography of Turin converge in a politics both postcolonial and Italian-European.

In the early 1990s, a group of Italian feminists allied with migrant women to construct a women's interethnic cultural and political organization, Alma Mater. The organization was intended to address the specific troubles encountered by women migrants, which some analysts have described in terms of double or triple forms of gendered subordination (Phizacklea 1983; Morokvasic 1991). Through an ethnographic study of Alma Mater and the urban context in which it emerged, this work explores growing heterogeneity in Europe and the spatial politics of race and gender. What makes Alma Mater unusual is that it was formed on the basis of an alliance between women from diverse ethnic groups, countries of origin, and religious and class backgrounds for the purpose of defending or promoting women. The participants decided that they had to organize part of their struggle around the issue of cultural difference because pervasive ideological misconceptions of migrants had become increasingly problematic and would presumably become worse if left to fester. They strove to create an alternative space for women characterized by the practice of "Speaking Subjects"—that is, postcolonial and Italian women whose lives and struggles are frequently silenced. But to what extent have they succeeded? In a world dominated by Western European ideas of social and economic progress, can postcolonial subjects truly be heard by anyone? Or are women, as Gayatri Spivak contends, complicit in the muting of other women? Is there a fully recoverable postcolonial female consciousness that can operate as an interethnic feminism? There is continuing contest over the meaning of the term *straniere*, or "female migrant," but can the Subject as straniere, or immigrant, really speak (Spivak 1987, 1999)? By examining Alma Mater I hope that we might learn something about how and to what effect a politics of difference might emerge among postcolonial subjects and Europeans, and how the struggle to construct unity among diverse women may intersect with racialist discourses and practices at various scales.

In academic literature, migrants have often been viewed as devoid of political significance because they are temporary and have allegiance to external nations (Castles 2000). Yet whether contemporary migrants intend to settle in Italy for the remainder of their lives or to return eventually to their places of origin, they are political actors in their own right. In Italy, they now play a significant role in a shifting political culture that includes immigration as a central social and political issue (Merrill and Carter 2002). Many civil society and nonprofit organizations currently claim to represent migrant interests, and all over Italy associations promote immigrant rights and social and cultural differences (Mudu 2002; Riccio 2003). Alma Mater is one of the most prominent interethnic associations in the country.

To understand this increasingly complex social world, I have adopted an interdisciplinary theoretical lens that forefronts human geography's contribution to our knowledge of place and space, and cultural anthropology's approaches to the study of how patterns of meaningful practices and social relations are produced, rejected, or acquired. What distinguishes anthropological from geographical research, suggests anthropologist Henrietta Moore, is that the respective fields tend to work at different spatial scales. Human geographers have (with some exceptions) until recently focused primarily on the broad scales of urban and national environments, economies, and so on, leaving the analysis of symbolic, linguistic, and cultural practices and the microspecificities of day-to-day social organization to anthropologists (Moore 1996). I would suggest that to grasp the impact of contemporary migratory processes on local societies within the context of global restructuring, it is necessary to approach places and cultures as interactions between a wide range of spatial scales. Or, as Doreen Massey suggests, "What we need is a global sense of the local, a global sense of place" (1993, 68). This requires moving well beyond disciplinary boundaries and incorporating approaches from a wide range of fields, juxtaposing a variety of analytical perspectives (McDowell 1999).

As an anthropologist, I strive to give attention to broad contexts of power, inequality, and racism, and, as a human geographer, to use ethnographic theories and methods to explore how these contexts affect the construction of social and political subjects. The question of how to study local cultures and places in a tightly knit global world has occupied social scientific inquiry for well over a decade (Marcus and Fisher 1986; Appadurai 1990; Gupta and Ferguson 1992; Pred and Watts 1992; Keith and Pile 1993; Marcus 1998; Burawoy 2001; Trouillot 2003). Geographers have explored approaches to concrete geographical and historical circumstances—for example, the Los Angeles riots in 1992—as expressions of abstract social relations or global restructuring and time-space compression fueled by capitalist relations of production. Allan Pred and Michael Watts describe the problem as one of "how the 'outside' is an integral part of the constitution and construction of the 'inside'" or how the "local becomes the global becomes the local" (1992, 2). With a focus on racialist processes and grassroots feminist politics, this work seeks to offer an approach sensitive to local and place-specific character, historically and culturally generated in a contingent manner: in other words, to explore ethnographically the subtle details and patterns of behavior in everyday life in a place in relation to a broad and sedimented historical context. Adopting a comprehensive approach to the study of social life allows us to move farther away from the study of places and cultures as bounded and with shared identities, toward an understanding of their multiple identities and social relations stretched beyond an immediate spatial context (Massey 1993; Pred 1995a). This work represents an effort to develop an approach to the study of human societies that is aware of the politics of its own surroundings, and to move away from essentialist, monolithic, and often racialist uses of the concepts of culture and place (Trouillot 2003).

This study examines how migrants actually cope with life in a particular place, how a particular place and people cope with migrants, and how the local positioning of various migrants and Italians is informed by what Massey has referred to as "multiply scaled relations" within a specific location (1994). The concept of spatial scale suggests that social relations are stretched beyond particular places. In other words, power relations that constitute the social relations of space are entwined at different scales, from global finance to national power, to social relations in the city, neighborhood, church, household, workplace, and body. And these power relations are continually shifting, so that instead of envisioning places as static, bounded, and fixed sites of real or "authentic" cultures, this is a view of places as dynamic, formed out of ever-shifting social interrelations at multiple scales. Each location represents a particular articulation of these relations, and the specific mix defines, in part, the uniqueness of a place.

An important aspect of this formulation is that different social groups and individuals are positioned in distinct ways within the flow of connections that spread across spatial scales (Massey 1993; Pred 1990; N. Smith 1992)—different social groups, that is, not merely in terms of identity construction, but as the product of struggles and negotiations around socially demarcated boundaries established at specific scales (N. Smith 1992). Some groups have more power than others; for example, some initiate movements and flows while others do not. There is a great deal of mobility in the contemporary world, yet different social groups have distinct relationships to this mobility—or, as Massey put it, "some are more on the receiving end of it than others; some are effectively imprisoned by it" (1993, 61). This work explores some of the ways that racialized differences intersect with differences classified by gender, for example, or social class. Our gender and race, I suggest, are constituted differently according to our differential location within multiscaled relations of power and the way these relations are marked in specific places and at particular times.

Feminist geographers who have long challenged fixed and unchanging notions of what it means to be a woman are now turning to new ways of studying people whose identities are in the process of becoming rather than being a woman, or the making and remaking of identities (McDowell 1999). The identities of migrant women shift continually as they struggle with different sorts of power relations. For example, in relation to established Turin feminists, migrant women are "women," while in other instances migrant women may identify themselves as "Africans," as, for instance, they unite cross-nationally in distinction from "Arabs" or "Latin Americans." Or, in relation to the Italian state, migrant women might proclaim a number of different cultural markers as they seek to construct work spaces for themselves within public offices.

In the struggle to find belonging in Turin, migrants often engage in spatialized politics, involving the making and remaking of space across different scales, and the expansion of the scale of their own meaningful practices (N. Smith 1992; Merrill 2004). The postcolonial women at the center of this discussion are actively engaged in a spatialized politics in which they contest various forms of differentiation—challenging, for example, gendered and racialized spaces of the city, local labor market, neighborhood, and body.

One of the framing concepts of this study is that race is historically contingent, and therefore its meanings are not fixed at the scales of the body, community, city, and nation, but it is also continuous with, if not fixed in, modernity at the global scale. Racialization, or the construction of racial identity, is a set of practices and discourses that began with European colonial expansion in the fifteenth century as a justification for European domination and gradually became part of common sense understandings (Goldberg 1993; Gilroy 2000; Castles 2000; Gilmore 2002). Ruth Wilson Gilmore suggests that the modernist concept of a hierarchy of fixed differences that displaced royal and common knowledge required coercive and persuasive forces to come together in the service of domination (2002). Space and scale are deeply implicated in the modernist project of racialization, for example, in that the regulation of territorial boundaries is an intrinsically "racial" issue linked with the construction of racialized national identities (Gilroy 1991; Miles 1993; Hall 1991a; Liu 2000). The racial classification of migrants in Italy is to a considerable extent determined by the migrant's social-spatial location of origin within a global political economy.

The racialization of people and places in Italy is produced in and through multiple cultural social-spatial processes, including the local, national, and international economy, media and popular culture, historically sedimented ideologies and practices, state policies, the Catholic Church, colonial discourses, urban politics, communities, and social services and education, all of which are articulated with common sense, taken-for-granted, everyday practices. These different processes produce geographies, situated forms of domination and contestation based on gendered, sexualized, and racialized class and ethnic identities that intersect with one another in ways that may appear contradictory. I am suggesting that social practices are contingent on intersecting matrixes of power that operate at various social and spatial scales, and that identities are constructed through practices that position or locate people as subjects within complex hierarchies of power and meaning.

In Italy as in other parts of Europe, there is a popular tendency to regard migrants as alien intruders whose presence poses an economic, cultural, and social threat to local society (Campani and Palidda 1990; Wieviorka 1993; Burgio 2001; Castles 2000; Colombo and Sciortino 2002; Gallini 1996; Carter 1997; Cole 1997). Much of popular racialist discourse adopts a relatively indirect strategic posture, employing a logic of "cultural difference" to justify practices and establish a distance between Europeans and people from developing countries (Balibar and Wallerstein 1991; Ward 1997). According to this perspective, although there may be no scientific basis for the classification of the world's populations into distinct and essentially unequal racial species, this does not mean that territorially located human groups are all the same. Differences between historically and geographically rooted cultures are believed to be so vast and insurmountable that if the barriers between "us" and "them" should collapse, conflicts would erupt and, even worse, the integrity or purity of all cultures would cease to exist. Cultural or differentialist racism suggests that the mixing of cultures is unnatural, but that ethnic groups have the "right to be different"—and to remain in "their own" countries (Taguieff 1990). Racism is hidden under a veil of difference that postulates absolute group identities and splits human species into self-contained territorial and culturally fixed totalities. This variant of racialist discourse often presents itself as egalitarian and democratic by claiming that the exclusion of migrants and minorities is not based on any natural inferiority among migrant groups or any superiority of Europeans, but that societies ought to protect their populations by respecting "tolerance thresholds." Throughout Western Europe, the "new" cultural racism has been incorporated widely into mainstream discourses.[1] Racialist discourse permeates political narratives from the extreme right to the left and every other spatial scale, and therefore the effects of racism are far greater than may appear if measured solely in terms of the discourses of the extreme right (Hargreaves and Leaman 1995; Caponio 2003).

In an effort to effect change in gender—another hierarchical discourse— feminist scholars have reconceived the dominant Western epistemology of a "non-gendered, unified, and universal subject" as an active maker and user of culture while also being heteronomous and subjected to social constraint. This inquiry has contributed to the development of new ways of thinking about culture, society, language, and knowledge itself—that by redefining the nature and boundaries of the political, it at once engenders the subject as political and addresses woman as social subject (de Lauretis 1986). But epistemological critique is incomplete unless it includes a re-imagining of spaces and mapping processes in different ways (Blunt and Rose 1994). Feminist geographers understand gender as constituted according to the subject's differential position or location within relations of power, and these relations themselves produce space (Pred 1990; Hanson and Pratt 1994, 1995; Blunt and Rose 1994; McDowell 1999).

Feminism makes the important argument that instead of figuring prominently in historical accounts, the history of dominated and nonelite people, including women, has until recently been taken as relatively incidental to the lives of the people who occupy the center of historical narratives and exercise power over social and symbolic wealth (McDowell and Sharp 1997). Yet beyond making women and other dominated populations visible, it is crucial to analyze and understand why specific groups of people remain socially and spatially subordinate. I suggest that analysis of the socially created distinctions between women and men is incomplete without attention to differences between women and other women, based on various other axes of power. Subject position is marked by the geographies of power relations and the "situatedness of knowledge" (Haraway 1991). Feminist geographers Blunt and Rose suggest that the politics of difference is not only the politics of difference between two genders, but also the politics of diversity among women (1994). This work explores the way that hierarchical gender and race relations are affected by and embedded in space.

By attending to the actual complexity of migrant populations in Turin, and the complex manner in which they are situated within a local context in Turin, I wish to stress the social and cultural heterogeneity of contemporary Europe. Turin is an industrial city where recent restructuring has had considerable effect on the local working class, and it is a city with several grassroots activist traditions. These cultural-historical practices are informed by the climate that emerged when new migrant populations began to arrive in greater numbers during the late 1980s. Racism is experienced differently in Turin than in other Italian cities, for example, where the history of labor struggles were never as pronounced. Throughout my work, my approach is to examine the problems of racialization in Turin, and of a politics of difference, by examining everyday practices.

The growing presence in Europe of people from economically underdeveloped parts of the world represents a new phase in international migration, linked with the internationalization of national economies, both within the European Union and between it and other parts of the world.[2] The disintegration of the Soviet bloc and the end of the cold war, combined with rapid economic and social change in many countries, has also prompted vast, new population movements (Castles 2000). Ethnic and national diversity, a high proportion of female as well as male workers, and an emerging polarization of skills characterize contemporary migrants with both unskilled and highly qualified personnel participating. Where in France and England there is a history of limited labor and other migration from former colonies, Italy and a growing number of European countries now face large-scale immigration.

International migration to Turin, a northern Italian city in the Piedmont region, is unprecedented. Until the end of the 1960s, Italy was a country of emigration, where population movements were directed primarily from southern Italy to the United States, France, Germany, and Switzerland, and in the post–World War II period to northern Italy (Gabaccia 2000; Gabaccia and Iacovetta 2002). Several hundred thousand southern Italians migrated to Turin after the war to work in an industrial labor market where there was full employment. Not until after the oil crisis in 1973, and after other Western European countries had responded to the economic downturn by banning the entry of non–European Community workers, did international migration to Italy begin to increase (Castles 2000). The earliest migrants to Italy were university students and women, predominantly from Cape Verde, Ethiopia, and the Philippines, contracted through Catholic organizations as live-in domestic workers for Italian families (Andall 2000; IRES 1992). In the absence of immigration legislation, most migrants were compelled to remain in a clandestine legal status.

Until the early 1990s, Italy lacked a strong immigration policy. Debate on immigration legislation began in the mid-1980s, when expressions of

---

racism and intolerance were still unusual (Ferrarotti 1988). In 1986, the government proposed Law 943, which came into force in January 1987. The principal aim of this legislation was to prohibit illegal immigration, consistent with the trend elsewhere in Europe. The Italian borders were officially closed after Law 943 was enacted, but in practice illegal immigration continued to accelerate. Then, in the context of European unification and in preparation for monetary union, European governments accused Italy of becoming a gateway for third world immigrants wishing to enter European countries. The Dutch, French, and German governments threatened that Italy would have to create a stricter immigration policy for it to become a signatory of the Schengan Treaty. It was thus that Minister of Justice Claudio Martelli proposed a new immigration policy that was signed into legislation in 1990.

Law 39, or the Martelli Law, as it is called, marked a watershed in Italian immigration history. The law sought to terminate immigration, yet to recognize migrants working in the informal economy by granting them the possibility of proving that they were already living in Italy before December 31, 1989. By this time, there were antiracist mobilizations among some members of the trade unions, Catholic organizations, and migrant ethnic associations. Law 39 dealt with some issues not resolved in Law 943—for example, self-employment. The new law permitted migrants to be self-employed and to create cooperatives, but it was far more restrictive than the previous law in that, apart from "programmed flows," it prohibited the further entry of migrant workers. As if to demonstrate its commitment to the control of populations from non-EU member states, in August 1991 Italy expelled some twenty thousand impoverished Albanians attempting to enter the country (Campani 1993). Since February 1990, when the Martelli proposal passed into legislation, the law has been modified several times, usually in the direction of greater state repression of migrants.[3]

Until the late 1980s, when immigration began to take on the status of a social problem, Italy had a reputation among African students as a socially tolerant country in comparison with other European nations (Mottura 1992). Intolerance spread throughout the country at a rapid pace, and violence against immigrants became part of Italian social life. The first well-publicized incident occurred in August 1989, when a South African migrant, Jerry Masslo, was killed near Naples by some youth who were stealing his meager earnings from a day's work in the tomato fields (Campani 1993). This incident prompted intense political discussion over the need for a clear immigration policy; at the same time, public opinion began to turn widely against the growing presence of immigrants. Italian market traders and various neighborhood associations organized anti-immigrant demonstrations throughout the country. The government's response to these demonstrations and the growing hostility toward immigrants was to impose harsher controls and repressive measures on immigrants, particularly the Senegalese, Moroccan, and other itinerant street vendors, the most visible of migrants popularly referred to as *vu cumpra* (Carter 1997).

Italian right-wing political parties, including the former Fascist Party, or MSI (Italian Social Movement), currently the AN (National Alliance),[4] have seized the opportunity to fan the flames of anti-immigrant sentiment to maneuver themselves into positions of authority (Harris 1994; A. Smith 1994). The Italian Leagues, consolidated into the Northern League directed by Umberto Bossi, which had for years campaigned against a centralized Italian state that it viewed as favoring the south, in the late 1980s began to support hostile attitudes toward immigrants and to demand that immigration cease (Cheles, Ferguson, and Vaughn 1995). Political space for right-wing and anti-immigrant ideology opened in the late 1980s when, as in other European countries, labor unions and left political parties were weakened, exacerbated by the disintegration of traditional Italian parties and neoliberal political and economic policies of the 1990s. Traditional Italian regionalism has found new political expression in the Northern League's claims to defend northern Italy against a centralized state and a far less economically developed south. The league expresses a traditional parochialism quite pronounced in the region of Piedmont, where local identities are defended.

Despite the spreading violence and more subtle anti-immigrant sentiment, Italian reactions to the increasing presence of foreigners have been mixed (Dal Lago 1999; Cotesta 1999, 2002; Fedeli 1990; Marazziti 1993; Magni 1995; Björgo and Witte 1993; Rattansi and Westwood 1994; Balibar and Wallerstein 1991; Miles 1993; Miles and Satzewich 1990). Certain Italian feminist, labor, and Catholic organizations have sought to embrace migrant cultural diversity, while the predominant political and popular sentiment has been one of fear and rejection. Racist, anti-immigrant ideologies that were relatively quiescent after World War II and the decolonization of Africa have taken on a new character, encouraged by the opening of new political spaces and parties following the decline of the labor movement and traditional Italian political parties (Tabet 1997). Throughout

Europe in the 1990s, extreme right-wing groups successfully mobilized over immigration and supposed threats to national identity (Solomos and Wrench 1993; Harris 1994).

A popular question is why West African and other postcolonial migrants are attracted to Italy, a country with which they did not have a direct colonial relationship. Common explanations include the overwhelming poverty in countries of origin, demand for workers, and zero population growth in Italy. But I do not believe that the presence of newcomers can be explained in terms of demand for cheap labor or the economic conditions in developing countries alone. While it is true that corporations and many Italian families demand cheap, casual, immigrant labor, we ought to remember that the majority of today's migrants originate from places that have for more than a century had a variety of colonial and postcolonial social and economic connections with the European social formation (Matteo 2001). Only in relation to a history of ties with Europe as part of a broad capitalist economy can the migration of postcolonial migrants be fully understood. Those now migrating from postcolonial societies have, in fact, been to Europe symbolically for centuries: in the transfer of raw materials such as coffee, cocoa, and peanuts, and in the imaginations fed by stories about the great achievements of European countries such as England, France, and Italy (Fazel 1999). As Stuart Hall argues, there is no European history without those other histories of the peoples and places on the backs of which European social identities were constructed (1996a).

Before their arrival in Europe, migrants were already situated in an international division of labor that has acquired some peculiar global contours over the past several decades. Alterations of investment patterns and the spatial redistribution of industrial plants have exacerbated and further complicated the uneven distribution of development sites that were established during European and American colonialism and that did not disappear after decolonization. The liberalization of trade restrictions on American, European, and Japanese firms wishing to invest abroad, together with the consequent integration of new sites into the manufacturing processes of the advanced economies, has produced many indirect effects. Among the most prominent of the indirect consequences of global capital mobility is the changing structure and distribution of the labor force, which encourages migration.

While considerable emphasis is placed on the loss of employment in the industrial sector of advanced economies and on the movement of jobs from industrialized to third world countries, another crucial aspect of global economic restructuring is the increasing import of labor in many advanced economies. Some scholars suggest that the number of jobs lost in core economies has been exaggerated, and that if one examines different sectors within the industrial economies, the share of certain kinds of work has, in fact, steadily increased. While agriculture and employment in some industries has shrunk, many places have seen spectacular growth in other areas, including the information and service sector (Dicken 2002). Some 90 percent of the world's manufacturing is still done in Europe, the United States, and Japan, while the burden of poverty lies heavily across Asia, Africa, and Latin America. The world economy has been unequally structured since the sixteenth century, and systems of surplus appropriation, or the transfer of wealth from satellites to metropolitan areas, have continued to fuel growth in some places at the expense of others (Knox, Agnew, and McCarthy 2003).

Contemporary economic development is guided by principles of neoliberalism, popularly termed "globalization." This is a political-philosophical doctrine of economic liberty for the powerful, which insists that an economy must be free from the social and political restrictions placed on it by states trying to regulate in the name of the public interest. These restrictions include labeling national economic and environmental regulations, social welfare programs, and labor protection barriers to the free flow of trade and capital and to the freedom of multinational corporations to exploit labor and the environment in their best interests. Increasing demands for cheap labor and decreasing national spending on health, education, welfare, and work, along with increasing labor demands, have combined to encourage international migration to Europe.

Employment demand in the growing services sector is a feature of the contemporary gendered international division of labor (Sassen 2001). Along with considerable job shrinkage resulting from industrial flight in core areas, there has been a pronounced increase in domestic and international demand for services in high-income jobs requiring specialized educational training, as well as in low-wage jobs. As middle-income blue- and white-collar jobs have diminished, the demand for laborers in the lowest earning sectors has expanded—a labor force of the dispossessed sectors, including women, "blacks," and migrants. The technological transformation of the work process and the decentralization of manufacturing and office work have also contributed to the consolidation of new kinds of economic places, primarily cities, where the world is managed and serviced. Cities such as Turin, which provide the base point for industrial production and marketing as well as for the accumulation of capital, are points of destination for international migrants. Along with the expansion of low-wage activities directly related to the expansion of advanced services for professionals and managers in Turin has come an expanding demand for workers in low-wage service jobs, such as waiters/waitresses, cleaners, chambermaids, even prostitutes. In Italy, many of these laborers represent subordinate labor power from former European colonies.

In the 1960s, large parts of Africa and Asia decolonized, joining Latin America as part of a largely nonindustrial and ex-colonial but still dependent world. Africa currently generates significant outflows of intercontinental migrants, mainly to Western Europe, but also to North America and the Middle East. Sub-Saharan Africa in particular has had the poorest record of economic growth of any place in the world over the past twenty years. Among the many obstacles to the region's economic development is dependence on global exchange rates, particularly the falling prices of raw materials. The terms of trade—that is, the ratio between the prices of exports and the prices of imports in relation to many basic commodities exported to the core—have also deteriorated. Most African countries experienced declining or stagnant export earnings in the 1980s and 1990s. They are heavily dependent on foreign aid and investment by the World Bank and the International Monetary Fund, and are therefore heavily indebted. The cold war also encouraged militarization and political instability in former colonies, which were zones of superpower competition. In sub-Saharan Africa, superpowers have specialized in military aid and technical assistance rather than direct economic assistance (Knox, Agnew, and McCarthy 2003). It is impossible to understand the contemporary migration from parts of Africa to Europe without considering the profound historical, economic, and political links between the two continents.

Migrations usually arise from the existence of prior links between sending and receiving countries, based on colonization, political influence, trade, investment, and cultural ties (Castles and Miller 2003). Although Italy was not one of the foremost European colonial powers in Africa, the country did colonize Libya, Ethiopia, Eritrea, and Somalia. Italian firms such as the Agnelli family's Fiat of Turin have established operations in African countries, and other Italian companies market a wide variety of commodities. Pope John Paul II made numerous visits to sub-Saharan Africa, where millions were converted to Catholicism during the colonial and precolonial epochs. Today, numerous Italian Catholic associations, such as Caritas, engage in missionary work throughout the continent, and many of these associations are linked with other nonprofit, third-sector organizations and with various Italian political parties. The idea of Italy as an attractive European site that is part of the European formation as a whole draws many African migrants to study in Italian universities and, more recently, to search for a reasonable standard of living for themselves and their families. The interconnections between migrant countries of origin and destination are a starting point in analysis of the contemporary migration, indicating that complex transnational identities probably existed before the migration itself (Daly and Barot 1999).

Chapter Outline and Methodology

Alma Mater represents a form of both cultural merging and boundary delineating, or the construction of what Stuart Hall has termed "new ethnicities," a politics of difference concerned with new forms of identity formation but within the constraints of established languages of cultural "racial" differences or ethnicities (1996b). In chapters 1 and 2 I examine the emergence of an antiracist feminism in the context of an Italian crisis over immigration and its embeddedness in Turin political culture. Chapter 1 presents the social history of the alliance between migrant women and Turin feminists, and the construction of a spatial politics. I was involved in discussions about the formation of a migrant women's center before its full realization, returning several times to study the ongoing struggles of Alma Mater after an interval of years, and this chapter traces the concept of Alma Mater to its appearance in 1992. Chapter 2 discusses more specifically the components of Alma Mater and the establishment of its Center for Cultural Mediation.

To understand this politics of difference, in chapters 3 and 4 we examine the nexus of economic and power relations in which subjects are situated. Alma Mater seeks to expand the scale of women's labor practices, but its participants are faced with a daunting set of urban and global economic forces that may compromise the terms of their politics. The political economy of Turin and its division of labor in relation to the restructuring of the Fiat automobile company is examined in chapter 3. My aim here is to delineate the changing labor structure of the city, and in chapter 4 to explain its relationship to the immigration. In chapters 2, 4, and 7, I point out that migrants have historical agency, but this agency is situated in the historical geography of Turin and of Italy.

In chapter 5 I turn to the historical context of race and anti-immigrant politics. Discussing a Turin neighborhood populated by a number of African migrants, I explore the simultaneous construction of racialized space and spatialized race. The scale of this discussion stretches well beyond the confines of the particular neighborhood to levels of urban, national, and international politics, as well as the smallest scale of the individual body. The chapter examines a series of events that contributed to the development of anti-immigrant and immigrant politics as well as modification of the Martelli Law in 1995. By contrast with Alma Mater, this neighborhood represents an urban space in which migrant voices are almost entirely muffled.

In chapter 6, I discuss Turin feminism in relation to labor politics from the 1970s to the present. Beginning with an image of migrant participants in Alma Mater, I go on to discuss Turin feminism and the forms it has taken over the past several decades. Alma Mater may never have come to fruition as an alliance between migrants and Italians if it were not situated within the peculiar workerist tradition of Turin. Nevertheless, migrant women challenge Italian feminism to expand and reconstitute itself as a postcolonial and global feminism.

Chapter 7 returns to the internal workings of Alma Mater and its role as an NGO, or nongovernmental organization. The chapter discusses the multiple social positions represented in the organization and played out on a daily basis. I discuss the problems encountered between participants as they actually cope with life in the various social spaces of Turin. The story of Alma Mater is one of both cooperation and conflict, of new forms of cultural merging, the stretching of spatial scale, and the reconstruction of boundaries.

In a brief epilogue, I describe the Gender and Globalization Conference held in Genoa, Italy, in 2001, organized in anticipation of the July G8 conference. Some members of Alma Mater participated in the conference, giving speeches and voicing their views in small group meetings around specific topics. The epilogue is intended to give the reader an indication of the global direction in which Alma Mater has been developing, and suggestions about global gendered alliance.

Finally, I offer a few statements about the methodology. The study of migrant subjectivities in a large urban context with a population of nearly one million people was a complex undertaking that presented a host of difficulties. Migrants lived and worked in dispersed sites and it was not always easy to arrange a time to speak with them. Many lived and worked in precarious conditions and were vulnerable to deportation, which made them hesitant to speak to an unknown graduate student or college professor from the United States. My experience living in Cameroon and spending several months in Niger and the former Zaire gave me a certain amount of confidence and ease with African migrants. But the research was also greatly facilitated by my relationship with a first generation of migrants who gave me credibility through word of mouth.

This research was carried out during one and a half years in Turin, between January 1990 and May 1991, and during three two-month visits in 1995, 1996, and 2001. My methods included archival research, participant observation, and semistructured and unstructured interviews with approximately 150 Italians and migrants, with interviews conducted in French, English, and Italian. Most of my field research was gathered through participant observation informed by classical and contemporary social theory in geography, anthropology, and other fields. Given the conditions in which migrants lived during 1990–91, formal interviews would have been inappropriate; I therefore chose not to use tape-recording devices because they might have interfered with the research process in a delicate context in which few migrants easily trusted Europeans or North Americans. I selected informants whom I met by chance in a variety of settings, such as open markets and small bread and meat shops and at meetings about migrant problems, or to whom I was introduced by other migrants. My interviews were conducted on urban streets, in markets, on trains, in migrant homes, and at our apartments in Turin. In 1995, 1996, and 2001, I returned to conduct additional research more specifically on Alma Mater, race, and the political economy of Turin. During these visits, I tape-recorded and later transcribed semistructured interviews with Italian officials such as city council members, Turin feminists who belonged to Alma Mater, members of the Casa delle Donne, and a first generation of migrants with whom I had established long-term working relationships.[5] When I first began research in 1990, Alma Mater was only an idea, but by the time I returned to Turin in 1995, it had become a thriving organization.

My informants during all of these visits ranged widely in age, legal status, educational background, national origin, and social class. A first generation of migrants, many of whom attended the University of Turin, had acquired considerable knowledge of local political culture and played a prominent role in gathering Italian support for migrant rights between 1990 and 1991. Their numerous discussions and debates often left out the voices of more recent migrants with the most limited access to resources, and I therefore sought to form close participant-informant relationships with women migrants from very modest educational backgrounds and means. Some of my closest informants were women with few economic resources and little political knowledge who were from such countries as Cameroon, the Ivory Coast, Kenya, Ethiopia, and Senegal. Their ages ranged from early twenties to late thirties, and encompassed single and married women. Other close informants between 1990 and 1991 included men from the Ivory Coast, Morocco, Senegal, and Italy. During subsequent field visits, my informants ranged even more widely, and included Italian feminists, scholars and intellectuals, shop owners, migrant activists, and trade union representatives, along with migrant women. Some of my closest informant relationships during the latter years were with migrant women of various educational backgrounds from Somalia, Cameroon, Senegal, Ethiopia, Kenya, Brazil, Nigeria, and Italy.

My research was also facilitated by a number of circumstances that made it easier for me to earn the trust of migrants, including their knowledge of my husband, an African American anthropologist who did extensive research on Senegalese in Turin. Many migrants mistrusted Italians and were reluctant to speak with them, but being North American, I was considered a bit removed from Europe. People were also predisposed to speak with me because our young children were either with us or I was pregnant, which tended to humanize us and to make me less threatening. Finally, my research was influenced by connection with the IRES Piedmont group of migrants and Italians conducting research on migrants and labor issues between 1989 and 1991. Through this group, the majority of whom were migrants, I was introduced to many of my first informants.

CHAPTER 1

The Spatial Politics
of Race and Gender

The Europeans have to deal with us being here now.
They came over to our countries, so now it's our turn
to come to theirs. They were uninvited.
—*MaryAnn Akinyi, a Kenyan migrant*

GEORGETTE WAS A HEADSTRONG YOUNG WOMAN in her early twenties from the Ivory Coast. She had lived in Italy for several years, having made the journey for the purpose of improving the life she would have led had she remained in Abidjan. Arriving in Turin with a minimum amount of secondary schooling but fluent in French, she rapidly learned Italian by "watching television soap operas." An observing Catholic, she and her husband belonged to a church in their neighborhood and participated regularly in church activities. Georgette was a woman of many trades, driven by the desire to improve her social position in relation to other Europeans and Africans. She enrolled in evening courses to obtain a middle-school certificate and took a sewing course with a compatriot. To support her training and to help pay her rent, she cut and braided hair for a host of regular customers and worked part-time as a domestic, caring for children and cleaning house for an Italian woman who, she complained, did not wish to *regularizzare* (regularize) her employment.

Georgette and her husband rented a small, one-room flat, where they shared an external toilet and took hand baths from a large bucket placed on the kitchen floor. They lived in a Turin neighborhood where anti-immigrant protests had been organized and conflicts between Italian and migrant residents had erupted on several occasions. She had met her husband in Turin, and he too was determined to improve his social position by taking courses to earn the certificate that would make it possible for him to work as an automobile mechanic. Georgette's husband was Ivorian, some

1

ten years her senior, and from an ethnic group different from her own. He had an angry, arrogant air and an apparent disdain for Europeans and most university-educated Africans. He claimed that his experiences on the Ivory Coast had led him to distrust Europeans intensely. Frequently, he expressed frustration with Italians for "deliberately keeping him from acquiring the specialized knowledge of his trade" or for showing a "polite smile, while harboring the secret desire that he fail at his every endeavor."

Georgette's husband did not want his wife to travel around the city unaccompanied, unless it was for the purpose of receiving training or to earn money. He sent his younger brother to monitor her social visits with us. Georgette never seemed to mind this, accepting her husband's distrust of Europeans. Her enterprising spirit kept her from closing herself off entirely from others, although her efforts to improve her position were hampered in an Italian society not yet prepared to accept and accommodate a large foreign presence. Social classifications of "insiders" excluded migrants from developing countries, who were assumed "different" from Europeans and "out of place" in Italy (Douglas 1966; Carter 1997; Tabet 1997).

When she first arrived in Turin, Georgette worked in a small hairstyling salon owned and managed by Francesca, an immigrant from Martinique who had lived in France before moving to Turin. Married to an Italian man and from an island that is part of France, Francesca was a French or Italian citizen, and her husband owned a photography studio. When Francesca opened her salon, she hired Georgette and two other African women as hairstylists. After one of the stylists allegedly stole money from the shop and lured customers away to earn income on the side, Francesca decided to close the business. A year or so later, Georgette had established her own informal network of clients, and, with African migrants entering Turin by the hundreds, wanted to open her own business to support this new clientele. She decided to approach Francesca about using the site that she had already established as a salon, but felt that she needed my husband and me to mediate because "you are Americans," a status that carried considerable symbolic capital (Bourdieu 1977, 1984).[1] Georgette's social class position and ethnic status in Turin silenced her, and she knew that without a high-status mediator, Francesca would not take her seriously.

Wishing to support legal immigrant businesses, and aware of the need for and absence of hairstyling salons for Africans in Turin, we agreed to help represent Georgette. When Georgette contacted Francesca, she immediately asked to speak with us and then identified herself as "French, from Paris," remarking that Georgette's French was not very good. This meant that in Francesca's estimation, Georgette, who spoke French with her natal family and husband, did not speak with a "correct" continental accent and idiomatic expressions. Francesca considered Georgette uneducated, which in French society meant that she belonged to a low social class (Bourdieu 1984). After arranging a meeting time, we accompanied Georgette to speak with Francesca, who quickly expressed her expectation that *we,* and not Georgette, might reopen the hairstyling business, and that Georgette would work for us. In Georgette's presence, Francesca explained to us that, "like so many other Africans," Georgette was "incapable of running her own business" and that, based on her own experience with them, "these women" would "just not do right by her." Francesca was a French citizen and was also able to obtain Italian citizenship, and she treated Georgette as a social inferior. Georgette retorted by accusing Francesca of paying her employees low, "exploitative wages." We decided to research other ways to support Georgette's vision.

Georgette knew little about the legal requirements for opening a business in Italy, so we tried to help her gain this knowledge by connecting her with people who might have an interest in helping a young, enthusiastic African woman. She did not have formal training as a hairstylist, but had acquired the skill informally as an apprentice to family members. We thought we might find a way for her to acquire the formal training she needed to work legally in an Italian salon. Italians learn this trade as teenagers, apprenticed in salons and mentored by shop owners until they receive a certificate, which finally allows them to earn full salaries as stylists. We thought we might be able to find a Turin salon with an owner interested in supporting immigrants, someone willing to permit Georgette to work as an apprentice and learn the skills required to style Italian hair. This, we hoped, would be a step toward operating a shop on her own. We approached the president of the Artisanal Association, which is a kind of trade union association for autonomous artisans. The president, Silvio, was a member of the Italian Communist Party (PCI, Partito Communista Italiano),[2] which we expected would make him much more likely than others to feel sympathy for immigrants as workers and potential trade union members. Silvio was, in fact, receptive to the concept of creating several paid apprenticeships for African migrants in local hairstyling salons.

A few weeks after we spoke with Silvio, he referred us to another man, the assistant president of the Artisanal Association for this category of work, who trained Italian hairstylists and owned a salon. This man, Marco, asked that we bring Georgette and one of her customers to the salon so that he might observe her while working and speak with her about an apprenticeship. Georgette's husband agreed to permit her to visit Marco's salon, but only after an Ivorian man with elevated social status among Ivorian immigrants had explained to him that he could trust us and that this might be an excellent opportunity for his wife.

When we arrived at the salon, Marco was cordial while offering to teach Georgette and explaining that he couldn't hire her just yet, because she didn't have the skills to cut and style Italian hair. He suggested that she might be able to obtain a scholarship from the local government to pay for her training. Marco and Georgette worked out a schedule in which Georgette would maintain her morning cleaning job and in the afternoon train at his shop. She was not worried about being paid little as an apprentice, because she had already established a number of her own clients and Marco had agreed to allow her to style their hair while in his shop. At an arranged time on two occasions, Georgette went to Marco's shop, expecting to begin a kind of apprenticeship. She later described what happened:

> I really wanted to do this, really. I had even decided to stop the sewing classes to devote myself only to doing hair. But I cannot work with that man. He is not married, and when I went to see him, he would not talk with me until the shop was empty of customers and employees. After the others had left, he put his hands on my shoulders and asked for the phone number of the Brazilian woman who I brought to his shop the last time I was there.

She explained that Marco asked her what she wanted from him, and her response was that she simply wished to work in his shop to learn. He protested that this would not be good for her, because she would not make any money. But she explained to him that the money didn't matter; she simply wanted to learn. Marco told her that he didn't have time to train her on a regular basis.

Fearful of his covert sexual advances, a discouraged Georgette decided not to pursue the apprenticeship with Marco, whose actions were subsequently condemned by all concerned. A formal complaint was registered with the Artisanal Association and the Italian Communist Party. After this experience, and until she and her husband moved to France in the late

1990s, Georgette continued to freelance as a hairstylist in Turin, to clean Italian homes, and to hope for a better tomorrow.

Francesca's and Marco's practices in relation to Georgette were informed by their respective positions in European society and understandings of African women, migrants, and "outsiders." Their practices might be described in Bourdieu's terms of bodily disposition, or *habitus*, that encodes cultural understandings of social position mediated by such cultural differences as race, gender, and ethnic distinction, marking the Other as an outsider (Bourdieu 1977). Despite her apparent African origins, Francesca identified herself as a European insider by virtue of her French citizenship, social status as a property owner, and marriage to an Italian man. She perceived Georgette as an outsider to the European world, an *extracomunitari* from the colonies, with which she shared little common experience. Francesca classified Georgette as an outsider for several reasons, including the belief, as she commented to me, that Georgette spoke French poorly, that is, with an Ivorian and African accent. Other markers of her status included the fact that she held only temporary legal status as a migrant, had a relatively low level of educational training, and was connected with an African continent whose populations were metaphorically associated with the underdeveloped space or territory where they lived. Marco's position as an Italian man, the representative of a major worker association, and a shop owner was clearly marked with relative power in relationship to Georgette. She was a woman, a foreigner without citizenship, and a wage laborer. For these reasons, Marco was disposed to conceive of Georgette as easy prey and someone to whom he owed absolutely no social or political obligation. She seems to have been lumped by Marco into the loose and easy-to-dismiss category of African women who are often assumed to be in the business of selling sex. For either Francesca or Marco to have responded differently to Georgette's needs, they would have had to classify her as an actual or potential social-political insider, which neither of them imagined.

In early 1990s Turin, many migrant women were humiliated in situations similar to those experienced by Georgette. In the popular imaginary, such women were assumed to be on their own and unsupervised, traveling freely without traditional familial or other institutional support. Their physical movements on foreign land, outside their own recognizable social structures, and the added dimension of phenotypical distinctions or dark-colored skin, foreign clothing, and hairstyles, led to their virtually automatic cultural classification in Italy as sexually available or promiscuous. Entering Italy and searching for work with increasing frequency, migrant women were positioned on the precarious margins of "female work" in Italy, associated with household and sexual services. With employment opportunities almost entirely limited to formal and informal domestic work and the illicit world of prostitution, for which there was a growing market, these migrant women rapidly became part of a peripheral stratum of the working class. Many of them distrusted Italians and expressed the feeling that they lived in a racist environment. A Nigerian woman told me, "I can't stand most Italians. They're racist. These Italians hate me. The women give me evil stares on the buses, and they ignore me when I'm in the market or in a store. The women are the worst because they're jealous, and the men just think we're prostitutes."

Despite the generally unwelcoming climate, in the relatively politically active context of Turin there were organizational precedents for newcomers to confront perceived social injustices. For them to make use of these political structures, and to challenge their growing social marginality within Italian society, migrants had to gain practical knowledge of Italian institutional culture and rework it. Faced daily with various forms of discrimination and vulnerability, a number of Turin migrants formed ethnic and interethnic associations and cooperatives in an effort to stretch beyond the social-spatial scales that acted as confining boundaries. The most successful of these grassroots efforts, Alma Mater, was achieved through an interethnic alliance between a diverse group of migrant women and Turin feminists.

When Alma Mater opened its doors in the early 1990s, there was nothing else like it in Italy or in many other parts of Europe where international migrant populations have been part of the social geography for decades. Since this time, other interethnic feminist groups and youth social centers that include migrants have appeared throughout the country, but none at the scale of Turin's Alma Mater.[3] Feminist scholars, criticizing essential notions that generalize "womanness" across a variety of differences, have discussed the possibility of a feminist politics and theory of social justice articulated by differences (Mouffe 1992; Harstock 1998; hooks 1990). But alliances among women of different ethnic and social class backgrounds, or among "third world," "black," and "white" women are rare (Twine and Blee 2001; Sandoval 1991; Hanson and Pratt 1994; Mohanty 1991). Alma Mater, an alliance between postcolonial migrants and women of an advanced industrial economy in different subject positions, can be understood only in relation to a specific time and place. The cultural and political geography of Turin encouraged the emergence of political alliance, and was also a medium for fixing identities and hardening conceptual boundaries. Local practices are not, however, entirely fixed, but change continually as they are articulated with global processes and their side effects, or, as Massey suggested, "The 'character of an area' is no more the product of an internalized history than are the recent fortunes of its manufacturing history. The global is in the local in the very process of the formation of the local" (1994, 120).

Spatial Politics of Scale

Alma Mater facilitates the seizure of space by a group of migrant and Italian women who have felt marginalized in mainstream society and contained in prescribed gender roles (Hanson and Pratt 1995; McDowell 1999). Through this space, they may expand the physical and metaphorical boundaries that confine them to the social and economic peripheries of local society. For migrant women, Alma Mater may be a site of safety and hope in sharp contrast to Turin neighborhoods, streets, and work spaces. Their spatialized politics involves the making and remaking of space and the expansion of the scale of meaningful practices. The very building in which Alma Mater is housed stretches the neighborhood or community scale of women's influence and seeks to contract the urban scale of popular and official power over women's bodies and movements (Merrill 2004).

As global capitalism works at various scales extending from the global to the national, community, home, and body, it does so by way of producing and reproducing differentiation (Hall 1991b, 1996a). Difference, as I use the term here, does not have the same meaning as "different subject positions" (N. Smith 1992). The differences that members of Alma Mater struggled to overcome can best be understood not as individual identity-level constructions, but rather as the products of struggles and negotiations around socially demarcated boundaries established at particular scales. The cultural identities often expressed through various Alma Mater initiatives were formed in continual interaction with the socially constructed scales at which they were established. Racial and gender classifications were constituted according to one's differential location within multiscaled relations of power and the way these relations were marked in specific places at particular times. The women of Alma Mater actively engaged in a spatialized politics in which they intended to contest and re-constitute differentiation. Migrant women struggled to transform the negative gendered and racialized spatial scales in which they traveled—in the local labor market, state, and neighborhood, and in their bodies.

The Emergence of Feminist Antiracist Politics
in a Changing, Modern-Provincial Italian City

All modern urban dwellers are, according to Simmel (1971), strangers, because they are constantly in contact with people who are both spatially near yet socially remote, and from whom they must detach themselves to avoid sensory overload. This detachment and edgy nervousness Simmel described are ways of life both culturally perfected and evaded in Turin, one of Italy's most modern provincial cities. Luisa Passerini described Turinese as taciturn and little given to gesticulation, but capable and willing to work hard (1984, 45). As a collective sense of self, the Turin character is counterposed to other stereotypes—for instance, of the "passionate Italian." Turinese see themselves as not given over to enthusiasms, a people who do not get carried away or even excited, but who are instead objective, or "see things as they are" (Passerini 1984).

In this busy industrial center of just fewer than one million inhabitants, acquaintances, friends, and family members regularly frequent the same cafés, markets, bakeries, butchers, and restaurants, mapping daily life along well-known routes. Eating *una pasta* or a brioche and coffee in a familiar café is at least a once-daily ritual. Local owners of bread, meat, and other small shops resist efforts to expand their hours of opening to Sundays and late nights for the convenience of visitors or a few Turinese residents willing to succumb to the rapid pace of English or American life. Social life revolves strongly around core family members and an extended family of friends, although many Turinese are friendly to newcomers. For all the political, economic, and social change that Turin dwellers have experienced over the past thirty years, the city remains a tightly knit nexus of traditional familial, social, and political relationships, where strangers include anyone from outside of Turin or the region of Piedmont (Levy 1996). Social distance is generally greatest between Turinese and postcolonial migrants or those from the most economically undeveloped parts of the world.

The arrival of immigrants from the third world and countries outside the European Union seems to remind Turinese that life lacks predictability and knowable boundaries (Cresto-Dino and Fornaris 1993). The presence of foreigners signals that the life of the past has been disrupted and is deteriorating. An Italian term for immigrants is *straniere* or *stranieri,* translated into English as either "stranger" or "foreigner,"[4] but which often carries the connotation of "stranger" as it is used in Turin society. Strangers are different from us and potentially dangerous; they oblige us to question the habitual way we do things (Melossi 2000). Almost a century after Simmel suggested that differences must be negotiated in the modern metropolis, the rhythm of modern capitalism has accelerated considerably. Turin dwellers must now deal with job uncertainties, the presence of diverse newcomers, and increasing economic connections with other European countries and nations around the world (Harvey 1989; Pred and Watts 1992).

The physical geography of Turin has not, however, kept pace with the social and economic transformation, with at least one exception. At the southern end of Turin sits part of the old, abandoned Fiat factory, Lingotto, redesigned in the late 1980s into an international concert hall, hotel, and upscale shopping plaza. The renovated factory still has a commanding presence along a block of Via Nizza, its concert hall flanked with colorful flags representing nations in the global landscape. Farther to the north and west, Turin's architecture appears somewhat more uniform—eighteenth- and nineteenth-century, with a small mix of some postmodern-style buildings. The city's international texture is marked more by its diversity of populations and growing number of immigrant businesses than by a bold, modern architectural style.[5] People travel through the city using private automobiles—typically compact Fiats—or a fairly reliable system of trams that run on rail lines through the center and out to the urban peripheries. Wide, straight, or slanted paved streets and avenues intersect with narrow cobblestone roads and open piazzas, many of them surrounded by small boutiques, bakeries, ice cream shops, restaurants, and cafés where elderly men can be seen milling about during the day, chatting with family or friends over a cup of coffee. The colors are muted grays, browns, tans, and yellows, with an occasional splash of a rosy Mediterranean pink or orange pastel. The absence of color in Turin relative to other Italian cities is echoed in a certain cool social reserve that the Tunisian migrant Salah Methnani described even among African and South American immigrants (Fortunato and Methnani 1997).

A central feature of everyday practices in this industrial town includes the visit to one of the neighborhood open markets, where fresh fruits, vegetables, and other consumables can be purchased from regular vendors to whom the newcomer should be introduced. A central market is located on Via Madama Cristina in the historical San Salvario neighborhood, near the train station, which until the 1980s attracted customers from the wealthy *colline,* or hills. In the 1990s, it came to be associated with African migrants from Nigeria, Senegal, and Morocco, who were not welcomed as vendors and customers by resident Italians. To the north of Turin is the old, expansive Porta Palazzo market in Piazza della Repubblica, where fresh produce is purchased in bulk and where one can find almost anything, from clothing and shoes to kitchen appliances, dairy products, meats, and household decorations. During the 1990s, the Porta Palazzo market became the site of a growing number of migrants and the traditional flea market, called the *balon,* which is open on the weekend and became characteristically multiethnic. In the surrounding neighborhood, numerous migrant-operated shops have opened, representing specifically African and Chinese cultural tastes. To the west of the city, where the Polytechnic University is located, is the Crocetta market, known primarily for designer clothing, bags, and shoes. Over the past decade, this market too has had a growing migrant presence, although several informants have told me that "Italians don't want migrants there."

The river Po runs along the eastern corridor of Turin, where nightclubs and restaurants cater to wealthy members of the old nobility and their children. Many such families reside in freestanding homes on the hills along the eastern side of the river, while the majority of Turinese own and live in old apartment flats called *case,* or homes. The hill side of the Po River is almost a separate place, with its own markets, piazzas, parks, and churches. But on the western, urban side of the Po, the Murazzi has become the site of a diverse and lively nightlife, attracting Italian as well as North African and other foreign youth. The Valentino park is also located along the urban fringe of the Po, where children may play soccer and where Italian families take their *passeggiata,* or stroll, after their Sunday meals, eating gelato, feeding ducks, and watching boats or performances. Over the last decade migrants have begun to use the park to play soccer, perform plays and musicals about migrant cultures and their experiences in Italy, and participate in festivals, featuring "ethnic" crafts.

International migrants represent culturally diverse populations, not only because of the wide range of countries from which they come, but also because of the differences between migrants from the same nation. There are abundant points of religious and political contrast and even contradiction between newcomers who engage in grassroots political organizations. Among Moroccan and Tunisian migrants, some were active in secular-based antigovernment politics in their countries of origin, while others are practicing Muslims uninterested in politics. The majority of these migrants maintain a wide range of religious affiliations, frequently connected with political activities. Some Islamic migrants from the Middle East and Northern and sub-Saharan Africa take assistance from Catholic charities and may even borrow Catholic church facilities to host religious services (Carter 1997). Many sub-Saharan, South American, and South Asian migrants are closely affiliated with Catholic or Protestant Church and voluntary organizations in Italy. In a context with a high level of political interest, consciousness, and activity, a number of migrants describe themselves as politically neutral, wishing to avoid affiliation with Italian political parties. Other newcomers, particularly those who arrived in Turin before the migration began to accelerate, willingly ally themselves with local political parties and trade unions. During the 1990s, several migrants became representatives for the CGIL (Confederazione Generale Italiana del Lavoro, Italian General Federation of Labor) and CISL (Confederazione Italiana Sindacati Lavoratori, Italian Confederation of Workers' Unions) trade unions. In the early 1990s, Italian women from the feminist organizations in the Casa delle Donne, historically connected with Italian left and extraparliamentary political parties, began to construct alliances with women migrants. Many voluntary organizations associated with the Catholic Church—for example, Caritas—have played an active role in helping to accommodate newcomers to Italy.

Although the labor movement is relatively weak today, traces of its passion remain in the activist culture that is a living feature of Turin. When migrants began to arrive in considerable numbers, many Turinese active in trade unions, feminist organizations, and Catholic and lay voluntary groups responded relatively quickly. These groups took some sort of action to better understand how migrants might fit into Turin society or sought to create places for migrants to sleep and eat and ways to receive some sort of health care. The majority of migrants worked in precarious jobs and lived in dilapidated housing, and many Turinese were inspired to challenge these social conditions. The category of "immigrant rights" began to emerge, becoming a new issue in grassroots and national Italian politics.[6]

Alma Mater became an idea when an interethnic group of migrant women who were members of an Italian African women's association,

AIDA (Associazione Italiana Donne Africane), floated the concept among friends and political acquaintances. AIDA was an association officially registered with and kept track of by the municipal government. The migrant women members from Somalia, Morocco, the Ivory Coast, Ethiopia, and Iran had attended universities in their countries of origin or the University of Turin and had lived in Italy for a number of years. For them, as for many other first-generation migrants in Turin, the arrival of migrants in the 1990s signaled a kind of cultural rebirth. They felt that their claims to cultural heritage and community had been stifled in an Italian society uninterested in and unaware of their rich cultural backgrounds. The concept of a grassroots women's political and business organization represented for them an attempt to develop an alternative space of respect for people of non-Italian social origins. The interplay of this first generation of migrants to Italy, who understood from their own experience what the meaning of standing apart from Italian society might be for newcomers, and the newcomer community most in evidence since the 1990s formed the basis of interethnic coalition (Merrill and Carter 2002). In Turin, they were located in a peculiar position, with insider knowledge of Italian cultural and social life as well as identification with their countries of origin.

The first generation of migrant women began to formulate the idea to design an intercultural space, where migrant women would teach the local population about "Other" cultures around the world and contest racism. They believed it necessary to teach Italians about diverse forms of cultural knowledge and to engage migrant women in work that deployed their skills and artistry as hairstylists, seamstresses, cooks, and traders. AIDA had acquired knowledge of Italian legal and bureaucratic procedures and contacts with Italians concerned about the rise of anti-immigrant sentiment and racism in Italy. In 1990, AIDA began to write a proposal to ask the municipal and regional governments for financial and physical support.

Several AIDA members were also participating in a research project sponsored by the Institute for Social and Economic Research (IRES) of the CGIL trade union. Vanessa Maher, an anthropologist at the University of Turin, along with Francesco Ciafaloni, an economic and labor historian working for IRES, and Jean Marie Tschotscha, a Rwandan political activist and French instructor, designed a unique research team from a diverse group of migrants living in Turin. The IRES team consisted of an interethnic group of researchers who studied the relationship between immigration and the Turin labor market. Many of the researchers had participated in local political actions at the University of Turin and in relation to the Italian trade unions, and some were politically active in their countries of origin. The first generation of migrants had considerable influence on a second generation that began to arrive during the late 1980s. They represented different cultural, political, and religious backgrounds, but were united by a common concern about the social and economic position of migrants in contemporary Italy. Many held political views to the political left of the CGIL trade union, which frequently operated according to policies of the Italian Communist Party (PCI) (S. Hellman 1988). IRES researchers included a mixture of first- and second-generation migrants who were sociologists, anthropologists, labor historians, engineers, political refugees, activists, civil servants, Catholics, and Muslims from diverse parts of the world, including Italy, the United States, Somalia, Ethiopia, Morocco, Cameroon, Rwanda, the Ivory Coast, and Egypt.

IRES researchers were often members of ethnic or other associations and initiatives designed to improve the position of migrants in Turin and had considerable ties to local migrant communities. The IRES team had a high social standing among Turin migrants, and many were active in efforts to win migrant representation, protection, and rights. The AIDA women who participated in the IRES research incorporated many IRES themes and concerns into their proposal for an immigrant women's center, including expressions of cultural difference, Italian racism, and the need for knowledge of Italian society and politics. AIDA also adopted a similar understanding of migrants as social actors with particular histories, political orientations, and cultural practices faced with Italian cultural and political hegemony. The researchers believed that migrants were exploited in the local labor market, denied rights to housing and health services, and misrepresented as culturally homogenous, with an Orientalist logic as too strange and poor to be considered members of Europe (Said 1978; IRES 1992).

When AIDA began to develop its proposal to create a migrant women's space, the IRES research team was in the process of interviewing migrants and listening to their stories about work experiences in Turin and other parts of Italy. Many migrant women from Somalia, Ethiopia, Senegal, Cape Verde, the Philippines, and other countries, employed as live-in domestic servants for Italian families, complained about working in demanding, tightly ordered Italian homes. Working environments varied, but there were stories of unjust conditions, such as heavy workloads or lengthy hours, caring for children or elderly parents, cleaning, doing laundry,

Jean Marie Tschotscha, 2001

shopping, and cooking. More than a few migrant women complained that they endured forms of exploitation and abuse, and were poorly treated by employers, denied heat in their rooms, or not given time to rest or eat meals. Other problems among these domestic workers included low pay, the absence of health care benefits due to the frequently "informal" status of the work, and sexual exploitation by male household members (IRES 1992). Many said that while living in Italian households, they could not live with their own children (Andall 2000), spend time with friends or family, or participate in language and other educational courses to acquire skills and knowledge of Italian society. Many domestic workers had acquired secondary or even university diplomas in their countries of origin, and others had firsthand experience operating small businesses, but the officers working at the Turin registry office *(anagrafe)* systematically refused to record these and other categories of specialization on their work documents (Carter 1997). Europe rejected their training and skill (Fortunato and Methnani 1997), and, like increasing numbers of young Italian women, many felt humiliated by the low-status nature of domestic service.[7]

A sharp division of labor in Italy occurs across gender lines, and women migrants have been relegated to positions in the labor market identified with "women's work" and the service sector. Domestic work represents only a portion of the work of migrant women, although it remains perhaps the most visible. Other areas of the hidden work world of migrant women include nursing, retail, various kinds of piecework and textile employment, agriculture, and caregiving, particularly in home care of the elderly (Merrill 2001; Andall 2000). Despite the drawbacks of domestic work, it is readily available and frequently offers more security than, for example, informal trade or short-term contract work in agriculture.

An additional problem for migrant women, particularly in the early 1990s, was the rapidly expanding local market for African female prostitutes, and there were many frightening stories about the seizure of passports, with young women forced into sexual labor.[8] African women with experience as traders, hairstylists, or seamstresses lacked the social and political networks and starter funds necessary to meet the social and legal requirements for establishing independent businesses, or even to work in local markets or for shop owners. Many women complained that if a straniera wanted to have a good job or to own her own business in Turin, "she'd have to be married to an Italian man." But a basic knowledge of and willingness to accept legal regulations may have been sufficient. For example, Italian law requires that a hairstylist work for two years as an apprentice to procure a license. The apprentice learns to cut and style European hair and to operate according to the culture of an Italian hair salon, with its own peculiar hygienic practices and other cultural mannerisms. Italians enter the training stage at a very young age, usually fifteen or sixteen. This is partly because during the apprenticeship period, when wages are too low to generate self-support, a young Italian can live at home with her or his family.

While family labor sustains Italian hair salons, migrants are unable to survive at extremely low wages. Women with specialized training in their countries of origin may be able to bypass the two-year apprenticeship period in Turin, but some find it difficult to procure translation of their documents. Other migrant women believe that, even with the appropriate documents, there is so much prejudice toward migrants that salon owners will not hire them. One West African woman told me, "Every time I go into a hair salon to ask for a job, they think I'm a prostitute." In 1990, there were no hair salons in Turin owned or operated by immigrants capable of styling African hair.[9]

Accounts of the many work-related and other social problems experienced by recently arrived migrant women prompted members of AIDA to search for solutions, hence the idea of a physical space to serve as a practical and symbolic locus. The association members debated the idea, drafted a proposal to the municipal and regional governments, and opened their idea to interested parties. The participants never reached full agreement about the design of Alma Mater. They debated the differences between migrant cultural practices, and some meetings ended in ethnonationalist arguments about the meaning of "collective migrant identity" and what it meant to be "African." Those with the most educational training and greatest command of Italian, often with considerable local knowledge and access to economic resources, made an effort to include some of the recent migrant women like Georgette, who had had little formal schooling. The less educated and newly arrived migrant women were not part of the social and political networks established between migrants who had studied at the University of Turin and who were often leaders of ethnic associations.[10]

At a meeting in spring of 1990, a small group of women and men from Kenya, the Ivory Coast, Cameroon, Senegal, Venezuela, and Somalia debated the idea. Georgette, who was present at the meeting, voiced her objection to the project, which, in her view, "could not work." She argued that the several hair salons would compete directly with each other, and suggested that African women could never work together cooperatively. Georgette said that she would prefer to remain "on her own," freelancing, with the ultimate goal of owning her own business. She referred to "jealousy" and "individualism" among African women, offending an East African woman who argued that this was a "personal" quality that did not characterize the majority of African women. A Senegalese man argued that people from the Ivory Coast (like Georgette) were so deeply assimilated into French society that they turned their backs on their compatriots. He suggested that Africans from the Ivory Coast had lost the African cultural practices of mutual assistance and solidarity described by the former president of Senegal, Leopold Senghor, and other Pan-African intellectuals, which many Senegalese migrants believed were still very much alive.

The women's center was conceived as a reference site for migrant women, a site where they could actively construct their own livelihoods and struggle against popular representations of migrants as sexually loose, morally corrupt, and untrustworthy. The space was envisioned as a place to promote, instead of reject, migrant women and their myriad cultural differences. They would construct work sites for women in the center itself and throughout Turin, including the production and sale of goods representative of diverse cultural backgrounds or crafted by migrant artisans. At this site, migrant women would sell African cloth, design clothing, and operate hairstyling salons and catering businesses representing diverse culinary traditions.

Turin is a city with numerous family-owned businesses, but it has needed to expand its entrepreneurial scope beyond local borders. The members of AIDA wished to contribute to a reversal of the trade patterns established when European countries colonized Africa and parts of Asia by selling their cultural commodities in Europe, and on their own terms. They hoped that, with the growing presence in Europe of people from former colonies, those from less economically developed areas were in a position to influence the distribution of goods and ideas within a wider Italian and European market. As Giovanna Zaldini (1992) wrote:

> We have imagined ALMA MATER as a place where women can carry out work activities derived from their own cultures, which immigrants want to make known and appreciated, and other activities that will only have the function of responding to the work needs of women, and to the exigencies of the market.

Another important aspect of the Alma Mater plan was to create formal recognition of the practice of "intercultural mediation." The first generation of migrants were frequently called on to play the role of informal mediator (cultural/social/political) between their community and Italian society, as well as between various factions, classes, castes, and/or ethnic divisions within their own community. Migrants had offered their services as mediators to Italian government offices free of charge, but now proposed a series of formal training courses for "cultural mediators" who would be able to work for gainful employment.

Expanding Boundaries

After months of planning, the leadership and other interested women reached a loose consensus about the formation of a migrant women's center. Many participants envisioned themselves as part of a grassroots politics, contesting Euro-Italian racism. The women defined themselves not as a special interest group posed against men, but as migrant women who were at an even greater disadvantage than their male counterparts in Euro-Italian society.[11] The majority of migrant women did not at this time define themselves as "feminist," which some equated with a form of "Western imperialism" that concerned itself only with equality between white women and white men. Even after the leadership had drafted an agenda and charter, there were never any clear ideas of a collective feminist migrant identity. The women united on the basis of their common experiences of cultural and economic alienation within Turin society, living daily in a world in which they were both present and invisible.

Referring to themselves as "ignored soldiers,"[12] AIDA members wrote a proposal to the municipal and regional governments, signed by nineteen migrant women from such countries as Morocco, Somalia, Kenya, the Ivory Coast, Yugoslavia, Spain, Germany, and Tunisia. Their use of the term "soldier" implied a global sense of identity, which contested the nationalism associated with the idea of a soldier fighting for the honor of a national territory. These were by contrast multiethnic postcolonial migrant women, describing themselves as political soldiers struggling for social justice *between* nations, in defense of multiple ethnicities, and against their relegation to the social peripheries. Their proposal outlined a project for a Centro di Donne Immigrate (Center for Immigrant Women), first presented to the Piedmont Regional Commission for Equal Opportunity for Men and Women (Piemonte Regionale Commissione Pari Opportunita' Uomo-Donna). They argued that life was especially difficult for migrant women who had left behind familial networks of support and were confronted with new cultural and religious practices that compelled them into struggle at every turn. They suggested further that migrant cultural diversity was ignored in Europe, or that their differences were used to justify exclusion from local society:

> This all occurs in a society that ignores our own cultures, marginalizes us because of our diversity, because of our origins, because of our color, and sees our diversity only from a negative point of view and never as a form of cultural enrichment. (Zaldini 1992)

The founding members described Alma Mater as a space for cultural exchange and *accoglienza,* a mediating space for migrant women who were isolated and without access to urban resources. They redefined the term *accoglienza,* commonly used in Centra di Accoglienza, to describe a space where migrants live when homeless and awaiting review of requests to enter Italy. Alma Mater used *accoglienza* to encompass a much wider idea of entry than to simply have a bed in which to sleep while waiting for formal processing. The women urged the Commission for Equal

Opportunity to sanction a proposal supported in the Martelli bill, which designated spaces of accoglienza for migrants. They argued that no centers had yet been designated specifically for migrant women.

The Commission for Equal Opportunity for Men and Women is composed of fifteen women appointed by the regional council *(giunta)*. Usually appointed every four years, these women represent the majority political parties in the regional parliament. The commission has a certain amount of funding at its discretion, which it might apply to various initiatives on the topic of women and work. It can also formulate proposals and present them to the regional or municipal council. When migrant women proposed Alma Mater, one of the members of the Commission for Equal Opportunity was also an active participant in the Turin feminist organization, Donne in Sviluppo (Women in Development), a subdivision of Produrre e Riprodurre (Production and Reproduction), from the local Casa delle Donne (Women's House). Donne in Sviluppo had expressed interest in organizing initiatives for migrant women, but Italian feminists were having difficulty establishing social connections with more than the "elite" or least disadvantaged among migrant women. Some complained that they did not know how to approach migrant women, because often when they

Giovanna Zaldini, 2001

met someone and sought to create a connection, they were greeted with a cold shoulder. The Alma Mater project provided Turin feminists with the opportunity to create an alliance with migrant women.

When the Commission for Equal Opportunity presented AIDA's proposal to the municipal government *(consiglio comunale),* all female council members voted favorably. The city council members agreed to sponsor the project by awarding it access to municipal property and providing funding. The project is reputed to have had considerable support from members of the PDS (Democratic Party of the Left),[13] who were interested in broadening its social base. Approval of the project could earn the political left the favor of two social categories: women and migrants. To go forward, the project had to be approved by the president of Reggio Parco, the industrial neighborhood on the northern fringe of Turin where it would be located. The neighborhood president was a woman and a member of the PDS who had taught at the abandoned school designated for the project. It was called Alma Mater, a girl's school for the children of female tobacco factory workers. Immigrant women decided to retain the original name of the school because participants could not agree on a name representative of ethnically and religiously diverse migrants.

To the considerable disappointment of the AIDA members who designed the conceptual framework for Alma Mater, the local government denied them the right to direct the organization's finances. The project had received approval from the mayor, city council, and neighborhood president, but a legal stipulation required an association to be more than five years old to direct such a large project, and AIDA did not meet these criteria. They rapidly created another association, with an even more culturally diverse membership, and waited for more than five years to direct Alma Mater. But for the organization to be funded by the government, the participants would have to find an older association willing to handle finances and other administrative matters. For this support, they turned to the Casa delle Donne.

Turin feminists in Donne in Sviluppo enthusiastically embraced the Alma Mater project. Several members of the organization were already volunteering their time and vehicles to help deliver North African meals ordered via telephone during an immigrant radio show. Others were indirectly involved with migrant women through international initiatives on behalf of female victims of the Gulf War and the war in Somalia. The association Produrre e Riprodurre, dedicated to issues of women's work and reproductive health, was particularly excited about the Alma Mater project. Forming an alliance of interethnic migrant women from AIDA and beyond, Turin feminists from Produrre e Riprodurre and Donne in Sviluppo put together the first Alma Mater directive body, composed of two Italian feminists, two Somalians, two Moroccans, and a Lebanese woman.

In a political context ripe for peaceful solutions to the growing immigrant crisis, migrant women and Italian feminists had persuaded the local government to donate a school building that other social-political organizations also sought to use. The municipal and regional governments provided funding to renovate the building and to finance a small but full-time administrative staff. This was an extraordinary feat of social and political maneuvering. At one point, when financial support promised Alma Mater by the government was insufficient, more than one Italian woman in Produrre e Riprodurre mortgaged her home. It was not uncommon for the urban and regional governments to give financial support to Catholic voluntary organizations that represented populations in need of social benefits, such as the drug addicted, desperately poor, and mentally disturbed, but this was the first time they had recognized anything like Alma Mater, an interethnic migrant women's group designed to challenge Italian racism and cultural hegemony.

Alma Mater members struggled to expand the spatial and ideological boundaries of the workplace, community, city, and nation (Merrill 2004). Migrant women designed the organization to challenge racist stereotypes of migrant women, create new forms of work or places in the local labor market, and educate the local population about migrant cultural backgrounds. The first migrant participants imagined a more equitable division of labor and distribution of symbolic power across both gender and racial lines. Alma Mater was intended to contribute to the remapping of cultural, political practices among migrants and Italians in Turin.

After obtaining financial and political support from the Italian government, Alma Mater applied for and received funding from the European Economic Union for several international initiatives. Early on, the European Union funded a training course for women entrepreneurs and to encourage the establishment of micro-enterprises and a three-year project on maternity practices in Italy and the Maghreb. One of these courses was administered by the United Nations organization NOW (New Opportunities for Women). The maternity project linked Italian with other European cities. Another course, funded by the municipal and regional governments, trained fifteen migrant "cultural mediators" *(mediatrici culturali)* as linguistic and cultural brokers between Italian institutions and migrants. The administrative staff at Alma Mater, who initially included four migrant women from parts of Africa and South America, was selected from the trained cultural mediators. In its first year, research and training sessions placed Alma Mater in a nexus of relationships throughout Turin and with other Italian cities such as Milan and Bologna. In its second year, the training programs linked women in Italian cities with the Maghreb, Barcelona, and Marseilles. From its earliest inception, Alma Mater was a multiethnic, international, and antiracist women's organization. Its objective was to "elaborate an innovative strategy of social politics." The organization's location, in an old working-class quarter on the outskirts of Turin, has become a microcosm of complex backgrounds and negotiations among Italians in this industrial city.

CHAPTER 2

Alma Mater: The Architecture of an Interethnic Social Politics

> [Alma Mater is a] place that is a kind of grand market of exchange relationships, a place not only of our voices, but of things, income, money, hopes, illusions, dreams, in order to reinforce our cultural and gendered identities.
> —*Giovanna Zaldini, "Il Centro Interculturale delle Donne di Torino"*

Aᴸᴹᴀ Mᴀᴛᴇʀ ᴏᴘᴇɴᴇᴅ ɪɴ Dᴇᴄᴇᴍʙᴇʀ 1993 in a large, brown and white stone, three-and-one-half-story building with a handicapped en-trance.[1] In the basement there is a Turkish bath (hammam), a laundro-mat,[2] a seamstress shop, an office, and a kitchen. Coming up a flight of stairs to the first floor are colorful posters of Alma Mater events, images of women, and a large office, which always appears to be private. Up an-other flight of stairs to the main floor is the Office of Cultural Mediation, a day care center, a library, a central office, a sitting and meeting room with an adjoining kitchen, two restrooms, and a long, spacious room for meetings and ethnic dinners. There are also rooms on a third floor with beds and for storage that victims of spousal abuse may temporarily oc-cupy. Alma Mater's now well-known theater group, Almateatro, which rehearses in the building, has written several interethnic plays and per-formed them in various parts of Italy and other parts of Europe. Civil servants working in social services for the municipal government and volunteers in nonprofit Catholic organizations regularly send migrants to Alma Mater. The Office of Cultural Mediation works directly with the Ufficio Stranieri e Nomadi (Office of Foreigners and Nomads). Local of-ficials regularly ask Alma Mater participants to help organize seminars and meetings about immigration issues; the organization frequently con-tributes to discussions organized by the local and national governments or trade unions about topics related to migrant women, such as genital

23

mutilation, the adoption of Eritrean and Somali children, and prostitution. In 1995 the CGIL (Confederazione Generale Italiana del Lavoro) trade union and Alma Mater organized a national forum on immigrant women that drew thousands of immigrants and other visitors from throughout the country.

The cultural mediators produced two work cooperatives, Mediazione and La Talea, both initially allotted space in the Alma Mater building. In the mid-1990s, Mediazione had a membership of approximately twenty migrants from various parts of the world, including a few men. Mediazione took charge of the laundry business located in Alma Mater's basement and specialized in a customized service of *ricette esotiche,* or exotic meals. Mediazione also offered language translations and services to youth, the elderly, and the disabled. This cooperative struggled for several years to make the laundry business a success, but because it was located far from most migrant residences in Reggio Parco, it was unable to acquire a stable clientele and was eventually removed from Alma Mater.

Mediazione was described as a cooperative of social solidarity, and its leaders decided early on to require that all its members have "black" skin pigment. This meant, for example, that only Moroccans, Tunisians, and Brazilians with dark skin color were invited to participate. The director, a Zairean woman, explained her view that black African women and men were treated with a greater degree of discrimination and prejudice in Italian society than "socially preferred" light-skinned people—for example, people of Hispanic, Middle Eastern, or Asian origin. Many Alma Mater members were taken aback by the racialized separatism in Mediazione, but the director argued for the necessity to mandate color classification to give darker-skinned persons a chance to succeed in a European world. In the end, Mediazione moved out of Alma Mater, but many of its members remained active members of the women's center.

The second Alma Mater cooperative, La Talea, administers the operations of the Turkish bath, also located in the basement of Alma Mater. This cooperative has been quite successful in a number of areas. Its membership of between twenty and twenty-five members is fully female and multi-ethnic, without chromatic distinction as a membership qualification. La Talea offers a variety of services to the public and private sector, including language translation and interpretation, nursing, and elder care. The cooperative was awarded several long-term contracts for paid full- and part-time migrant cultural mediators with municipal services such as the Ufficio Stranieri, hospitals, and schools. La Talea has produced several

Hammam, the Turkish bath in Alma Mater, 2001

films about immigrants, including *Semi di Zucco* (Pumpkin Seeds), shown to Italian elementary schoolchildren. It is also in charge of the highly successful Alma Mater theatrical group, Almateatro.

Most of Alma Mater's initiatives for empowering migrant women are geared toward bodily practices and representations, including health, birthing practices, sexuality, clothing and hair, dance, and food. The body holds considerable symbolic power in Italian society, as well as in many migrant cultures of origin. Alma Mater women seek to employ their bodies to represent the meanings migrants bring to the Italian context, expressed through movement, design, clothing, and health practices. Through this small but resonant spatial scale of the body, the women contest negative images of migrants in the mass media and popular and political discourse. They hope to substitute commodified images of migrant bodies as exotic and erotic with images of migrants as active, thoughtful beings with histories, curiosities, and feelings. Bodily health, a traditional concern in the American and European women's movements, is also of concern to these migrant women and Italian feminists. Alma Mater has sent many cultural mediators to local hospitals, especially the maternity hospital, to help Italian doctors and nurses understand the bodily concepts of immigrant women. A number of immigrant women, for example, have had clitorectomies (surgery to remove or alter the clitoris), and migrant women that give birth in Italian hospitals with particular Italian birthing practices have often found it difficult to adapt to medical expectations quite different from those with which they were raised. Cultural mediators have been charged with explaining to Italian medical specialists how to approach these migrant women. The Turkish bath also centers on women's bodies and their communicative capacities. The bath is one of Alma Mater's most successful projects, attracting Italian women from all over the city. Unfortunately, the bath employs only a few women, and for a long time part of its earnings was devoted to Alma Mater maintenance.[3]

During the first few years of its operation, Alma Mater was supported by grants from the local and regional governments and the European Union. By the mid-1990s, these funds had run dry, and the center could no longer employ a full-time administrative staff. Alma Mater was forced to generate its own income, and its members were forced to offer their time as volunteer workers. While struggling to remain afloat, it had, as one East African migrant put it, become a "feather in the cap of the local government," which continued to send many migrants to its door for free advice and cultural mediation. Alma Mater sought a number of small grants during the mid-1990s, but greater resources were sorely needed. In 1998, the organization received a large grant from the Center-Left national government, on which it thrived financially until a new administration cut back this funding.

When I purchased an Alma Mater membership card in September 1996, I was member 598 for that year. In June 2001, when I renewed my membership, I was member 3,108 for that year alone. I was one of a growing group of Alma Mater members from all over the world. By 1995, it had become an interethnic organization widely known throughout the nation, which many other Italian cities sought to emulate as an example of women's intercultural solidarity.[4]

Many Alma Mater members actively promote antiracist initiatives and migrant rights. Some participate in political activities in Turin, and others are connected with political and social activities in their countries of origin. A number of Somali women, for example, have played a role in their country's post–civil war reconstruction. Some Moroccan women in Turin are also active in promoting migrant women's rights both in Italy and in Morocco. Many other migrant women, like Georgette, are simply too preoccupied with the daily effort to feed and house themselves to exhibit much interest in abstract or long-term political issues. This at times puts them at odds with Italian feminists and with other immigrants who

Sonia Oduware Aimiumu, Laura Scagliotti, and Giovanna Zaldini in the Alma Mater meeting room during a workshop on racism, 2001

urge postcolonial migrants to participate in political actions for the sake of their compatriots in Europe.

Identity and Space: Intercultura and the Emergence of Mediazione Culturale

Maria Viarengo, an Ethiopian-Italian woman who has lived in Turin for more than twenty-five years, said in 1995:

> Until the migrants arrived in great numbers just a few years ago, Turinese had absolutely no knowledge of anyone outside of Italy. Everyone else was just "out there somewhere," and they didn't have any interest in knowing anything about the world that people live in outside of this small place.

Her statement expresses a widely felt sentiment among newly arrived and first-generation migrants in Turin. In the mid-1990s, many described experiences of cultural alienation within a context that Anna Belpiede of the Ufficio Stranieri refers to as Italian *monocultura,* or monoculture. The

Maria Viarengo, 2001

term "monoculture" refers to a spatial location culturally identified as strictly "Italian" (Belpiede 1995). Cultural and historical memories are inscribed in the physical and social geography of Turin through buildings, piazzas, monuments, and daily practices. Certain piazzas, for example, demarcate major Italian working-class and student demonstrations of the 1960s and 1970s. Streets are named after male historical figures like Cavour Garibaldi and Antonio Gramsci. Shops and markets sell Italian cheese, wine, bread, sliced meat, pastries, clothing, and shoes.[5] Large factory buildings, even those that stand idle, are a visible testament to the workerist culture of Turin. Residents identify various neighborhoods with southern or northern Italian working classes and the bourgeoisie. Castles, areas of the Turin hills, leisure activities such as opera attendance, and some restaurants are associated with the Italian nobility of the House of Savoy. There are a series of places infused with such an immediate sense of local meaning and memory that the unseen and unfelt web of connection to people or places beyond Turin's physical boundaries is forgotten, excluded, or denied. In popular discourse, newcomers are automatically classified outside of local historical memory, belonging to worlds far away, different, unknown.

Naturalized representations of seamlessly unified, culturally homogenous, and coherently structured lived spaces (cities, villages, nations), claiming to represent "the one identity," render peripheral and exclude real heterogeneities (Jones and Natter 1997; Hall 1991b). In daily practices, space and identity are frequently contested, although many discursive histories tend to obscure differences and antagonisms. It is arguable that before international immigrants arrived, Turin was already a culturally heterogeneous place, and that workers and managers, southern and eastern Italian as well as local Turinese and "Piedmontese," and Catholic, Jewish, Protestant, and atheist political traditions and identities crisscrossed and conflicted with each other. But by the late twentieth century, Turin had become a field of even greater social contestation and negotiation with the arrival of postcolonial migrants in growing numbers and with the self-conscious effort among the first generation and their Italian allies to construct more inclusive forms of social politics. Contemporary migrant women and men strive for inclusion in urban spaces previously reserved for some Italians, and to infuse these spaces with their interpretations of culture, work, and sociality.

With the appearance of international populations in Turin, regional and municipal administrations began to support the training of a new category of employee to act as mediator between administrators and migrant populations. Postcolonial migrants designed an experimental category of work, called cultural mediation, to create spaces within Turin public offices in which migrant cultures might be represented and included without necessarily becoming "assimilated." Migrants also planned to create a category of migrant employee that could work legally for the Italian state. Until then, it was legally impossible for noncitizens to work in public offices because employment is permanent and guaranteed within the Italian state. Cultural mediators could not become permanent employees, but could instead work on a contractual basis for state agencies. Membership in cooperatives and associations made it legally feasible for migrants to work for the Italian government on at least a temporary basis. Cultural mediation was intended to address numerous difficulties faced by migrant populations in Italy, including the relaxation of rigid Italian bureaucratic procedures. Through cultural mediation, postcolonial migrants struggled to pry apart static Italian rules governing access to knowledge and resources, and to insert a fluid category of worker to negotiate between public institutions and private migrant social networks.

Another purpose of cultural mediation was to help prepare civil servants to deal with migrants. At a meeting held in Alma Mater, Piergiorgio

Maggiorotti of the Turin Department of Health Education (USSL, Settore Educazione Sanitaria USSL Torino) stressed that Italian civil servants are not even trained to communicate with *Italian* citizens—limits that are magnified when such persons are confronted with diverse migrants. Maggiorotti explained that the Italian organizational model and philosophy is based on the presentation of official documents. When civil servants are faced with stranieri who may not possess the precise documents, or with those that have them but appear different, the civil servants become nervous and do not know how to respond to unknown persons who introduce new and unprecedented elements into established procedures (Maggiorotti 1993).

In the late 1980s, newly arrived migrants, many unable to speak Italian, were not informed about the complicated bureaucratic procedures required to live, work, and acquire health care or other social benefits in Italy. Turin social services were unprepared for the sudden influx of migrants, and personnel were not trained to receive them. Instead, many first-generation immigrants volunteered their time as informal cultural mediators to various state agencies such as the *questura* (police station), Ufficio Stranieri, schools, hospitals, and prisons. Beginning in 1982, when the Ufficio Stranieri was created, Italian officials asked migrants in ethnic associations to volunteer their time on an informal basis (Belpiede 1995, 1996). These volunteers translated languages, in many instances acting as temporary bridges between one set of meanings and another. According to Anna Belpiede of the Ufficio Stranieri, there was a "fertile interlocution" between public services and immigrant associations in Turin. Without the help of first-generation migrants, newcomers frequently met with hostility from Italian civil servants who had never before been faced with so many immigrants, and who were in the habit of treating even Italian citizens in a harsh, often demoralizing manner.

The Italian bureaucratic system has been described as labyrinthine, with its apparently endless procedural rules (Haycroft 1987). It is not unusual for Italian citizens to become frustrated with the system, despite being accustomed to living with it on a daily basis. Postcolonial newcomers are at an added disadvantage. While, for example, the Martelli legislation was being put in place, it was not uncommon for civil servants to claim not to be aware of or to deliberately ignore these laws when faced with a migrant. For example, health care privileges were frequently denied (Carter 1997).

To address these problems of translation and interpretation, several migrant groups, including Alma Mater, proposed to train cultural mediators to act as formal brokers between Italian state institutions and migrants (Belpiede et al. 1999). In addition to the Alma Mater association Produrre e Riprodurre, the multiethnic association Harambe was awarded government money to teach several courses (Varagliotti 1993).

The model that migrants drew on to propose government-supported training programs for cultural mediators was that of the "150 hours" of courses *(cento-cinquanta ore)* created by the Italian labor movement. In 1973, Italian trade unions won the right for workers to take 150 hours of courses on any topic during company time without losing pay. The labor movement designed this program as a way to break down class distinctions based on educational differences and to give some workers the opportunity to earn their basic educational certificates while broadening the intellectual horizons of others (Barkan 1984; Lumley 1990). The unions ran the programs and employers paid their employees while they took courses for up to three years. The course offerings represented a wide range of topics and were open to housewives, students, and workers. Feminists from New Left groups designed some of the courses for women—for example, in health education, the history of women, and women's work. Students, feminists, unionists, and workers were drawn together in the 150-hour courses to discuss their experiences and specialized knowledge (Lumley 1990).

The cultural mediation courses were also taught with the goal of providing quality instruction for workers. The training staff drew from a range of health and social services practitioners, university professors, and migrants with cultural knowledge. To follow courses on the topic of foreign cultural practices, civil servants took time out of their workdays. Produrre e Riprodurre courses trained professional cultural mediators to work in Alma Mater. The intention was to create a category of immigrant civil servant to be hired as cultural mediator in Italian public and private institutions.

The Alma Mater courses were intended to promote intercultural understanding in Turin. Training-program documents emphasize the importance of professional mediators to encourage and exemplify equality between Italians and immigrants. The women who organized the first training programs were concerned about transforming Italian society into a place tolerant of and open to learning from cultural differences. As an Italian feminist described the courses, "They intend to capitalize upon the resources of female immigrants, to construct a more just and richer society from the meetings and exchanges between different people." And in a rather zealous statement, one of the original members of Donne in Sviluppo (Women in Development), who played an instrumental role in promoting Alma Mater, described the courses and Alma Mater as intended

> to contribute to the creation of Turin as a civil society organized dif-
> ferently, in which all women, including immigrant women . . . can find
> space. Only in this way can one work toward the construction of a truly
> new and multiethnic society. (Battaglino 1993)

To win the funding from the Turin municipal government for Alma Mater cultural mediators, Produrre e Riprodurre argued that women play a critical role as cultural mediators, trained as negotiators in disputes and relationships within families and schools and among medical profession-als and neighbors. This "women's knowledge," Italian feminists argued, was not systematically developed, yet was particularly useful in a context of international immigration with an absence of institutional structures to receive migrants (Battaglino 1993; Scagliotti n.d.). These Italian and migrant women of Alma Mater attempted to legitimate hidden aspects of social structure throughout the world, the area in which women act as so-cial gateways or barriers to the private world of families (Goddard 1987). Instead of advocating the restriction of women's familial knowledge to the private, familial realm, Alma Mater women suggested that a woman's informal role as mediator ought to be used and expanded within the pub-lic sphere. Cultural mediators would represent entire migrant and ethnic populations instead of small familial units.

The Alma Mater courses in cultural mediation were taught by uni-versity professors, civil servants in social and health services, immigrant women with social work experience, feminists in Produrre e Riprodurre, and women involved in social cooperatives. The UNESCO center offered Italian language courses to trainees. Migrant and Italian women attend-ed seminars on such themes as the history of the Italian women's move-ment, the family of *extracomunitari* (people from non-European Union states), women's health, and genital mutilation. Strategies of intercultural communication were taught and one-month apprenticeships arranged for trainees. Migrants apprenticed in the Sant'Anna Maternity Hospital, a pediatric hospital, the Ufficio Stranieri, the Informazioni Salute per Immigrati (Center for Information on the Health of Immigrants) of the De-partment of Health Education, elementary schools, and a nursery school (Battaglino 1993; Scagliotti n.d.). Apprentices were expected to acquire knowledge of Italian institutional practices, including how to interpret verbal and nonverbal forms of communication.

The theme central to all courses was that of cultural translation, or methods to exchange intercultural knowledge and understanding. Mediators would interpret multiple forms of expression to bridge understandings between persons from two or more different cultural backgrounds. In this way, migrants could institutionalize some degree of migrant control over the flow of human knowledge from Africa, Southeast Asia, and Latin America into Western Europe. Within a Turin Gramscian tradition, Alma Mater sought to attack key sites of state power and authority, sites of power as knowledge where hegemony is produced and where the inequalities are reproduced with migrant women at the bottom of the social hierarchy (Balbo and Manconi 1992).

Between 1992–93, when the courses were taught, and 1996, a relatively small number of migrants obtained temporary contracts as cultural mediators in, for example, the Ufficio Stranieri, the Sant'Anna Maternity Hospital, and the Office of Cultural Mediation within Alma Mater itself. The Ufficio Stranieri's office for minors from non–European Union member states works regularly with Alma Mater cultural mediators. Anna Belpiede, the director of that office in 1996, was enthusiastic about cultural mediation, describing it as an innovative form of modern bureaucracy that brings a degree of flexibility to an otherwise rigid system. Each day, Belpiede works with migrant women who need help locating secure housing, who understand little about Italian society, and who are in turn barely understood by the majority of Italian civil servants. Cultural mediators facilitate communication between the Italian state and migrant populations, which is often very difficult given the differences between bureaucratic practices in Italy and in other parts of the world:

> It is increasingly apparent that there is a contradiction between the way that services are provided in Italian institutions, and the organizational models and diverse cultural codes employed by the foreign populations living in Italy. (Belpiede 1996, 59)

Belpiede further argues that mediators promote equality and act as pathways into a complex set of personal networks between migrants, with the sort of access to understanding that the Italian state does not have:

> In Turin, there are many ways to understand the function of cultural mediation, but we are currently in agreement about the need to utilize

cultural mediation for the promotion of access to equal opportunity among foreign persons that contribute to Italian institutions, and on the fact that inter-cultural mediators are actively engaged in the inner world of immigration. (1996, 59)

Belpiede, who hopes for a local world with solidarity between Italians and migrants, sees migrant interfamilial and friendship networks as infrastructures, accessible to Italian civil servants through the mediation of immigrants (1995).

Despite its hopeful beginnings, problems have arisen in connection with cultural mediation. The social conditions that prompted Alma Mater and the association Harambe to propose the formal training of cultural mediators do not seem to have been at the core of state and official interests in the courses. Harambe was eager to train migrant cultural mediators as well as Italian civil servants ill-prepared to receive newcomers for the purpose of demarcating permanent representative structures for migrants in the Italian state. Alma Mater, with its philosophical stress on interculturalism and multiethnic society, was not as clearly dedicated to establishing a site of migrant representation inside the Italian government. Traditional Turin feminism maintains a distance from state institutions and political parties, based on a philosophy of opposition to state authorities instead of reform and co-optation. It was for these reasons that 1970s Italian feminists worked through extraparliamentary organizations. However, Alma Mater was designed to create work sites for unemployed or marginally employed migrant women. With their ambivalent relationship to state institutions, Italian feminists in Alma Mater had not made certain that the public services established clear policies about employing cultural mediators, and for this reason the services were not committed to sustaining these work sites (Maggiorotti 1993). Some civil servants did not want to share their designated work space with migrants or to forfeit their principal position as knowledge brokers for migrants whom they considered outside the social and political geography of Turin. Several civil servants may have been willing to learn something about migrant cultures, but to move over and make space for newcomers, to give up something to which they had laid claim, seemed to ask for more human flexibility than the system was designed to encourage.

In the early 1990s, the Ufficio Stranieri began to hire cultural mediators on a part-time basis. These migrants received salaries of approximately one thousand dollars per month, commensurate with the income of low-skilled Fiat workers. Associations and cooperative organizations of migrants won contracts for mediators to work in public institutions. The Ufficio Stranieri eventually hired migrants from countries such as Morocco, China, Senegal, Somalia, and Nigeria in positions guaranteed for two years with the possibility of renewal. But in 1996, the municipal government decided to open competition for mediator positions, asking all interested associations and cooperatives to submit proposals, including plans to improve mediator tasks and to designate a salary bid. What developed was a sort of bidding war, with competition between migrants running high, or, as a CGIL official said, the policy had created a *guerra dei poveri,* or "war among the poor."

A cultural mediator trained in one of the Alma Mater programs lost her job at the Ufficio Stranieri and was replaced by a man from her country of origin with a university degree who had not taken a training course to become a professional cultural mediator. This incident demonstrates the absence of established standards about what does and does not constitute qualification as a cultural mediator, and exposes the precariousness of migrant cultural mediation in Turin, even in what was assumed to have been one of the most stable employment sites. The social service administration created a highly flexible practice of hiring, which made it possible for them to easily replace cultural mediators whom the managerial staff did not like personally or who may not have worked well or may not have known the "right" people in positions of authority. In the end, some higher-income bidders lost positions, joining the ranks of the immigrant marginally employed.

There is a great deal to admire about the creative efforts of Alma Mater and Italian feminists. They have committed themselves to social change in Turin, contributing to a more equitable social world tolerant of and with perhaps some knowledge of cultural differences. But one needs caution about an intercultural world as a solution to all sorts of social problems. The expression of different identities, if possible, is not in itself a sufficient method with which to challenge established institutional practices with access to resources and knowledge limited to Italian insiders. When the finances tighten as the Italian welfare state continues to roll back expenditures, those newcomers added to a system in a temporary and ambiguous space of cultural mediators may be the odd ones out.

CHAPTER 3

Limiting the Laboring: Industrial Restructuring and the New Migration

This is still an industrial city, but based on different sorts
of industry than thirty years ago. It's now more like Seattle
than Detroit in the sense of more high tech firms. . . .
There's a demand—there are 5,000 jobs, without
the workers. There's been a downgrading of skills.
—*Francesco Ciafaloni, labor historian*

Alma Mater isn't going well now because no one has
any income, and how can you justify this to your family?
The state gives little money, and that only late. People have
gotten frustrated and discouraged. The Caritas associations
have other income; they have many private donators
so they don't have to wait for the state's money. Anyway,
for non-Catholic organizations there is not much money.
The Catholic associations have more money. People
give their money to get a piece of Paradise.
—*Giovanna Zaldini, Somali immigrant*

A FTERNOONS IN ALMA MATER are often buzzing with intense activity. The Almateatro theater group may be dragging props into the large third-floor conference room in preparation for a rehearsal. In the library, there is frequently a meeting between staff and trade union representatives, civil servants from public social service offices, or university professors. Young children may be heard playing in the *nido*, or day care room. And visitors may be milling about in the hallways and sitting room or reading wall postings, such as articles about immigrants or leaflets about courses, initiatives, ethnic dinners, or African dance courses. Most days, the office phone is ringing frequently, and the woman designated to handle the reception desk responds to queries and problems that require her to enlist other Alma Mater staff with special knowledge or areas of expertise.

It is not unusual to see migrant women from places as diverse as

Argentina, Peru, Somalia, Senegal, and Yugoslavia seated in the main office, expressing their difficulties in languages translated by mediators, usually members of Alma Mater. Newcomers often hear about Alma Mater from other immigrants or Italians working in public offices like the Ufficio Stranieri. Many migrants are homeless. On one occasion, two Romanian women sit with tears in their eyes as several members of Alma Mater seek to help them locate a place to sleep. For the past few nights, they have slept in the train station. Alma Mater's director manages to find them a couple of beds in one of the local charity organizations directed by Catholic nuns. The Italian director turns to me and asks, "What am I supposed to do? They don't have anywhere else to stay!" Her defensive attitude is prompted by a wish to justify the use of Catholic voluntary networks, viewed by many as enemies of progressive or left-wing feminism in Turin. Alma Mater frequently contacts, and is contacted by, Catholic networks. In 2001, a cultural mediator, a Yoruba woman from Nigeria, was contracted to help Catholic nuns and former Nigerian prostitutes communicate with one another. After submitting the names of the prostitutes' "sponsors" to the Italian authorities, the Catholic Church provides them with a place to live for six months.

Many migrant women visit Alma Mater hoping to find a job. Although Alma Mater was never designed to function as an employment agency, many staff are reluctant to turn away migrant women with few, if any, social contacts in Turin, and who, it is believed, risk being swept into the network of prostitution if left without other recourse. Therefore, should a family or private firm phone Alma Mater to ask for a female worker—usually a domestic servant or an elder care provider—the request will, most likely, not be turned down. The information will be taken, and if a migrant woman comes into the Alma Mater building searching for work, she may be referred to the potential employer. The work offered is more often than not in the formal sector, which means that to be eligible for it, a migrant woman must have a legal document authorizing "permission of stay" *(permesso di soggiorno)*. Although referring women to undocumented work in the informal economy is discouraged, sometimes Alma Mater staff will put aside their law-abiding principles to help migrant women with no other apparent means of survival. As one of the Italian feminist administrators of Alma Mater remarked: "I've given up living by ideals. In this context, people are in need of basic things to survive, so that ideology has to measure itself against the reality of daily practices."

Regarding labor, one of the central concerns that motivated the creation of Alma Mater was to establish an actual place where migrant women would engage in small-scale entrepreneurial activities. Many migrant and Italian women considered self-employment as a productive alternative to domestic service and the illicit activities surrounding the sex trade. Divers migrant women were already engaged in informal trade within their own migrant networks, but these exchanges tended to remain closed to the Italian public. To begin with, Alma Mater was supposed to constitute a tangible space for women to conduct economic activities representative of their cultural-historical backgrounds and to develop a local market for their goods. The act of performing domestic service was anathema to some, and became a source of conflict even within the Alma Mater organization itself. There was considerable tension during Alma Mater's initial years around the need to keep the Alma Mater building clean and tidy. When the building was opened, few members volunteered to do any cleaning, an activity associated with domestic service and, for many, a form of servitude and exploitation. No one wished to be seen clearing tables after meals, washing dishes, dusting tables, and so on. A local scholar and activist described some of the effects that disdain about household or cleaning work had on the daily functioning and success of Alma Mater in 1996:

> The immigrant women feel they have to get something out of Alma Mater, but they don't have to contribute anything. Who is to pay the light bills, etcetera? Now there are only two bills paid by the *comune* (city council). The comune doesn't give as much money to them as to other associations, and Alma Mater is not making any money. The laundromat is not making any money because everyone argues about the type of work it is, i.e., *cleaning*. The immigrants don't want to give up any money from the co-ops, from the Almateatro, from the baths. They ought to give some 5 percent of their earnings to the place for upkeep, etcetera, but they refuse to even think of it. Instead, they blame the city government for everything. They take money to live on, OK, but then how is Alma Mater to be maintained?

To set an example, Alma Mater members with the most formal schooling began to clean, and the issue was brought up for discussion during meetings. However, many migrant members continued to complain, either openly or secretly, that Alma Mater's Italian administrators wished only to maintain the position of migrant women as third world "servants" to Europeans.

Setting aside the intrinsic flaws that may exist in Alma Mater's effort to engage in entrepreneurial activity as oppositional practice, the issue of how an organized group of migrant women might gain rewarding entry into the Northern Italian urban political economy requires examination. At its inception, Alma Mater's cooperatives, particularly Mediazione, sought for their members whatever contracts they could obtain in Turin. Mediazione's flyer advertised a "cooperative of social solidarity" that offered services to children, the elderly, and the disabled in homes, hospitals, day care centers, retirement facilities, or mental asylums. The cooperative members hoped to procure well-paid and skilled or semiskilled social service employment, but the very framework of their self-descriptions could be easily construed as suggesting that members would eagerly engage in domestic services of all kinds. Mediazione, which operated the Alma Mater laundromat, encountered considerable difficulty locating work for its membership, and most of them were employed in some variety of part-time domestic service. It is simply not easy for migrant women to locate diverse forms of employment in Italy: "They are lucky to have anything at all," is a common expression. Another Italian volunteer in Alma Mater commented, "They come here thinking Italy is a rich country, and it is not . . . that they can find work here, a better life. So many are coming in, every day—the poor, the desperate, the needy." Among the eighteen members of the Alma Mater cooperative La Talea, nine acquired contracts that provided stable work at the end of 1996. A tenth had lost her contract as a cultural mediator in the Ufficio Stranieri. Five of the ten women worked at night doing cleaning and care work in an elderly community. Two others were employed to oversee and perform massages at the Turkish bath, hammam. The eighth was retained as a cultural mediator at the Ufficio Stranieri. And the ninth and tenth were the director and assistant directors of the cooperative itself. Thus, it was extremely difficult for migrants to locate employment that was not in some measure a form of domestic or caretaking service.

In the 1990s, distrust and competitiveness were rife in Alma Mater, in part traceable to the basic fact that money was so scarce. Many early administrators were not paid the monies promised by the local administration, which may be attributed to government inefficiency. It is common to search for someone to blame, including state agencies, "Italian feminists," or other migrants. To understand the frustration that many migrant women and men experience in an effort to improve their lives, we must examine the manner in which they are situated within a Turin labor mar-

The Gran Madre di Dio Church as seen in 1996 from Piazza Vittorio Veneto, where the IRES CGIL office was located

ket that has been in the process of rather dramatic transformation since the 1970s. The growing demand for domestic service, including elder care, is in some measure a side effect of shifts that have occurred within the local labor market during the past twenty years. There is a considerable amount of tension between frequently held migrant expectations and the realities of Turin's economy, which cannot, ultimately, be distinguished from the racialized manner in which international migrants are situated in Italy and which inform local hiring and dismissal practices. As flexible work forms and increasing job segmentation become the orders of the day in Turin as elsewhere, migrants are swept into a system not of their own making, and which they may or may not prove able to significantly alter.

Fiat in Turin: A Company Town in Transition

From 1945 until the 1980s, Turin was characterized as a company town, where economic and demographic growth was driven by Fiat, one of the most prominent family-owned businesses in Italy. With the postwar rise of Fiat, Turin became home to the largest industrial proletariat in Europe and a quintessential worker city (Carter 1997). The economies of Turin and of the Piedmont region overall depended almost exclusively on the production of automobiles and the accumulation strategies adopted by

Fiat managers and the company owners, the Agnelli family (Corsico 1987). The city hosts other industries, but until recently few were independent enough not to have been in some manner linked with Fiat. The company has generated much of Turin's private sector employment, either directly or indirectly through multiplier effects. Along with automobiles, Fiat also produces industrial and agricultural machines, parts, and systems for trains and trams. Arnaldo Bagnasco points out that the importance of Fiat for the Turin economy far exceeds the income generated by large, mass-producing automobile plants (1986). The indirect influences of the firm are far-reaching. Fiat has always been linked to hundreds of small contractors and subcontractors and, on a more abstract level, to financial concessions. Castronovo writes:

> From metallurgy to rubber, from the construction of machinery to spherical cushions and of varnish, from the production of loose and spare parts, the major part of the system of production in Turin was formed or developed around the automobile industry. (1987, 367)

Beyond its grip on the economy of Turin and the region of Piedmont, Fiat has dominated the direction of local political administration, urban development, class composition, and the very texture of Turin society and culture (Bagnasco 1990; Locke 1995; A. Segre 1994). Gallino (1990) describes Turin's political administrative system as bifurcated between the community and a vast zone of diluted and blurred politics mediated by the parties and unions, with little in between. The everyday lives and identities of a substantial portion of the local labor force were until the past decade drawn inexorably into the orbit of dependent and primarily unskilled factory work. Under the hegemony of Fiat, Turinese society developed along relatively simple class lines, polarized between an industrial bourgeoisie and a proletarian working class. Donald Carter describes Turin as a place of contradictions, a working-class city with a premodern social world, which in the evening "closes up like a small provincial town" (1997). Paradoxically, Turin is also home of the former Italian monarchy, once an international center of court society with private clubs for the aristocracy. The city continues to be comprised of two worlds: the first, an elite center of art and music, and the second, a restricted world in which social life is characterized by the centrality of work in the day-to-day lives of Turin inhabitants. A central feature of the dual class division is a pronounced regional-ethnic differentiation demarcated by the concentration of southern Italians in inferior, low-skilled jobs, with a pronounced ceiling on southern social mobility (Gallino 1990; N. Negri 1982).

From the early moments of the great postwar expansion, Fiat drew workers from a national labor market, stimulating mass migration and urban growth. Lured by the promise of stable employment, migrants traveled to Turin from the rural hinterlands of Piedmont, the northeastern province of Veneto, and above all from the Italian south, or mezzogiorno. Between 1945 and 1973, employment at Fiat increased by an average of twelve thousand workers per year (Michelsons 1989, 440). From 1951 to 1971, the population of Turin grew by 63 percent, a dramatic figure, considering that during the same period population growth for the entire country was 13.7 percent (Castronovo 1987, 383). Between 1951 and 1971, the number of manual workers in Turin industry expanded from 271,000 to 514, 370 (Castronovo 1987). And in 1961, almost two-thirds of Turin's workforce was employed in industry.

During the early 1950s, production plants were located along the central axes of Turin's metropolitan zone, but Fiat progressively expanded its activities to the urban peripheries. The company's expansion prompted development of two *cinture,* or industrial belts, including the new site at Rivalta that employed approximately twenty thousand workers (A. Segre 1994, 99). This new production site, as well as a series of subcontracting firms located in the belts, triggered the beginning of a residential shift from the urban center to the peripheries. The Turin peripheries now constitute some 90 percent of urban space (Dematteis, quoted in Cresto-Dino and Fornaris 1993, 17).

Following the Second World War, Fiat was able to incorporate Fordist strategies of mass production, leading it down a path of growth that contributed significantly to the so-called Italian economic miracle (1958–1963).[1] Years earlier, the company was already among the first in Europe to adopt the Fordist organizational style and production strategy. But during the late 1970s, Fiat entered into another phase of radical organizational transformation, when the Fordist system of centralized, hierarchically organized assembly-line production, which concentrated labor in large plants, began to lose efficiency. Fordism was too rigid and cost-inefficient to sustain high levels of profit under slackening demand, increasing international competition, the diffusion of new technologies, and the need to respond to or to create new market niches.[2] Almost all automobile producers were experiencing difficulty as a consequence of high energy costs and decreasing consumer demand (Harvey 1989). But Fiat's troubles were intensified by the company's highly centralized organizational structure, its lack of investment in new technologies, and the disruptive consequences of the labor movement during the 1960s.[3] Like many other large manufacturing firms around the world, Fiat began to restructure its organization of production, replacing Fordism with a version of what David Harvey has referred to as a system of "flexible accumulation" (1989).

The industrial restructuring and downsizing of Fiat began during the mid-1970s, and in various phases has continued into the present. The company has sought increasing flexibility and speed in response to market "needs" (Michelsons 1989).[4] The main features of the organization's restructuring process have included investment in new technologies, a new and more flexible production strategy, rationalization of the company's network of suppliers, massive worker layoffs, and further weakening of trade union strength within the factories (Comito 1982; Volpato 1996).

During the 1980s, Fiat invested heavily in new process technologies such as industrial robotics and computer-assisted design (CAD). The company installed more than two thousand robots in its various plants. The introduction of these new technologies had a considerable impact on the composition and organization of work. For instance, with the introduction of Robotgate, an electronically controlled welding system in one of Fiat's shops at Mirafiori,[5] the need for workers decreased by almost 50 percent (from 247 to 137 workers). And while semiskilled workers had composed more than 70 percent of the labor force in the 1970s, after the introduction of Robotgate the proportion of these manual workers decreased to only 15 percent of all employees. At the same time, the employment of highly skilled workers grew from 16 percent to more than 64 percent of the shop's workforce (Locke 1995, 110).

To diversify products, Fiat revamped its product strategy, further decentralizing production by reconceiving the automobile as a modular system of interchangeable components shared among Fiat's different models. This approach enhanced the variation of models and made it possible to achieve greater economies of scale. Fiat was able to produce the two million or more cars annually that, it decided, were required to show a significant profit (Locke 1995). This reconceptualization of the automobile made it feasible for parts, such as brake systems, engines, and seats, to be produced by specialized suppliers. To enhance greater flexibility and efficiency, the company rationalized its supplier network, reducing its supplier base from thirteen hundred firms in 1979 to approximately eight hundred suppliers in 1986 (Locke 1995). Suppliers were selected on the basis of their reliability, technical capacities, and prices. In cooperation with Fiat, the chief subcontractor now draws up technical specifications for the subassembly that is to be produced (for instance, transmissions), and it assembles the simpler components produced by Fiat's own suppliers and subcontractors, thus increasing specialization and decentralization of production. Fiat also altered its rigid hierarchical structure by subdividing into eleven units responsible for distinct operations. This decentralization provided the possibility for more direct response to the external market and fostered greater competition between subholdings (Bagnasco 1986). The need for access to new technologies led Fiat Auto to turn to new suppliers, which supplied the company with new know-how and stimulated design capacity.[6] In 2000, Fiat formed a joint venture with the General Motors Company for the purpose of increasing efficiency and further expanding its role in information services. Although there is concern that the presence of General Motors may rupture Fiat's control over suppliers, the merger consolidates Fiat's international influence (IRES 2000).

In the aftermath of the great wave of labor protests that spread over much of urban Italy during the 1960s, and the radical industrial restructuring initiated in the early 1970s, Fiat began to lay off a substantial number of workers. This period represented the onset of a process of contraction within the production base and the introduction of a model of work in which, as one commentator put it, "We cannot find a motor for new struggles, nor the instruments of their socialization" (Belforte et al. 1978). From 1973 onward, stable jobs began to disappear. Nine to 10 percent of Fiat workers were laid off every year between 1973 and 1975 (Belforte et al. 1978). In 1961, 61 percent of the Turin workforce was employed in industry, 62 percent in 1971, 51.5 percent in 1981 (Bagnasco 1986, 37). Some of the successes achieved by the labor unions had included the considerably enhanced power of shop-floor union delegates. But a central feature of Fiat's restructuring was management's effort to regain control over the shop floor and to eliminate "redundant" workers.

The layoff process was most dramatic in 1980, when the company announced that it would have to put twenty-four thousand workers on *cassa integrazione*, a state- and employer-financed wage supplement fund, for fifteen months. The announcement was followed by a ten-week labor strike that was brought to a crushing end by the "silent march of the forty thousand" through the streets and piazzas of Turin. Fiat foremen, supervisors, and some blue-collar workers organized this demonstration against the trade unions,[7] signaling the rupture of a string of gains won by an Italian labor movement unable to halt Fiat's determination to downsize and reduce its workforce. Although workers were not immediately laid off, the agreement reached between the union and management signaled a major defeat. With the union in effect out of its way, the company intensified its process of reorganization, including the continual reduction of its labor force. In the end, Fiat had reduced its workforce by one-half (Locke 1995, 111), cutting the number of blue-collar workers from 113,568 in 1979 to 60,283 in 1986 (Locke 1995, 112). A worker interviewed in 2001 who was forced onto casa integrazione in 1980 described his frustration with the trade union's failure to protect him and his fellow workers:

> I was forty-two years old when they laid me off. I couldn't find another job, because I was "too old." It was very difficult, and the unions didn't do anything to stop the closing of the factory. Thirteen thousand workers were left without work. The ones under the age of thirty were able to find jobs, but those who didn't have second forms of work or were old were simply out of luck. They drank. They sat around the house collecting pensions, doing nothing. I was able to scrape by, fixing electrical appliances.

The reorganization of production and the introduction of new technologies rendered many traditional union rules and practices obsolete. Labor—for instance, in chassis welding and engine construction—was reorganized for production in a number of different specialized shops, so that previous accords became irrelevant. The new technologies also rendered some traditional jobs redundant and created positions for people able to operate and service the new technologies (Locke 1995, 113). Accordingly, the old skill requirements and responsibilities within traditional job classification schemes became outdated, and many workers were considered redundant. The majority of laid-off workers were middle-aged, unskilled, poorly educated men of southern Italian origin. Many disabled and female workers were also dismissed.

Over the past several decades, real wages have been gradually reduced; "at one time Turin had a per capita income of 17–18 percent over the national average; today we have fallen to 12 percent" (Zangola, quoted in Cresto-Dino and Fornaris 1993).[8] The *scala mobile*, a wage-indexing system implemented after World War II in which the government agreed that wages would be indexed according to prices, was abolished in July 1992 (Scobie et al. 1996). Some of the effects of income reduction have been cushioned by the central economic role of the Italian family. Able to rely on strong familial bonds, children now tend to stay at home far longer (IRES 1995). Beginning in 1999, the Turin and Piedmont economies began to pick up a bit, and an IRES study reported that many families had more disposable income and increasing faith in the local economy (IRES 2000).

A persistent loss in union membership since the 1980s can be attributed at least in part to the feeling among many workers that their pay scales and working conditions were not protected by the trade unions (Gall 1995).[9] In 2005, approximately one-third of union members in Turin were retired Fiat workers. Fiat's policies over the past two decades have included the softening of relations with workers. Since the early 1980s, Fiat management has managed to circumvent the unions by negotiating directly with workers over such issues as retraining, flexible hours, and job modifications. Neoliberal policies have been adopted, and in 1993 employers, union confederations, and the Italian government signed a new agreement on industrial relations and wages. This agreement, or "social contract," comprises an income policy that its proponents claim is capable of controlling inflation and stimulating economic growth. The theme of the agreement is "cooperation and compromise." Under its terms, workers suffer reduced hours (and pay) to prevent redundancies (Gall 1995). The contract is also part of a sustained effort to ensure that labor costs remain lower than projected rates of inflation, guaranteeing decreased real wages.

The effect of Fiat's many reorganizational efforts since the 1970s has been increased productivity and profits for the firm. Between 1979 and 1989, the average number of cars produced by a single worker more than doubled. By the late 1980s and into the 1990s, Fiat had reemerged as a serious competitor in the European market. The expanded export of Fiat automobiles within the European Union in the 1990s is a significant gain for a company whose internal market played a crucial role in retaining its competitive edge into the early 1980s.

The 1970s economic crisis led to the proliferation of small- and medium-sized firms in Piedmont. Small industry has had a rebirth, not only in the central and northeastern regions known as the "Third Italy,"[10] but in Turin as well (Bagnasco 1986; Sabel 1989). Following the decentralization of production and decision making, there was a vast growth in the number of small firms hiring twenty or fewer workers, and in medium-sized firms employing between twenty and one hundred employees, but a consistent decrease in the number of firms with more than one hundred workers (Contini and Revelli 1992). In the 1990s, firms gained increasing autonomy from the automobile market and began to diversify—for instance, by manufacturing capital goods such as machine tools, electronics, and computers. Technological developments have encouraged smaller businesses to enter a broad market beyond the geographical confines of the Turin metropolitan area (A. Segre 1994). The local success of many small- and medium-sized firms can be explained in part by the fact that micro-activities are less easily penetrated by international competition (IRES 1995). However, recent patterns in Turin show that, although an increasing number of small and medium enterprises are born each year, a substantial proportion of these firms are unsuccessful, and there is a considerable amount of employee turnover, with more employees fired than are hired on a regular basis.[11] This may be partly a result of the fact that Italian laws protecting workers are limited within firms employing fifteen or fewer workers.

Global economic trends indicate a generalized growth of the tertiary or service sectors in most advanced industrial economies (Sayer and Walker 1992). While the rate of tertiary-sector growth in Turin has accelerated, the overall picture is of a minimal degree of steady tertiary-sector expansion (Belforte et al. 1978; Bagnasco 1990). The traditional tertiary sector is in the urban administrative system, where any new employment is guaranteed for life. Turin's local tertiary sector is highly industrial-dependent, with most economic growth in the expansion of industrial services, which guarantees industry a determining role in technological development (IRES 2000). With growing investments in Turin during the 1990s, there was considerable development in transportation and industrial services, communications, credit, and insurance (IRES 2000). The most recent industrial growth has occurred in the area of construction, in which there is a substantial proportion of temporary work. Some of this can be explained by investments in infrastructure, prompted by preparations for the Winter Olympics, which took place in Turin in 2006. The region has continued to develop its technological and productive capacities, with greater specialization in information services (IRES 2000). An IRES study suggests that Turin's economy is dynamic, particularly in relation to the growth in business services. With an image of the Fiat factory built in 1939, IRES researchers reflected on the city's recent growth in services: "It is as though in the past two years in the Turin area, a 'Mirafiori of Services' was created" (IRES 2000, 18). The Piedmont region, with its capital city of Turin, seeks to become a leader in innovative business activities and expertise and a center for research. Its preeminence in research and development entrepreneurship gives it the hope of becoming one of the most technologically and industrially advanced regions in Europe (IRES 2000, 85).

International migrants exert a significant effect on local society and population stabilization in Turin. In the late 1990s, immigrants accounted for a slight growth in the Turin population, which had not happened in twenty-five years (IRES 2000, 17). Most migrants work in low-tech or private social and other services for individual families and firms that have also proliferated in Turin and throughout the country (Sciarrone 1996). Labor demand is most pronounced in areas that require high levels of technical expertise and educational training or in retailing, commerce, and low-skilled personal services (Dematteis and Segre 1988). There is also considerable demand for labor in low-paid and often dangerous forms of construction work (Ciafaloni, personal communication).

The Shifting World of Turin's Workers

The intensity of racism and forms of intolerance in Turin—a workerist city with a historically strong labor movement and recent history of internal migration—can be understood, in part, in relation to the perceived threat posed by immigrants in the context of economic and labor market uncertainty. The post-Fordist processes of economic restructuring have prompted many Turin residents to question accustomed ways of living that emerged after the war. The center of production is gradually moving from the industrial to the service sector, and the centrality of factory-based production is lost in favor of decentralized and more flexible electronic, information-based production technologies. These shifts are magnified by the loss of the centrality of the male, trade union–dominated working class and the appearance of a sharply segmented, poorer, and precarious immigrant class of worker. The working class is also being taken apart by higher levels of educational training among the young, the spread of consumerism, and middle-class living styles.

With economic restructuring and the disappearance of the Fordist work regime, there are indications that the social class composition of Turin has begun to shift. Between 1981 and 1991, the percentage of industrial workers decreased by 5 to 6 percent, although such workers still constitute approximately 45 percent of the urban population (IRES 1995). The number of middle-class white-collar workers increased by 1 to 2 percent between 1981 and 1991, but continued to represent a lower proportion of

residents, only 23 percent. The urban petty bourgeoisie was up 2 to 3 percent, to 18 percent of the population, while the most significant growth
occurred among the most privileged, bourgeoisie class, up 30 percent since
1981, to constitute 8.6 percent of the urban population in 1991 (IRES 1995,
10). The 1995 IRES regional economy report suggests that Turin's future
will include continual transformation of the urban social base, along with
possible changes in political attitudes, modes of association, and identities. Carter describes a recent confusion about identity in Turin culture,
related to a loss of the worker's centrality (1997).

Unemployment rates hovered at around 10 percent from the 1980s until
the late 1990s, when they decreased to some 6.3 percent. However, on the
whole, occupational losses in industry have not been absorbed by new
jobs in the tertiary sector (Bagnasco 1986). The transformation of local
labor requires a younger and highly skilled worker, which Turin, as labor
historian Francesco Ciafaloni has noted, simply has not been producing. The labor context in the 1990s called for a great number of laborers
to undertake the technical transformation of the city, and yet Turin has
been forced to look to sources other than its own population. The sons
and daughters of a first generation of factory workers often do not wish
to take blue-collar jobs, yet they are often unable to find anything better.
Most Turin youth simply have not been schooled to take on the new forms
of employment requiring a highly educated, computer-literate cohort of
workers. According to Ciafaloni, sometimes the children of factory workers "have too many hopes and too few achievements." There has been little
fit between Turin's educational institutions and labor market demands.
Nevertheless, the sons and daughters of older workers seek to people the
world of intermediate white-collar positions, leaving the manual work and
precarious jobs in welding, masonry, and construction to immigrants.
Such employment options seem unattractive to many young people for
whom education and the seductions of consumption have fanned the
flames of a hope of inching beyond the world of manual labor (Merrill and
Carter 2002). There is also the question of working conditions, including
income, safety, and social prestige, which may be unacceptable to young
job seekers (Reyneri 1998). Many older Turinese lament that young people
are spoiled by the *benessere,* or good life, provided by their parents. As one
retired worker commented:

> The young people, like my son, now twenty-two years old, have had a lot
> of trouble finding work. They refuse to do any kind of work except the

kind that they have training to do. My son is trained in graphics, but if he can't find work in that profession, he won't work. When we were his age, if we didn't find the perfect work for which we were trained, we simply took anything to pay the bills, but now these young people refuse. They're spoiled and lazy.

Preparing workers for the current high-tech labor market is daunting in a city with a workerist cultural history. During the phase when Fordist-style production was dominant, only minimum levels of skill were required of most workers (Gallino 1990). Even recently, 39.5 percent of Turin workers were low-skilled, as compared with 29.5 percent in Milan (IRES 1995). Regarding the reskilling of workers, Bagnasco asked, "One is thrown into the water in order to learn to swim, but does one have the resources to manage it?" (Bagnasco, quoted in Cresto-Dino and Fornaris 1993, 58). Most workers laid off in the 1980s were unable to find new jobs, at least partly because they were trained to work in forms of industrial labor that no longer existed or that required only a small number of workers. The percentage of high school and college degrees awarded in Turin is lower than in other metropolitan areas in Italy, and is particularly low among southern Italian migrants (ibid.). Educational levels reflect class differences, as 50 percent of the children of the managerial and professional classes, and 40 percent of the children of entrepreneurs and white-collar workers, attend universities; this is true of only 10 to 20 percent of the children of working-class and petty bourgeoisie families.

Even in the more favorable Turin labor market of the early twenty-first century, many have difficulty finding work. Even for Italian youth willing to accept factory jobs, stable and well-paid work does not come easily. This is partly because of discrimination against the young, which is high in Italy. Most Italian job seekers are women and young people without working experience (Reyneri 1998). An elderly electrical worker laid off from a Fiat subsidiary firm explained that it is difficult for young people to find any factory work, and, when available, the jobs are poorly paid and offered only with temporary contracts. Many Italian firms, including Fiat, have gone abroad to countries with less costly labor—for example, Brazil, Poland, and Romania. Without stable earnings, few Turin youth can afford to marry and purchase their own residences. There is an overall tendency for Italian youth, even those without the necessary educational qualifications, to seek prestigious and well-paid nonindustrial work in the tertiary sector (IRES 2000). As one union official said, "When I was a kid, my father worked for Fiat and we all expected that I would work there too and become some sort of a manager. Now, no one has such expectations anymore."[12]

Not only have the number of available low-skilled manufacturing jobs in large factories decreased, but there is a general sense that stable and guaranteed forms of work in sectors outside of state administration have, in effect, disappeared (Ambrosini 2001). As in other parts of the world, precarious forms of work on a contract basis, part-time employment, and work in the *economia sommersa* (informal economy) are on the rise. More and more people are being retained on a temporary, terminal contract basis—as many as 45 percent of those hired in Piedmont in 1994 (IRES 1995, 51). There is a great deal of rotation in positions as people change jobs frequently, especially in the vast universe of small firms. Recent legislation has liberalized the use of terminal contracts, which enable employers to try out workers before offering more stable employment (IRES 1995). Employers may also hire less-qualified workers with short-term contracts and let them go before their salaries have to be increased, or before they are required to obtain specialized on-the-job training. Even qualified workers are frequently hired on a temporary contract basis. The implicit logic of this increasingly "flexible" hiring and firing system is that employers save money by not keeping on workers unless they are absolutely necessary.

More than half of those hired in Turin in 1994 worked in unskilled forms of work, while almost all of those hired in 1999 were highly educated (IRES 1995, 2000). There are indications of an increasing degree of job polarization. Some populations are more vulnerable to the transformations than others, and there is considerable differentiation in the ability to access particular jobs and social positions. Until non-European migrants began to arrive, southern Italians, certain women, and youth had the least access to good, stable jobs. Today, with diminishing state resources, there are risks that a more acute polarization will develop between those able to withstand the changing labor market and others left outside or on the margins (Mingione 1993). The unemployment rate may have lowered in Turin, but this was primarily for those with the highest levels of educational access, leaving the rest in an even more marginal position. As the poorest 10 percent of the population becomes even poorer and the income of the middle strata increases only slightly, the greatest expansions in wealth are concentrated among the already wealthy (Bagnasco 1990).

Throughout the past few decades, an increasing number of Turin factories, once teeming with activity, closed their doors (Cresto-Dino and Fornaris 1993). An architect in Turin commented, "The abandoned spaces will grow. I don't know if in two, three, five, or ten years the enormous property that is Mirafiori, one of the largest of Fiat buildings, will even exist"[13] (Sergio Jarett, quoted in Cresto-Dino and Fornaris 1993.

As factories have disappeared, international migrants have become a feature of local geography in a city with a worker culture constructed by the organizational styles of a single industry (Bagnasco 1986; Michelsons 1989). But the migrant presence seems to have intensified the challenges faced by Turin dwellers within a shifting political, economic, and social climate. It is as yet unclear how the presence of newcomers, with their diverse cultural and ideological baggage, will affect the often rigid and hierarchical traditions of a city widely perceived as culturally "closed." There is consensus among Turin's scholars that if Piedmont is to expand economically, it will have to emerge as a more cosmopolitan social place, because elements of rigidity and inertia in local society tend to limit entrepreneurial innovation. In an effort to attract tourists by representing Turin as a "world class" city, local government has begun to portray the city as multicultural and cosmopolitan. How, if at all, might the presence of migrants contribute new ideas and incentives to this local world or introduce broader social horizons?

Turin sociologists describe the weakening of family bonds and social solidarity in a city once the center of the Italian labor movement (Gallino 1990; A. Negri 1996). Many Turinese have lost faith in unions and political parties. Not long ago, Turin was considered culturally homogenous, distinguished by the local emphasis on work, scientific, and technological progress (Bagnasco 1990).[14] Today, many Turinese question local "identity," unsure of how to describe the fast pace of change that seems to encompass their daily lives. Urban dwellers generally feel less secure, worried about the future, fearful of further plant closings. Turin's cultural texture has become uncertain and somewhat tense. Migrants are easy scapegoats for sometimes overwhelming feelings of fear, accused of posing a threat to wages and of increasing crime rates. However, wages have been in decline for years, and from the corporate standpoint there may be a financial incentive to maintain a weakened labor force to ensure maximum profit rates in existing businesses and to attract international investors for new business ventures.

It may be difficult to creatively imagine how third world and Eastern European migrants can be inserted into this city in economic crisis. The demand for migrant labor is not as straightforward as it was in the past. Labor costs were relatively high in Turin, particularly in the wake of a successful workers' movement of the 1960s and 1970s. But as this discussion has suggested, wages and union power have been declining for years, while local entrepreneurs and government officials seek to diversify the local economy and to attract foreign investors. In this context, it is possible that the presence of international migrants will provide an additional, highly exploitable reserve labor force for foreign investors wishing to take advantage of areas with established infrastructures, social organizations, and cheap labor supplies (Sassen-Koob 1984).

There is a considerable degree of incongruity between the hopes and expectations of the migrant women of Alma Mater and the growing demand in Turin for cheap, domestic services.[15] The desires of the present generation of migrants come up hard against, among other things, the kind of work available to the most vulnerable populations in the local labor market. Portraits of European free-market capitalism, assumed to include limitless possibilities for individual and familial achievement, compelled some migrant women to travel afar. But such images are often thwarted by the harsh realities of daily life in an urban industrial economy struggling to diversify and to de-industrialize.

CHAPTER 4

Extracomunitari in Post-Fordist Turin

Westerners always ask, "Why does the foreigner come here?
I would not leave my own country." That's because they
don't have to. They have food, clothing, materials, housing.
They never have to endure anything really difficult. But only
10 percent of the world lives like they do, while the other
90 percent suffers. Many who are leaving their countries
do so under grave conditions, crossing the desert
to enter southern Italy, because if they should die it
would not be worse than to remain at home.

—*Maria Viarengo*

[Referring to a job in a hairstyling salon:] I worked in that
salon one whole week and they never greeted me. I went there
in the morning and would say hello and no one would answer
me. They were stupid people. Very stupid Italian people. . . . All
they would let me do was wash hair. I could do more—I could
do the permanents and cut the hair—but they would never
give me the chance. Oh, it's so hard here. It's hard to find a job.

—*An East African woman*

Globalization and the International Division of Labor

Recent shifts in Turin's economy and occupational structure—its movement from an economy based principally on Fordist-style automobile production and stable, relatively unskilled employment toward decentralized
production and a more polarized labor market—can be understood as part
of one phase within the continual process of capitalist expansion. There is
a great deal of discussion today about what is often assumed to be a new
process of "globalization," a term employed to describe the free movement
of capital around the world, the implosion of boundaries between nation-
states, and the domination of transnational corporations. Although there
is little doubt that Turin's economy has recently been altered in response
to pressures connected with global capitalist restructuring, the city has
been responding to a similar capitalist rhythm for well over a century

55

(Harvey 1989, 1996).[1] Despite its provincial cultural texture embedded in local and regional identities, and familial and social networks, Turin's late nineteenth- and twentieth-century infrastructure, social class composition, politics, and culture were fostered in relationship to the expansion of Fiat.[2] Incorporated into a system of global capitalisms, the drive to innovate and to change was a feature of the very fabric of local society and economy, and with this impulse, the continual merging of styles and practices into new creations. Within modern capitalism, disintegration is an integrative force, or, as Marshall Berman described: "In this world, stability can only mean entropy, slow death, while our sense of progress and growth is our only way of knowing for sure that we are alive. To say that our society is falling apart is only to say that it is alive and well" (1988, 95).

The most recent phase in the development of global capitalist expansion began in the mid-1970s, when rising oil prices, labor costs, and oversupply in systems of mass production triggered a worldwide economic recession (Harvey 1989). One of the most remarkable by-products of the ensuing economic crisis was the increase in offshore investments in regions previously "peripheral" to, although already incorporated within, international capitalist production. The decreasing cost of moving people and commodities as well as the deregulation of financial markets made it possible for companies in advanced economies to further invest in export-led industrialization in some parts of the developing world. There was an effort to keep labor costs as low as possible, while boosting production and expanding trade. Many companies relocated to other, wealthy OECD (Organization of Economic Cooperation and Development) countries, where, for example, they were able to penetrate new markets or to manipulate tax laws and other state regulations that would have been applied to companies operating in their home countries (Dicken 2002).

Side effects of the radical dispersal of manufacturing throughout the world include massive, global proletarianization of women as well as men, and, as we saw in the case of Fiat, downsizing in the advanced economic areas with fierce reductions in the stable manufacturing labor force. Between 1966 and 1995, the global labor force doubled in size, though almost half of these workers live on a few dollars or less per day, lack representation, and work in unhealthy, dangerous, or degrading conditions (Harvey 1997). The "global international division of labor" has become increasingly segmented by migration, "race," and gender, and polarized between a growing number of professional jobs for high pay and low-paid unskilled work in services or manufacturing, especially in major cities (Cross 1994; Harvey 1997).

Low-skilled female work and migration have emerged as central components of the current phase of global capitalism. In economically developed countries as well as in the newly industrialized zones, women are concentrated in low-paid manufacturing and service jobs (Sassen-Koob 1984; Nash 1984; Ong 1987). In places as geographically diverse as Mexico, Haiti, and Malaysia, women workers have been massively recruited into labor-intensive manufacturing plants (Ong 1987; Fernandez-Kelly 1983). In some areas of the developing world as well as in Europe and the United States, there is an expanding use of female labor in subcontracting industrial housework and in sweatshops within textile manufacturing and other forms of commodity production.[3] These forms of labor for both male and female migrants are growing in Italy, especially in the Veneto and Emilia-Romagna regions. Many women migrate from rural to urban areas within their countries of origin, a throwback to early industrialization and the intense exploitation of women and minors. At the same time, more women migrate internationally than during previous periods of industrial boom. In Italy, a sharp division of labor occurs across gender lines, and women migrants have been relegated to positions in the labor market identified with "women's work" and the service sector. In the northeast, women migrants are often found working in low-level service jobs—for example, in restaurants, hospitals, or domestic service in places where these forms of employment have expanded as manufacturing has either shifted abroad or become less labor intensive.

The dispersal of laboring populations throughout the world is a central feature of the current phase in capitalist expansion.[4] The internationalization of labor is no less a fundamental aspect of the current phase of globalization than the internationalization of capital (Sassen 1994).[5] Since the 1960s, potential laborers have moved from the third world to the advanced economic zones—for instance, from the Caribbean basin, Asia, and parts of Latin America to the United States—but the scale of population movement began to take on far wider proportions in the 1980s. Never before have African populations migrated in such great numbers to Western Europe, joined by Asians, Latin Americans, and Eastern Europeans. The presence all over Europe of such a wide variety of diasporic populations will have far-reaching effects on European cultures that are only beginning to be felt (Carter 1997).

Local Migrants, Local Laborers

The growing presence of newcomers since the middle 1980s masks the declining population of Turin proper, which plummeted from 1.2 million in the 1970s to less than a million today. Stranieri contribute a more apparent cultural diversity to this industrial city, their often colorful clothing and design bringing into relief the faded grays and pastels of the Turin architecture. In 1995, a woman of East African origin commented that Turin "used to be a dead city that migrants brought to life." International migrants lived in Turin before the late 1980s, but not in substantial enough numbers to influence the local cultural landscape in a significant way. Official ISTAT (Istituto Nazionale de Statistica, National Institute of Statistics) 1995 figures for foreign residents in Turin enumerated migrants from 142 countries, including European Union member states.[6] These official figures, however, do not represent the untold number of unofficial, or *clandestine*, migrants living, working, and contributing to the local economy without state permission.[7]

Extracomunitari, the term for non–European Union citizens, frequently originate from nations without any apparent cultural or colonial connection to Italy. To understand their connections to Italy, it is useful to conceive of the peninsula as part of a total European social formation instead of a singular national territory. From the perspective of many migrants, Italy is just another European country that participates in a generally European-dominant geopolitical influence on their countries of origin. Some migrants began to travel for work well before they arrived in Turin, often journeying first to urban centers within their countries of origin and then to other parts of Africa, Europe, and Italy. However, some do not consider themselves permanent residents in Europe; they continue to maintain social and political ties with their countries of origin, to which they hope to return someday (Carter 1997). In many instances, a much-hoped-for return home is not in the making, as in the case of a forty-five-year-old Senegalese man, who in 2001 had been in Turin for more than a decade. About his predicament, including the need for him to send remittance money back to Senegal to support his immediate and extended families, he said:

> I am really fed up. I have lived here for eleven years, giving all of my money to my family. I am the third child—there are two older brothers— out of the eleven children my mother had, and yet I am the oldest because I have to give so much to the family. I even sent money for my older broth-

er in Paris to get married, and then gave money to my sister to buy cloth for her to sell, and for the very expensive drugs for her infertility problem. I have a brother in Senegal who has been married three times and who has five children, all living in my house. I have had eight months at home with my family during these eleven years. That is too little. I cannot stand it any longer. My oldest was ten when I left, and she is now twenty-one. I have not been able to see her grow up. My wife was young, now she is not so young anymore. I am not like many of the other Senegalese who take three wives. I don't want three wives; I will not do that. No, no, that's not for me. I have too much respect for my children. I want them to have a future. My mother would not let me off the phone today; she kept me on the phone for fifty minutes. I paid. She asked me to find a husband for one of my sisters, but how can I do that? The Senegalese men here, many are now selling drugs. What happens when you sell drugs? You go to jail, and your life is finished. I would never do that, and there is no one here for my sister to marry. I cannot do anything about this. I cannot solve all of these problems. I work seven days a week, and it's not enough. But now, after these years I have a pension coming, which in Senegal will be enough money to live on, to fix up our house a little bit, and to buy things to sell—to go to the U.S., to buy, to come back and sell, etc.—me and my wife. My mother asks me to go home. I want to go home. I am so tired of this. My family is getting old, and I am here. What is this? I cannot do this forever. But I cannot leave my sisters here like this.

This man lives in a small flat with several other Senegalese men. He does, in fact, work seven days a week at a factory that subcontracts with Fiat because workers are needed on Sundays, when Italian men have familial and other obligations. Afraid of losing his job, he does whatever the managers ask of him. Yet he is paid low wages, only enough for him to get by, to help the sisters in Turin under his care, and to send the rest of his earnings to Senegal.

International migrants experience much more job vulnerability than postwar Italian migrants encountered in the industrial north. They are at the mercy of a state institutional system with weak mechanisms of support and a host of voluntary forms of mediation, which, should they have any access to them, may or may not require returns from the migrant. "Good" jobs and safe and decent housing, difficult even for Italians to procure in Turin, are much more rare for stranieri, particularly those with somatic features and speaking styles that distinguish them as different from the local population. As a West African woman told me in 1995, "They (Italians), when we go for a job interview, think we're either domestics or prostitutes." Migrants are primarily employed in jobs with the toughest conditions as regards the number of work hours and night shifts, endurance, physical effort, and risk of accident. They carry out work in agriculture, construction, domestic service and elder care, street trading, small- and medium-sized manufacturing firms, and low-level urban services.

With or without legal residence documents, postcolonial and Eastern European migrants are at a greater disadvantage in the labor market than Italians. Migrant labor is widely demanded in the Italian underground economy, and they generally work in inferior and precarious forms of labor within an increasingly segmented labor market. They tend to have to accept whatever jobs they can get, which is rare among Italian job seekers (Reyneri 1998). Until the presence of international migrants became more visible at the end of the 1980s, southern Italians were the principal subjects of a system of institutionalized racialization and sexual discrimination (IRES 1992; Carter 1997; Cento Bull 1996). The jobs available to migrants are characterized by forms of "casual," low-skilled production, agriculture, and nonproduction or service work. These jobs are low-paying, offer little security, and are dead-end, without the chance of promotion (Edwards 1979; Form 1995). Many migrants work in the informal economy, where they change jobs frequently, are not protected by the trade unions, and are always threatened with the possibility of replacement. A Senegalese man who had not been in Turin for long in 2001, for example, had a temporary job working in a factory that made parts for refrigerators, bicycles, and automobiles. He explained that he was hired on a month-to-month basis:

> I hope I can keep this job. If they like you, they'll hire you again for another month. Before I had this job, I went around selling things on the streets, like sunglasses. My older brother also works in a factory here, but he'd like to become an architect.

The principal employment for migrant women is in domestic service (COLF, Collaboratrice Familiare), especially in cities throughout Italy (Andall 2000). Recruitment of foreign domestic servants began during the 1960s, but demand expanded in recent years for a number of reasons. As more Italian women work in paid employment outside of the home, domestics have become widely sought after among Italian families. The result is a growing polarization between women. The new social contradictions of the labor market include a broadening, increasingly female middle class (Ambrosini 2001). The employment of a domestic worker in Italy is a sign of middle-class respectability. Many Italian households seek cleaning and cooking services, child care, and at times tutoring or language training for their children. In 1990, thousands of illegal workers were regularized, which permitted many domestics who had been working without documents to become formally employed through COLF.[8] However, large proportions of domestics work within the informal economy. The costs of social contributions, which increased after the first *sanatoria,* or amnesty, in 1990, drive many Italian households not to register migrant domestic workers.

Catholic organizations in Italy have had a long tradition as employment agencies for domestic workers, and contracts between migrants and Italian households are frequently mediated by Catholic voluntary organizations (Andall 2000). Filipina women, for example, may first learn about their jobs by reading advertisements in church newspapers distributed in the Philippines.[9] Other women[10] ask for help from Catholic organizations after they arrive in Italy. Catholic structures also frequently offer support and assistance to migrant domestics who often live in the homes of their employers. The Italian state has established very few organizations for the purpose of receiving migrants (Balbo and Manconi 1992), and Catholic voluntary organizations play a central historical role in helping the poor, unemployed, drug dependent, psychologically disabled, and now immigrants. Church mediation is not always disinterested, however, and the 1992 IRES migration study notes that recent migrants are often brought to talk to "the faithful" about their poverty and their countries of origin. The IRES study also points out that religious mediators have not always been concerned about representing the interests of COLF, neither defending their levels of pay nor requesting regularization of their work. Many have felt they ought to accept any work conditions because the domestic jobs were presented to them as "acts of benevolence" (IRES 1992).

The demand for domestic servants is linked with certain cultural-historical features of Italian society and the weakness of the Italian welfare state. Young Italian women, even in southern areas where unemployment rates exceed 50 percent, are often unwilling to take jobs that involve grueling working hours and are symbols of social inferiority. Italian families nevertheless hire more domestic servants than in any other European country (Andall 2000). Enrico Pugliese suggests that the "arcane preference" for domestic workers in Italian households represents a certain "type of mentality" and willingness to reaffirm ancient habits that ought to have been superseded in a modern, "developed" society. Pugliese is referring to the premodern habit among the Italian nobility of maintaining domestic servants, which the new middle classes seek to emulate. The availability of a third world labor force satisfies the desire for prestige among the small and medium bourgeoisie (Macioti and Pugliese 1991). Servants are more easily affordable to working- and middle-class Italians than they once were, particularly with a large pool of female migrants without legal permission to remain in Italy.[11] Living within an Italian household is a way for migrants to avoid police controls if they have only a tourist visa.

Carolina, a Peruvian woman working as a CGIL representative, explained in 2001 that in Turin, some migrant women are being trained to do domestic work, which is a positive act because it professionalizes them and they learn about legislation designed to protect workers:

> Some of these women are exploited, but less than in the past because we're doing something about this by training them. Many more migrant women now know their rights and stand up for themselves in ways that they feared in the past.

From this trade union perspective, formal training of migrant women in domestic service will protect these workers against exploitation. Carolina also pointed out, however, that migrant women in these jobs often remain highly vulnerable. Many, for example, are working within contracts specifying four hours of work a day, and yet these women really work ten hours a day, while the family pays a pension rate at the daily part-time rate of four hours.

Italy has one of the lowest birth rates in the world and a growing aging population in need of care. Immigrant women are called on to fill a deficit in services for the elderly, especially for personal or live-in care. As retirement pensions have been reduced and living costs have risen, many elderly Italians find themselves without the resources to adequately care for themselves at the end of their lives. The availability of a low-cost postcolonial labor force supplements the shortages of an Italian welfare system that is not equipped to support the needs of this aging population (Mingione 1993). In Turin, where institutionalized care is expensive and rare, many families can look to immigrant women to care for their loved ones. Elderly persons frequently require round-the-clock assistance and live-in care. Some migrant partners divide their hours of work, with one person working the day shift and the other through the night.[12] These jobs are temporary, of course, because the elderly parent is not expected to live long.

Stories reported by women migrants who have worked as domestics are not uniform. Some recount experiences of trusting relationships, while others describe exploitation or forms of abuse. The 1992 IRES study documents cases in which employers inform themselves about how to obtain proper legal documents for domestics, and in which migrant women feel secure:

> I work in a family as a domestic. I do the shopping, the cooking, I clean and iron the clothing; in sum I do all the work of a housewife. There are four people in this household and they are very nice; the mother lets me run the household. (IRES 1992, 141)

In less fortunate and also common instances, migrant women are hired to perform designated tasks, and then expected to perform well beyond what was required of them according to the original agreement. Many report being very poorly paid, treated as inferior persons, and exploited within the household. In one instance, a Senegalese woman was put in a bedroom without heat while the rest of the family slept in warm comfort. In another instance, a Somali woman had been contracted to care for a man's sister at the rate of seven hundred thousand lira a month, but upon arrival in Italy was paid only five hundred thousand lira. She had also been told that she would care for the sister in Milan, which is where her own sister lived, but instead her employer brought her to Rome to take care of his mother and wife in addition to his sister. The family did not permit her to leave the vicinity, except to take a stroll in the garden next to the house (IRES 1992, 142). Migrant women also report sexual abuse within Italian households. One young Moroccan woman, for example, worked for an Italian family, but later decided to become a prostitute. She claimed that prostitution was a better way to live because she had to support sexual abuse at the hands of her employer anyway, but with the complication of being a dependent instead of an independent or autonomous worker (IRES 1992, 142).

Other areas of the hidden work world of migrant women include a wide range of jobs in the least-skilled services and in nursing. Many work in retail, various kinds of piecework and textile employment, and agriculture, and as caregiving professionals for the disabled, mentally impaired, or drug dependent (Merrill 2001). Wages are usually very low and the jobs unregistered. These are the low-skilled urban jobs typically needed to service the needs of wealthy modern cities. In Turin, migrant women have a difficult time securing forms of work other than domestic labor, elder care, and prostitution. A few migrant women work as nurses; some work in local seamstress shops. Others work in restaurants or bars, usually at night. Many engage in part-time cleaning or child or elder care, and are occupied in forms of trade, primarily, although not exclusively, through migrant networks. A few have documents stating that they belong to associations or cooperative groups of artisans, which permits them to sell in the open markets, but most do this on an informal basis, expanding trade activities from parts of Africa into Europe (MacGaffey 1987). Migrants sell African cloth, skin products from Russia, African spices, hand-carved hair combs, African masks, and other forms of art, such as paintings, baskets, jewelry, and crafts. Many other women provide services such as hairstyling and seamstress work. In a market previously cornered by Catholic charity organizations, the taste for ethnic goods has begun to expand, even in Turin.

Some African and Chinese men and women are self-employed traders, traveling regularly to purchase or sell cloth and other products. Some sell within households and informal networks, while others are street sellers. A Senegalese woman who lives in Turin travels regularly to Austria to purchase cloth she can sell in Italy. She says that there are no immigrants in this part of Austria, and that the Austrians produce a high quality yet inexpensive cloth. Some women travel as far as the United States to purchase jeans and other items of clothing for much lower prices than are

Mary Ann Akinyi, a Kenyan migrant selling at the Porta Palazzo Balon, 1996

available in Italy. Other, usually male migrants work as street sellers during the summer or when not employed in industrial firms or agriculture (see Carter 1997). The social impact of this activity is strong because of its visibility and illegality. Migrants are not allowed to sell on streets without a license, procured only if one is a member of an association with permission to street-peddle. Migrants are therefore allowed to sell on the street only by virtue of the absence of any controls or because of tolerance by the police. They are sometimes exposed to sanctions, including heavy fines and the confiscation of their goods. Moreover, those not in possession of proper legal documentation may be given a deportation order. Police controls may become more stringent under the recent Bossi-Fini legislation, which provides for the arrest of migrants who do not leave Italy when ordered.

The term *vu cumpra* (you buy) is popularly used to refer to ambulant sellers along Italy's urban sidewalks and sometimes in the open markets, with their blankets or tabletops covered with goods for sale (Carter 1997). The visibility of these men has marked them, along with prostitutes, as the symbols of the absence of work in Italy, the poverty of the migrant, and the out-of-place nature of the migrant as a sort of street dweller who occupies no real space. Some of these migrants are artisans by trade, but the majority perform this informal trade to survive when industrial labor contracts end or seasonal agricultural labor is finished. During the summer particularly, when most Italians vacation along the Atlantic, Mediterranean, or Adriatic shores, these sellers of various items such as watches, purses, sunglasses, and music cassettes travel there to capture the tourist market. Their place in the Italian labor market is driven by the increasing consumer demand for low-cost commodities.

While it is difficult for migrant women to find factory employment in Turin, many male migrants work in temporary contract jobs for small industrial firms or in the building industry. They work in trades such as metalworking, plastics, ceramics, marble cutting, shoe and textile manufacturing, and electronics. Many work as masons, builders, and diggers at construction sites, but most of these men are not officially registered workers. According to some early estimates, between one-quarter and one-third of male extracomunitari work in small- and medium-sized Piedmont manufacturing firms (A. Segre 1994).[13] However, in 1990 it was estimated that some 38 percent of these migrants worked on a temporary contract basis (IRES 2000). Few find the sort of stable employment offered in large factories, where the competition with Italian workers would be fierce (Sciarrone 1996; Reyneri 1998). Many migrant men work as parts cleaners in subcontracted firms, where southern Italians used to work. As one explained:

> There are no Italians working there in these types of factories and cleaning jobs. Only Italians work for Fiat, foreigners don't. Foreigners work for the subcontractors. They clean the machines. It's very dirty work and we have to wear masks, but the masks are filthy after an hour. And we also suffer because it's extremely hot in these places.

Reyneri suggests that the issue for firms employing migrants is stability, because they need to hire laborers willing to withstand poor working conditions over a long period. In some industries labor contracts are often regular, but many firms save on labor costs by placing migrants in the lowest positions and paying them at the lowest trade union rates. Italian workers doing the same tasks are placed in higher positions and receive wage benefits (Reyneri 1998). Many migrants working in small and medium factories in Turin turn to the trade unions for protection.

Agriculture is another major area of migrant employment, though less so in Piedmont than in other Italian regions. Most of these laborers work in the south, hired usually on a day-to-day basis, and are paid by piece (per box of tomatoes, grapes, apples, and so on), which is often less than half the trade union rates (Mottura 1992). Agricultural harvesters work as many as twelve hours a day and live in old huts without water or electricity (Pugliese 1993). A number of migrants, primarily in the north, have official work documents and are registered with trade unions. Increasingly, migrants work in pig and cow farming and in agricultural processing (Mottura 1992). Some migrants take seasonal agricultural work and street-sell or work in the building industry or low-level services for the rest of the year.

The Economia Sommersa

Migrant women have often been stereotyped in the Italian news media and popular imagination as sexually promiscuous or as prostitutes by virtue of their being socially marked as different and exotic (Merrill 1994; Maneri 2001). In a memoir of her experiences as a young Ethiopian woman in Italy, Maria Viarengo writes of her ride with an Italian taxi driver:

> The taxi driver took me from one side of the city to another, and he offered me a free ride if, in exchange, I would guarantee him a "great hand-

job" that, according to him, only "we" knew how to do. According to this man, Black women are great in bed. Black woman was the equivalent of a sexually easy, exotic animal. (1990)

While the vast majority of women migrants in Italy have never engaged in prostitution, in the past decade there has been a thriving local market for African (especially Nigerian and Ghanaian) and Eastern European prostitutes (Da Pra Pocchiesa 1996). As one Turinese client put it:

When they arrived, these Nigerians, the market went crazy. Everyone wanted to try the black woman; a little because of the novelty of it, and her exoticism, a little because these wretched women are the only ones willing to do it without protection, and this fact created growing demand for them.[14]

The expansion of trade networks in sexual services has a global reach, from Russia to New York City and Las Vegas, to the sex tourism industry in Thailand, to Filipina women in Hong Kong, and Eastern Europeans in Western Europe (Raffy 1993; Hornblower 1993; Ong 1990; Skrobanek 1990). In Turin, Nigerian prostitutes are highly visible, and their presence has been depicted in many a daily newspaper article, magazine feature story, or television show as representative of the "problem" of immigration in contemporary Italy (Maneri 1998a, 1998b). The image of the foreign prostitute signals illegality, criminality, and social deviance.

The 1996 film *Vesna va Veloce* (Vesna, Go Quickly) by Carlo Mazzacurati portrays a twenty-four-year-old Czechoslovakian woman, Vesna, who runs away from a tourist bus during a routine rest stop because she wishes to stay in Italy, where she survives by working as a prostitute. Vesna asserts that prostitution is better work than what she did in Czechoslovakia. After her passport is stolen by an Eastern European and a Moroccan pimp who work together, the young Czech woman cannot hope to find legal employment in Italy. Vesna cannot go to the hospital when she is ill, fearing deportation, so, when beaten by thieves, she is patched up by an African doctor connected to a politically left network. Vesna dreams of opening a massage shop with the money she earns as a prostitute. When penniless, she is treated with complete disrespect, harshly thrown out on the street. This is a world in which money, sometimes more than sexual behavior, demarcates the division between the socially acceptable and rejected.

Vesna va Veloce is a film that represents the condition of migrant prostitutes in Italy, whose passports have frequently been seized before they ever consider working in their new residence as prostitutes. Others are directly recruited into prostitution in their countries of origin. Not represented in Vesna's story are the extensive networks of organized crime into which numerous prostitutes are inserted. The majority of African prostitutes in Turin are Nigerian and Ghanaian. In 1995 the Catholic priest Fredo Olivero, the former director of the Ufficio Stranieri and now director of Caritas's immigration center, waged a campaign for the purpose of obtaining the documents of foreign prostitutes that had been seized in organized criminal networks or by migrant pimps. Olivero offered the prostitutes an opportunity to leave their trade and to become legally resident in Turin. His efforts were apparently fairly successful, and approximately seven hundred prostitutes sought help. On local as well as national levels, there are some judicial actions against the illegal criminal rackets into which many foreign prostitutes are inserted in Italy. In 1996, the government decreed that any foreign, clandestine prostitute who should denounce the man or woman who exploited her as a pimp, or who had unlawfully seized her passport, would, in exchange, obtain residency papers.

A structural feature of modern economies, the *economia sommersa,* or informal economy, is believed to be expanding in contemporary Turin (Reyneri 1998). This economic sector, also referred to as *lavoro nero,* takes a variety of forms, but is generally characterized by small-scale, unregulated activities that are highly flexible and may involve family labor (Castells and Portes 1991). The presence of today's migrants is often assumed to be prompted by expansion of the informal labor market (Hajimichalis and Vaiou 1990; Dell'Aringa and Neri 1989). In the Italian context, however, there is no direct causal link between the growth of the informal economic sector and the presence of foreign labor. It is important to keep in mind that the economia sommersa is well rooted all over Italy, in the southern regions as well as in northern and central Italy, all of which lead Europe in terms of high income and very low unemployment. Many Italians work in occupations where it is easy to ignore administrative and legal rules: agriculture, construction, domestic service, self-employment, appliance and automobile repair, and retail. In Italian society, moreover, a casual behavior prevails with regard to taxes and other monies owed the central government.

The Italian informal economy works through networks of personal relations, where workers are recruited by word of mouth. The term *doppio lavoro,* or "double work," refers to a form of informal, self-employed activity that thousands of Italians have engaged in as a means to supplement incomes derived from jobs within the formal labor market. Before Fiat and its subsidiaries began to lay off thousands of workers, many of these workers did other odd jobs to improve their standard of living. Some engaged in informal economic activities to make ends meet after being laid off, or perhaps as a means to achieve upward mobility (Gallino 1990; Paçi 1992). Doppio lavoro is a highly local practice, embedded in Italian forms of kinship, in which informal work is often contracted as services rendered to other family members or through friendship and work contacts. The popular association of informal activity with immigrants may be partly attributed to the mistaken assumption that it is only the poor who engage in informal economic activities (Castells and Portes 1991). A more widely known and even more historically embedded instance of the Italian practice of using family labor is illustrated by the highly successful industrial districts of central and northwestern Italy (Sabel 1989; Harrison 1997; Capecchi 1989; Vinay 1993). In these regions, where flexible and specialized subcontracting in small enterprises has led to considerable economic profit, informal and familial labor—including the use of Italian women and young workers—is widespread. The economia sommersa is even more segmented than formal forms of labor (IRES 1996).

In the present context of high levels of competition between international firms, informal activity is expanding. One explanation is that labor costs are generally lower in the economia sommersa. Even when workers are paid according to union rates, employers save because they don't have to pay social security contributions, income taxes, and other labor costs. In some cases, informal workers receive seniority pensions and other welfare benefits.

Highly vulnerable migrants are an easily exploitable population (IRES 1992). Many immigrants accept informal work for low wages because they are not aware of worker rights. Most migrants speak little Italian until they have spent a considerable amount of time in Italy, and very few are inserted into local social and informational networks. Often, Italian mediators locate work for migrants in the economia sommersa, and have been known to warn the migrant worker not to denounce the padrone (boss) if anything happens because he might be a Mafioso (IRES 1992). If something happens to the worker, he or she is unprotected. Often, the employer will feign ignorance, claiming that he does not even know the worker who has incurred injury on the job (IRES 1992).

According to the first IRES study, there are more migrant women than men engaged in informal work in Turin (IRES 1992). Lavoro nero in social services is a growing sector in response to demographic changes in Turin, the absence of elder care, and the pressure on the Italian welfare state to decrease health care costs. In small- and medium-sized industrial firms, informal labor is not widespread but it does exist, particularly in small mechanical cleaning or repair jobs that do not require the sort of numerical accounting procedures that make it difficult to hide informal forms of labor within industrial manufacturing. But a growing number of migrant men engage in informal contracting for small construction firms that have become more specialized in recent years (IRES 1996). Many migrants who do not plan to remain in Italy are sometimes willing to accept high levels of exploitation in a transitory and instrumental situation (IRES 1992).

It is increasingly difficult for both male and female migrants to find sustainable, registered work, even when they possess resident documents. Migrants have the highest occupational turnover in Italy, and should they lose a regular job during an economic crisis they would have to return to irregular work, except in the unlikely circumstance that another regular job could be found (Reyneri 1998). Also important is that once a migrant's permit expires, the key to its renewal is having a regular job. If the migrant has been working in the economia sommersa and his/her residence permit has expired, the only opportunity for further employment is in the informal domain.

When permissions of stay granted in 1990 expired two years later, for example, migrants were asked to prove that they were in receipt of a minimal income to renew their documents, difficult for those in the informal economy. In 1995 with a second amnesty, it was necessary for an immigrant to be employed and to persuade the employer to register the labor contract as well as to pay an advance amount of money to social security. Few employers were willing to do this, and when they were, the migrants usually had to pay the social contributions themselves (two months' salary). A case that illustrates the precariousness of the job situation for many migrants in the informal economic sector in Turin involved a Romanian couple in their fifties who shared a twenty-four-hour-a-day job, caring for an old, dying woman. Together they were paid eight hundred thousand lira per month, in addition to room and board. This is about half the current average wage for one person. When the old woman died, the couple did not find an equivalent arrangement, but they did find work waiting tables in a bar-restaurant. They had to find somewhere to live, which they did. In this restaurant they were also paid less than half of the expected rate for regularized workers. In 1995, when the national government decreed a second amnesty to enable working migrants to obtain legal documents, the Romanian couple asked their employer to provide proof of work for them, and he agreed to do so for one person. But in the end the employer cheated the couple, taking the money they had given him to pay for the regularization. Expressing anger and disappointment over this betrayal, they lost their jobs and any savings that remained. They had spent their money, were jobless, and had little hope of securing health or unemployment benefits.

Race and Labor Migration in a Declining Zone

Many migrants are employed in the economia sommersa, but this does not explain why they are becoming marginal within local economy and society. It is not enough to suggest that migrants work in the informal economy because they are poor and desperate. According to the 1990 figures for Piedmont, 79.4 percent of migrants were not educated at all and 90 percent were classified as *operai generici,* or generic, nonqualified workers. Since we know that many migrants are educated, these figures indicate that when migrants go to the police offices or the *anagrafe* (registry office),[15] civil servants record that they are uneducated, unskilled, and unqualified. There is in practice a growing, collective racial stigmatization, fueled by uneven practices of power. In Turin, artificial boundaries are drawn between migrant outsiders and local Italians, and power is exercised by demarcating and identifying the culturally different stranieri.

We cannot have a full understanding of the relationship between postcolonial migrants and the labor market in Turin without examining the cultural-ideological and representational practices informing their daily lives. Most postcolonial migrants are marked as physically and culturally distinct, particularly those assumed to be African (Melossi 2000). The working body is perceived and classified through the historically sedimented lenses of modern racialized stereotypes. Distinctions are made on the basis of preconceived assumptions about "natural" cultural traits or merits (Ciafaloni et al. 1999). Migrants are classified in relation to their assumed spatial origins: worlds of poverty and destitution characterized by strange, retrograde cultural practices, including the Islamic religion. Growing labor market segmentation in Turin and other parts of Italy is linked with the production of racial stereotypes about migrants. There is

Mary Ann Akinyi in front of her association shop, From the Nile, in San Salvario, 2001

a prevailing attitude of prejudice, in which the "good" worker is assumed to possess certain personal and cultural qualities that, it is believed, postcolonial migrants cannot by definition acquire (IRES 1992).

Finally, migrants are inserted into a set of social class relationships in Turin and, despite the efforts of some, into a precarious labor force marked by low pay, poor conditions, and the absence of union protections (IRES 1992). Those working in industry and construction generally perform manual or unskilled work, which is often physically onerous and dangerous. Migrants are at an automatic disadvantage as outsiders within a local system that operates through a series of internal political, familial, and friendship networks (Sniderman et al. 2000). Whether or to what extent the closed nature of Turin society will become more open to international cultures depends, to some extent, on the willingness of Turinese to set aside cultural and racial presuppositions when in the presence of foreign migrants. Migrants do not quite fit into the established working class in Turin, and conscious, concerted efforts are required to bridge the gaps.

CHAPTER 5

Race, Politics, and Protest in the Casbah, or San Salvario, Africa

> We all speak from a particular place, out of a particular
> history, out of a particular experience, a particular culture,
> without being contained by that position as "ethnic artists"
> or film-makers. We are all, in that sense, ethnically
> located and our ethnic identities are crucial
> to our subjective sense of who we are.
> —*Stuart Hall, "New Ethnicities"*

> Individual and collective repertoires are . . . inseparable from
> power relations that ultimately are a matter of who may
> or may not do what, when, and where; from power relations
> that govern place-bound project admission, project content,
> and project execution; from power relations that en-gender,
> class-ify, and otherwise simultaneously open up
> and restrict the (time)-spaces of human action.
> —*Pred, "In Other Wor(l)ds"*

> To endure, social inequality requires not only a
> material base, but also a degree of normative support.
> —*S. Smith*, Racism, the City, and the State

Racing Space

Racial stigma is ascribed directly to physical bodies and their locations, produced not only by the state, but also by the institutions of civil society (Jackson 1987; Hall 1996a). Gramsci's writings on modern Italy suggest that serious attention be given to the everyday world of civil society, including institutions such as neighborhoods and communities, ethnic institutions, and cultural and church organizations that play a vital role in producing and reproducing different societies in a racially structured form (Hall 1996b). For Gramsci it is in these institutions, as well as in state institutions, where power is produced and reproduced, where particular constellations of power relations in historically specific times and places penetrate everyday practices and make all sorts of ideas appear as natural or common sense. It is in the grounded terrain of practices, languages, and representations in any specific society that commonsense notions of race help shape social life (Crehan 2002; Hall 1996b; Tabet 1997).

Gramsci struggled to understand the insidious influence of modern nation-state formations, the subtle cultural-ideological forms of power channeled through institutions such as the mass media, capable of reaching into the pores of daily living and invading the soul of human expectation. He developed his concept of hegemony to explore relationships of power and the everyday ways in which these are lived. Although Gramsci believed that economic relations ultimately shaped societies, he was also critical of the often crude economic determinism prevalent among his generation of Marxists. Elaborating on Croce's concept of the "ethico-political" dimension of human practice, or *praxis,* Gramsci asserted that culture and ideology were integral to modern European forms of politics and state power. He wrote: "Croce's thought . . . has forcefully drawn attention to the importance of facts of culture and thought in the development of history . . . to the moment of hegemony and consent in the necessary form of concrete historical bloc."[1] Gramsci's main concern was with how the potential energy of subordinated classes could realize itself as a historical force, when dominant groups held this force in check through consent. People need to be made aware of the incoherence and inadequacy of the commonsense assumptions that they have absorbed, almost automatically and without critical thinking, from the social and cultural environments within which they have grown up. For Gramsci, cultural ideologies were real historical facts and instruments of domination.

During the 1920s and 1930s, Gramsci was concerned about the way that taken-for-granted community beliefs and sentiments were easily captured by right-wing political factions, even when the ideologies supported by these factions appeared to him to be against the best interests of Italian communities. Much of his attention was focused on understanding the social classes that followed Mussolini into the most repressive period in modern Italian history. Gramsci characterized commonsense ideas as the "folklore" of philosophy and as "fragmentary, incoherent, and inconsequential, in conformity with the social and cultural position of those masses whose philosophy it is" (Boothman 1995, 419). The problem of uncritical and taken-for-granted thinking is no less salient today, at the beginning of the twenty-first century (Foucault 1980).

Eric Hobsbawm suggests that, although the state maintains a significant degree of power, the "nation" is in the process of losing an important portion of its old function of constituting a territorially bounded national economy. The nation, Hobsbawm suggests, has been brought into question by significant transformations in the international division of labor, the development of international economic and political networks beyond the control of state governments, the mobility of capital, and international migration. The effects of these changes have been dislocations precipitated by new configurations of racism and by intercommunal frictions. In a climate of fear, the Stranger or Immigrant tends to be blamed for local troubles, an Other who rarely has to be invented, who is present and identifiable as a "public danger and agent of pollution, hating and conspiring against us" (Hobsbawm 1994). In Italian society, racism and xenophobia have entered new and reinvigorated forms of right-wing and mainstream political discourse, sometimes filling the void left by political parties that have recently disappeared or fragmented into new configurations (Kopkind 1991; Carter 1997; Campani 1993; Campani and Palidda 1990; Bocca 1988; Imbruglia 1992; Balbo and Manconi 1992; Cole 1997; Ferrarotti 1988; Gallini 1996; Zincone 1994). Paul Sniderman suggests that in Italy, differences of race now cut deeper than class, religion, ethnicity, and nationality (Sniderman et al. 2000).

Hobsbawm suggests that contemporary racism and xenophobia are but cries of anguish, reactions of weakness and fear fueled by rapid, fundamental, and unprecedented social transformation (1994). But he fails to recognize the structural-historical antecedents of contemporary xenophobia and racism through which some populations have been marked as "naturally" inferior for well over a century (Carter 1997; Tabet 1997). Colette Guillamin describes a system of "altero-referentiality," in which modern European societies define and redefine themselves by demarcating that which they are not, namely an Other. In an altero-referential system, it is the Other who is different, in contrast to whatever class, nation, gender, or race is perceived on the privileged inside. According to Guillamin, Self and Other are always opposed in a European system of signs that privileges the race symbol. Racism in contemporary Europe represents an expression of altero-reference in that it only recognizes Others, demonstrating a failure to recognize and define the Self group (1995). In a world that appears to increasingly operate through a few powerful and competing supranational blocs such as the European Union, the presumed danger of those considered culturally different has come to be perceived as a cause of social disorder (Maneri 1998).

This is illustrated by a series of events that prompted the organization of a major antiracist demonstration in the streets of Turin in which Alma Mater participated. In the 1990s, racial incidents had become frequent in Italy; for example, in 1995 there was a newspaper article on one of the many informational corkboards in the Alma Mater building that recounted a story about two Cameroonian women, twenty-one and thirty-five years old, who boarded a train in Genoa, headed for Turin. As they sat next to a window waiting for the train to begin moving, a young man approached their window from the outside and began pounding a finger on the pane of glass. The two women sat in silence, laughing. They thought he was joking. Instead, the man suddenly spat on the window and then boarded the train. He approached the women while screaming, "You whores, you're here looking for money." A conductor sent the man to the back of the train, but he later reappeared, with four friends. These five young Italian men began to attack the women verbally with racial slurs and insults, and as their anger escalated, they spat at the women, kicking and punching them while naming them as "only prostitutes."[2] While Alma Mater struggles against the common perception that migrant women are prostitutes, the organization has participated in outreach initiatives to instruct migrant prostitutes about threats to their health and how to obtain legal documents, as well as to direct prostitutes to clinics and other places where they may find protection and help.

Migrant women struggle in spaces of vulnerability against commonsense relegation to the marginal and highly expendable social classification as poor and prostitute. The prostitute who in Western ideology embodies both a fear of chaos and a longing for freedom has become in Italy a sign of the contemporary migrant woman (Gilman 1985, 1986). For many, wearing long-sleeved shirts buttoned to the top or loose-fitting dresses is not enough to avoid being mistaken for a prostitute. Prostitutes are popularly classified as streetwalkers, without a proper social place, yet never victims and usually criminals.

In the 1990s, the neighborhood of San Salvario came to be popularly associated with migrants and migrant prostitutes. Located in the heart of Turin's commercial and residential center and near the train station, San Salvario is, in fact, where many African prostitutes have lived. The migrant-woman prostitute, associated with San Salvario in Turin, has become a symbol of the transgressive and assumed potential criminality of the migrant (Carter 1997; Maneri 1998).

Crisis in San Salvario

It is no exaggeration to suggest that, from the late 1980s through the early 1990s, Italian society experienced an anxiety attack, mediated by official discourse about immigration and the media-projected figure of the dark-skinned migrant from the developing world, commonly referred to as *neri*,[3] or blacks. During a period of "social emergency," the city of Turin became a national symbol for the multitude of problems associated with immigration. Perhaps only through the image of Turin could political arguments about immigration truly reach into the hearts of the Italians throughout the country. Turin was the one remaining "real" Italian city, home of the House of Savoy and the country's principal industrial city, comprised of working-class Italians, many of them former southern peasants. Turin was the only northern Italian city that remained relatively culturally homogeneous while also relatively prosperous, a culturally "closed" place where residents rarely traveled and tourists seldom visited. If Turinese were being shaken by international immigration, the Italian nation was surely going to fall apart rapidly if something was not done to stem the tide.

In 1995, media attention turned toward the alleged problems generated by immigration in San Salvario, a central artery in Turin's historical, commercial, and residential zone. National newspapers and magazines produced an abundance of sensationalist stories about racial conflict and urban degradation, inviting readers with dramatic headlines that invoked images of slum conditions around the world—for example, "In the Casbah" and "San Salvario, Africa"[4] in the magazine *L'Espresso*, and "Turinese Mini-Bronx"[5] and "In the Ghetto of San Salvario" in the newspaper *La Stampa*.[6] An outpouring of stories associated immigrants with growing crime, the decline of a high-quality consumer market, degraded real estate values, and the erosion of a local Italian or Turinese community. The massive media coverage encouraged open expression of a rising sense of alarm that had been seething just below the surface of daily life in a neighborhood where migrants settled in ever-growing numbers. With attention drawn to the migrant presence in an identifiable place, San Salvario of Turin became the centerpiece in national and local debates about immigration legislation, sending political parties into frenzied argument while local tensions rose and protests proliferated.

Three consecutive events between 1994 and 1995 triggered media focus on San Salvario. Early in 1994, an alleged Nigerian prostitute was found murdered, and several more were discovered in subsequent months. Then in June 1995, police allegedly drowned a Moroccan boy. Finally, in September 1995 a neighborhood priest wrote a galvanizing letter that was published on the front page of *La Stampa*.

Six Nigerian prostitutes were killed, and some six others were proclaimed missing during a period beginning in March 1994, when the body of a Nigerian woman and her Bosnian client were discovered on the outskirts of Turin. Violent and apparently random murder is uncommon in Turin. In November 1994, another Nigerian was found murdered, one in early April 1995, and two others on April 19. Learning about the prostitutes' deaths, some African migrants living in San Salvario were greatly alarmed and their fears of violent acts against foreigners began to escalate. Someone left a menacing letter at the door of a neighborhood immigrant shop. The letter, which was addressed to a Nigerian man considered a leader among Turin Nigerians, threatened the shop owners, "If you don't stop it we'll kill you, your wife and your children."[7] In response to what many viewed as a generalized threat to migrant prostitutes, the Nigerian Association of Turin and the multiethnic center Kafila organized several meetings for the purpose of airing the fears of Nigerian prostitutes and offering assistance. Some migrants maintained that the murders were racially motivated: "For us this is about a maniac, someone who hates Nigerians."[8] The Nigerian Association agreed that the murders could be interpreted only as racially motivated crimes directed against their co-nationals.

Nigerian and Ghanaian prostitutes were particularly vulnerable to being erased from local history. Many did not possess official documents and were clandestine migrants. When the murders took place, a number of prostitutes expressed the feeling that they were not protected against human-rights abuses in Europe, and some threatened that their leaders would contact Amnesty International or the United Nations to report violent acts against foreigners in Turin. These migrants did not trust that the "forces of order" were making an adequate effort to investigate the murders. The fact that numerous Nigerian prostitutes did not possess official residency documents put them on the defensive when they needed protection, and many expressed fear of deportation should they report violent acts to the authorities. During the Nigerian Association and Kafila meeting for prostitutes, a Nigerian leader argued: "The Turinese must not continue to permit our women to be murdered like animals. Without 'Permissions of Stay' (Permessi di Soggiorno), prostituting oneself is a necessity, not an act that deserves the penalty of death."[9] This migrant man expressed the belief that without possession of state-sanctioned documents required to reside legally in Turin, migrants were living on borrowed time, vulnerable to treatment as other-than-human.

In June, Khalid Aarab was killed. He was an eighteen-year-old Moroccan boy *senza documenti* (without papers). During the warm summer months in Turin, it is customary for young people, especially the sons and daughters of Turin's bourgeois middle classes and old nobility, to frequent a series of nightclubs along the river Po in what is locally referred to as the Murazzi. Some of the most popular clubs are located along the urban corridor of the river, facing the hills on the opposite side, the exclusive domain of wealthy families of the old Italian nobility. Beginning around 1990, the Murazzi rapidly became a multiethnic site. While we were in Turin during the summer of 1995, friends were eager to show us the incredible changes that had taken place in Turin, best exemplified by taking a walk along the Murazzi. We observed an overwhelming presence of young North and sub-Saharan Africans selling their wares, cooking various African foods on barbecues, and frequenting the bars. It was astonishing to visit the Murazzi at night, a place peopled by what appeared to be hundreds of African men and some women milling about while engaged in conversations, the scent of Moroccan spices, cooked meats, and incense filling the air. Allegedly, there was also a considerable amount of drug taking and drinking, practices that began long before immigrants began to participate in the local scene. In 1995, the Italian newspaper *Il Manifesto* referred to the Murazzi as "one of the most important social centers in the city for migrants."[10]

During the early morning hours after a long night of clubbing in mid-June, the young Moroccan Khalid Aarab was killed while he engaged in a series of conflicts with a club bouncer, or *buttafuori,* and police. The private clubs hire bouncers, and some are referred to as "vigilantes" for the political right wing.[11] The police, the bouncer, and witnesses gave different accounts of the story. The most commonly held view among bystanders was that Aarab was beaten by the bouncer, then handcuffed by the police and further beaten, and finally thrown handcuffed into the river Po, where he drowned.

A few days later, Moroccan immigrants organized an antiracist protest that began its march in San Salvario and continued to the Murazzi site where Aarab died.[12] Some five hundred participants, many holding red roses, quietly walked in the rain on a Saturday afternoon, carrying a photo of the deceased, reciting prayers and consolations in Arabic. A newly formed group in San Salvario called the Comitato Spontaneo degli Stranieri (Spontaneous Committee of Foreigners) organized the manifestation. Migrants formed the Spontaneous Committee of Foreigners to oppose an Italian anti-immigrant organization, also located in San Salvario and also called the Comitato Spontaneo. This Italian Spontaneous Committee had already begun to organize a series of demonstrations against drugs and delinquent activities in the neighborhood, for which immigrants were held primarily responsible.[13]

The capstone event involving San Salvario took place in mid-September, when one of the local priests sent a letter to the newspaper La Stampa, in which he complained that the city and residents had to do something about the worsening "situation" (a euphemism for "immigration") in the neighborhood. One of the newspaper's editors, who lived in San Salvario, decided to publish the priest's letter on the front page of La Stampa's national edition. The priest, Don Piero Gallo, warned of the risk of a "civil war between whites and blacks." He urged residents to

> take pen and paper and denounce the landlords. Point out the small and large illegal acts that you are faced with every day, indicate the commercial abuses. Don't wait for everything to rain from above. Put yourself to work, shoulder to shoulder in the public exercise of the citizen's authority to render these streets newly livable. Changing this piece of the city is the job of those who live in it, before anyone else.[14]

Don Gallo expressed a sentiment widely felt among Italian residents of San Salvario that the neighborhood had become "unlivable" as a direct consequence of the growing presence of African migrants. The neighborhood priest, a man who had conducted missionary work in Kenya and who sang hymns in English during Sunday mass, asked Italian residents of San Salvario to report landlord abuses to the authorities. The landlords reputedly rented degraded apartments to foreigners at exorbitantly high prices, encouraging many more to live together in one room than was legally permitted by city housing codes. The priest was, in effect, ascribing the transformation of the neighborhood to the practices of overrenting to (African) foreigners, a transformation that included the housing degradation, criminality, and overcrowding that went hand in hand with overrenting.

After publication of the letter, some local Turinese accused the priest of being a Nazi sympathizer.[15] Don Gallo assured citizens that he was not urging Italian citizens to do anything akin to revealing Jewish persons to the Nazis, but that he was merely asking them to inform on criminals who controlled or mediated illegal activity in San Salvario. He remarked: "Informers were those who gave the Jews away to the Nazis. At stake here is instead the collectivity. The landlords are the true bloodsuckers of this quarter. Even if they are our neighbors. This is a big city, with a lot to give, which renders the act of informing an obligation." Don Gallo called for cooperation between Italian residents of San Salvario, the police, and the city government. He urged, "Make the forces of order and the city government understand that we want to give them a hand."[16]

The priest also expressed a need for the tightening of state control over clandestine immigrants. His letter was saturated with pleas for legality and police protection. Don Gallo voiced his anxieties at a particular historical moment in the early 1990s when millions of Italians were relieved after a few Italian judges had successfully, and uncharacteristically, exposed networks of corruption within the national political parties and state system (see Ginsborg 2003). At the core of Don Gallo's letter was criticism of what was commonly perceived as the growing open expression or shamelessness of criminal activity in San Salvario, especially among North and sub-Saharan Africans, and a plea for an intensified neighborhood police presence. He urged the police to take rigorous action against landlord abuses, while pursuing a far greater number of deportations of illegal immigrants.

Newspaper and television reporters flocked to the neighborhood, spinning stories recounting local grievances about drug trafficking, sex trading, overrenting, and other noxious, antisocial practices. Some Italian residents claimed they had once lived in harmony along these urban streets, but these criminal activities were now making the place unbearable.

The archbishop of Turin and other Catholic priests publicly supported Don Gallo's pleas. This was significant, because the church did not traditionally recognize state borders. The church generally followed a universal humanist philosophy in which the poor and needy (in this instance, immigrants) should never be turned away. After *La Stampa* published the letter, and the church and many San Salvario residents expressed their agreement with Don Gallo's concerns, a twenty-four-hour police force was established to guard the priest's church. When Don Gallo walked outdoors and mounted his bicycle, crowds of local residents greeted him with cheers of support, some adopting terms derived from the antifascist resistance movement: "Hooray, don Piero! Resist!"[17] The municipal government established an 800 number, or *numero verde,* for citizens to report criminal activities. The government also stationed a permanent police force in San Salvario, and the mayor appointed a special mediator to investigate the problems in the neighborhood.

The publication of Don Gallo's letter released a series of frustrations that were brewing just below the surface of daily life, awaiting the opportunity to be openly expressed. Months of rising tension surrounding the prostitute murders and Moroccan drowning reached a peak when anxieties were channeled through Don Gallo's words. With increasing regularity, San Salvario residents held spontaneous and organized anti-immigrant protests. The feelings of fear expressed in these protests were contagious, contributing to anti-immigrant demonstrations in other parts of what the newspaper frequently referred to as Turin's "hot" zones.[18]

These events converged in a national-level discourse on immigration legislation, which led to several new amendments to the Martelli Law. In the process, the neighborhood of San Salvario became the leitmotif of Italy's ongoing effort to deal with the growing presence of international migrants. For San Salvario and Turin, a massive antiracist protest organized by the Immigrant Consulta[19] and the trade unions was the dramatic finale to this particular crisis over immigration. When I returned to Turin in 1996, friends cautioned me not to live in San Salvario; for them, the mere mention of the place conjured notions of dangerous and unhealthy urban living. Locally as well as nationally, the neighborhood had become a symbol for crime, racial conflict, immigration—in sum, the urban crisis.

The conflicts surrounding the presence of immigrants in San Salvario evoke several issues. A situation of social alarm was created around a social imaginary of the migrant. The media portrayed clandestine migrants as synonymous with criminality and urban degradation, while Italian political parties deployed these images in a struggle for political gain. A particular urban space became racialized, associated with conflict, urban decay, and the root of the present evil. Representation (and counterrepresentation), or hegemonic commonsense thought, was a crucial element in the political contest. Not only local, but also national culture and identity were contested in a discourse about the way the neighborhood was going to be defined—as an "Italian" neighborhood, as "multicultural," or as an international and "European" place. And finally, the discourses and events surrounding San Salvario prompt one to ask how international migrants can be linked with the workers' movement in Turin. Just what kind of racialized or interethnic politics was being constituted, and what might the stories and mobilization around issues of community, rather than work, indicate about future forms of solidarity in Turin and elsewhere?

A major feature of what took place in San Salvario during the mid-1990s involved the racialization of space and the spatialization of race. To understand how space and race were produced, we'll need to adopt a highly complex lens capable of capturing the various registers of media, local and national politics, popular protests, and commonsense ideologies that constituted some of the building blocks of the "race-ing" of this urban European space. Before proceeding to an examination of these registers as they were played out between 1994 and 1995, I will outline the economic and sociological contours of San Salvario: the social class, religious, and ethnic composition of the quarter.

Ghetto or Latin Quarter: The Eight Streets of San Salvario

De Certeau (1998) wrote that landscape is produced when we walk along the streets, streets that in San Salvario come to life gradually while the newcomer becomes acquainted with particular market vendors and shop owners. It is a commercial zone located in the center of Turin, for urban dwellers the site of a daily market in fruit, vegetables, household goods, and apparel. Two of the city's most frequently used trams pass through San Salvario: one leaves passengers in front of the Madama Cristina Market, the other next to Turin's train station, the Porta Nuova. Every day with the exception of Sunday, San Salvario is a crowded area, bustling with people, cars, buses, and trams moving toward marked and unmarked destinations. To a newcomer, however, San Salvario can be a chilly, unwelcoming place. The transition is easiest if an Italian intermediary is willing to introduce one to a market vendor, humanizing both vendor and client and reducing the possibility that the client might be sold poor-quality goods at prices well above their market value. To the unidentified client, shop owners are standoffish; by contrast they are relatively warm and friendly to known Italian customers, who are likely to be served first even if they entered the store after a stranieri. In the coffee shop–bakeries, ritual sites where Italian customers take a morning cup of espresso *(caffè)* and a brioche, or an afternoon coffee or sandwich, an aura of friendliness toward newcomers is notably absent; the sort of welcoming attitude that one might expect from a shop owner whose livelihood depends on customer purchases is lacking. There may be a weak greeting of *buon giorno* or *buona sera,* one of the embedded practices of daily social exchange, but an aloof guardedness frequently replaces sociability, leaving the newcomer feeling as if she has entered a private domain instead of a public establishment.

The "eight streets of San Salvario" together have become a national symbol of racial conflict, but encoded in the sensory and experiential world of these streets is a far more complex portrait than the media and political parties were ever really interested in capturing. Long before international migrants arrived on the local scene, San Salvario was a relatively socially heterogeneous quarter. Built in the mid-nineteenth century in a geometric pattern designed to facilitate commerce, the quarter has never been associated with a single, dominant socioeconomic class. Its architectural style is relatively homogeneous, much like the historic center that it borders, but its social composition is far more diverse (CICSENE 1996). One of the most distinctive characteristics of San Salvario is that it is a quarter that may be expected to represent religious tolerance because it is home to two Catholic churches, a Protestant or Valdese church, and a synagogue. The neighborhood is now also the site of at least two storefront mosques. These distinct religious institutions have generated numerous schools, bakeries, clubs, and voluntary organizations in San Salvario.

The social-economic composition of the neighborhood has undergone many of the same processes of social and environmental degradation experienced in the rest of the city over the past fifteen or so years (IRES 1995). San Salvario is polarized socially between a population of residents living in buildings with well-preserved historical architecture and others living in degraded structures. Many wealthy professionals continue to live in the eastern corridor that overlooks the Valentino Park[20] (IRES 1995). San Salvario is home to an above-the-urban-average proportion of highly educated professionals, as well as a higher than average percentage of low-skilled, illiterate, blue-collar workers (CICSENE 1996, 34). Much of the central portion of the neighborhood was, until recently, populated by bourgeois middle classes, chiefly shop owners and commercial vendors. There is also a transitory population of single international students who rent spaces temporarily while they attend the Polytechnic University, part of which is located in an old castle in nearby Valentino Park (Valentino Castle). In keeping with the overall urban pattern, the elderly population of San Salvario is rapidly expanding. The high volume of prostitutes, delinquents, drug dealers, and addicts for which the neighborhood is well known is anything but new in San Salvario.

The western portion of the quarter, near the Porto Nuova train station, is a predominantly working-class area and was an initial settlement zone for thousands of Calabrian, Sicilian, Sardinian, and Venetian migrants after the war. The novelist Paolo Volponi described the rich social terrain of the area adjacent to the station:

> The first edifices are battalions of Calabrian immigrants from the years during the period called the "boom." The successive tidal waves, of Sicilians and Sardinians who arrived afterwards and didn't enter industry. And then, Lombardians, Venetians from the marches working in small localized industries, scattered among the body of the people. The buildings at the cross-streets, of distinct and indigenous small-bourgeoisie, overbearing and sick. The lowest houses of prostitutes, ambulant sellers, thieves, butcher-boys, a cast of characters as in a theatrical performance, drivers, porters, guards, students, apprentices, dancers, transvestites, models, restaurateurs, photographers, salesmen, encyclopedia sellers, police informers, cops, select errand boys, the early retired, prisoners on temporary release, jury witnesses, parking attendants. (Volponi, quoted in CICSENE 1996, 25)

The neighborhood has experienced several demographic shifts during the past twenty-five years. The San Salvario of the 1970s was polarized between a very wealthy class of residents along Valentino Park and relatively poor strata of southern Italian migrants around Via Saluzzo, south of the train station. Then, during the 1980s, the neighborhood became one of the preferred zones for the settlement of international migrants, the majority from Morocco, Tunisia, and Nigeria. Consistent with an overall urban pattern, many Italian workers have retired or moved to the peripheries, while the San Salvario working class is reportedly being predominantly replaced by extracomunitari, that is, those from a country outside the European Union (IRES 1995). CICSENE cites a population loss in San Salvario of 12.3 percent in ten years, which has accelerated since 1989, when immigrants began to collect in the area. The participants in the exodus are generally from the more wealthy socioeconomic classes. They leave behind "redundant" workers, including the elderly, low-income families, and extracomunitari (IRES 1995). A relatively strong proportion of people living in the neighborhood are transient residents, students, immigrants, temporary workers, or people with illegal housing contracts (CICSENE 1996). There is also a higher than average percentage of unemployed living in San Salvario, some 17.5 percent, compared to the urban average of 11.49 percent in 1996. Many of the unemployed are unskilled women over the age of thirty (CICSENE 1996). In an effort to encourage government and business investment, two local studies of the neighborhood have reported that San Salvario has the capacity to transform itself into a quarter characterized by market niches, which would be the potential site of a select consumer market for ethnic goods and specialties, a multiethnic urban quarter like the Latin Quarter of Paris instead of an urban ghetto of the United States (IRES 1995; CICSENE 1996).

Among the many popular complaints voiced by residents is the fear that violence and criminal activity are increasing, an apprehension that has allegedly compelled some residents to flee the neighborhood. But the sense of fear often far exceeds any actual experience of violence: "Even if there's an absence of personal negative experience, the perception of a diffuse danger remains" (CICSENE 1996, 29). Although a great deal has been made of an "increase" in violence, crime, and drug trafficking in San Salvario, the changes are not nearly as dramatic as commonsense wisdom suggests. Migrants are often more visible than Italian drug dealers or prostitutes, but the presence of migrants has not added any quantifiable difference to drug dealing or other delinquent activities in the neighborhood. The migrants may have merely replaced some of the Italian prostitutes and drug dealers (IRES 1995, 310). Furthermore, data from the Turin *questura* (police headquarters) reveals that criminality is not any higher in San Salvario than in other parts of the city. The proportion of burglaries and street robberies corresponds to the urban average (CICSENE 1996).

Although the modern architectural planning of San Salvario was intended to encourage high population density, crowded conditions have recently become a point of contention among residents. Some residents link property and commercial degradation to increasing population density as well as "the poor quality of many inhabitants," the diffusion of petty criminality, and the co-presence of diverse ethnic communities (IRES 1995). Congestion, overpopulation, traffic, pollution, and noise, as well as prostitution, drug trafficking, and other forms of crime, are commonly invoked by some residents to lament the "situation" in San Salvario. Underlying these discourses is a social-class tension between proponents of architectural and historical preservation, those who promote gentrification through such measures as reducing traffic, improving greenery, establishing park benches, and reducing noise, and others who are disenfranchised or underprivileged. Turin's historic center is represented by contradictory social interests: dual cities of diverse groups that live beside each other but do not communicate with each other, thus creating tension over the use of space and the social norms expected of those living in the neighborhood (IRES 1995). San Salvario has been characterized as the site of two worlds: one of stores and services, the other of drug sales and prostitution.

According to IRES, 27.01 percent of the population in San Salvario lives in substandard housing. Some Italian inhabitants have targeted blame on the augmented presence of extracomunitari. The problem with the buildings did not, however, appear recently. Real estate speculators purchased some of the degraded spaces, which they now frequently rent to extracomunitari (IRES 1995). Some proprietors do not maintain their buildings, but they readily maximize their profits by renting overcrowded rooms to newcomers at exorbitant rates. Increased police repression was adopted as a solution to what was popularly considered the practice of overrenting to immigrants by Italian landlords, but the presence of police has not begun to resolve the problem of urban degradation. Increased police controls have only reinforced the perception and treatment of neri as synonymous with crime and disorder (CICSENE 1996).

Despite concerns about decline, San Salvario remains a fairly economically dynamic commercial zone. It is the site of one of the city's daily markets, specializing in fresh produce and clothing. A host of small shops lines the eight streets surrounding the market. The quarter once catered to an upper-income clientele, many of whom traveled to the urban center from the surrounding hills to do their shopping. But declining incomes and demographic shifts have been a trend in Turin for fifteen or twenty years, and San Salvario has lost some of its most coveted patrons. When migrants began to settle in the area, some vendors modified their offering of goods to satisfy a more ethnically mixed clientele. Currently, some 40 percent of Italian shop owners on Via Gallior, Via Berthollet, and Via Madama Cristina serve mixed customers. Others have refused to diversify their offerings; for instance, some hair salon owners do not wish to hire African hairstylists, arguing that the presence of foreigners would only attract greater numbers of African customers (CICSENE 1996, 103). Some Italian clients have reportedly abandoned shopping in San Salvario because they "dislike black skin" (102).

Many shop owners complain that they have had to reduce the quality of their goods—their assortments of clothing, cloth, leather, and foodstuffs—because customers from the Turin hills are no longer willing to frequent the area. The contention among shop owners that the quality of offerings has been reduced for the purpose of satisfying migrant customers merits further scrutiny. It is not clear, for example, that Africans who are known to dispense considerable sums of money to buy quality goods that they send to families in their countries of origin would deliberately purchase low-quality items. And, contrary to popular opinion, migrants have made a considerable contribution to the Turin economy, with particular emphasis on neighborhoods such as San Salvario, where a disproportionate number of migrants live. As a migrant woman in Alma Mater argued:

> If you go to San Salvario or Porta Palazzo, you see shops that have clothing, often colorful, with sequins and the like that Italians never before bought, and now because of African migrants these stores are thriving. They have added different tastes, colors to this world. Not to mention how much they buy and send back, say, to Morocco, where this money helps to build the countries, just as the Italian migrants in Germany and those other European countries sent back money to Italy. Women buy hundreds of pairs of cheap Italian shoes to send back to their poor families in Africa. Also, young migrants frequent the bars in these Turin neighborhoods. So the fact that they are here has done a lot for the local economy.

In the early 1990s, a number of "ethnic shops" appeared in San Salvario. Thirty-three were operating in 1992, specializing in hairstyling, cooked and packaged foodstuffs, and clothing. These businesses sold to immigrant clients living in other parts of the city until many shied away from shopping in the neighborhood, fearing the effects of heightened police surveillance. By the early 1990s, San Salvario was the site of two noncompeting and fully separate markets: one by and for migrants, and the other by and for Italians (CICSENE 1996).

In an effort to defend their property and neighborhood, some Italian inhabitants of San Salvario began to organize. The strategy of one association of small shop owners in the area, Oasis, was to urge the city government to construct a parking lot under the Madama Cristina Market, to help alleviate problems of immense congestion and pollution.[21] Another group of vendors from the Madama Cristina Market opposed the project. The theme of crime among migrants prompted another group of shop owners to organize a Spontaneous Anti-Crime Committee (Comitato Spontaneo Contra-Criminalita). This is reported to be a politically right-wing, anti-immigrant organization. The group, which has held numerous public demonstrations, is not connected either with the Oasis group or with the Madama Cristina organization of shop owners, which both tend to

One of several African hair salons in San Salvario in 1995

play down the ethnic or racial tensions in the neighborhood. However, all three organizations have agreed that San Salvario needs enhanced police surveillance to reduce the growing rate of criminal activity. Another organization, called Coordination against Racism (Coordinamento Control il Razzismo), has objected to the Anti-Crime Committee, orchestrating anti–anti-crime demonstrations (IRES 1995). The group Coordination against Racism does not divide its membership according to religious or ethnonational identification. Instead, it represents itself as an interethnic group founded as part of a unified strategy to fight racism in San Salvario and throughout Turin.[22] Certain conflicts have erupted on the basis of religion, as when Muslims protested the obligation to use storefronts and private homes to hold religious services.[23]

For residents of San Salvario, it may be that the most dramatic transformation is the growing multiethnic composition of the quarter. The emergence of a highly visible degree of ethnic diversity, as well as the effects of wider economic restructuring on the neighborhood, seems to have triggered a defense of territory among some members of the local population, or a "turf war." For some, cultural difference signals collapse of the known world. Among many, there is an impulse to blame someone (the stranieri)—some entity that is identifiable, that one can point to with a modicum of certainty.

Graffiti in San Salvario, 1996

"We Are Not Racists; They Make Too Much Noise"

A San Salvario hairstylist of southern Italian origin who has lived in Turin for thirty-seven years asserts that he will not allow neri to enter his business. He explains: "(It's) exactly like the time here when they didn't let in southerners because we were ugly, dirty, and bad." Defending his prejudices, he adds, "This is not racism: they bring AIDS with them, they don't wash themselves, they are arrogant, they double-park, they don't pay taxes, the men get drunk on beer in the middle of the street, the women fight, they yell at you from the streets, and the police only make witty remarks."[24] For other, frequently elderly residents of San Salvario, there is an urge to instruct the extracomunitari about "community norms," to teach the newcomer to act "right." Another shop owner explains his behavior toward Africans: "Simply, in a couple of cases, I had to get tough, but it was not difficult to make them understand that here we say *buon giorno* and *buona sera*. We don't scream, we don't make a dirty mess, and we have to comport ourselves like civilized people. If an African steps out of line, I throw him out. But at this point no one steps out of line anymore."[25]

The Otherness or cultural difference marking Africans in San Salvario has become a point of justification, an explanation for why it is so difficult to live next door to "them." The discursive practices through which the term *extracomunitari* became a metaphor for crime can be understood in relationship to cultural characterizations of African migrants as noisy, dirty, and ill-mannered. Certain migrants are stigmatized with these characterizations by virtue of the fact that they come from poor countries located in the far south, and perhaps because many of them are Muslim. Africans may be stereotyped as ill-mannered (in ways that southern Italian immigrants once were), and their proximity to Italians may be rendered problematic because they speak different languages, understand diverse cultural codes, wear colorful and unusual clothing, or follow non-Italian religious practices.

Racism, according to the Italian sociologist Enrico Pugliese, is not socially acceptable in contemporary Italy, and few people will admit to being "racist." Instead, intolerance and racism have been fused under a veneer of "differentialism," or "new cultural racism," which carries the pretense of a nonracist stance toward migrant populations because it is presumed to operate without judgment about the intrinsic worth of other cultural practices. As nineteenth-century theories of biologically distinct "races" have been scientifically refuted, European racism has most recently been reincarnated in the language of "cultural difference" (Stolcke 1995). Hidden in assumptions in much contemporary racial discourse is the belief that cultures are constituted by irreconcilable differences. Thus, migrant cultures are portrayed as so different that it would be impossible to justify their cultural practices as in any way commensurate with the Italian "way of life." The notion of mutually incomprehensible cultural differences implies that cultures are fixed in bounded spaces, in the sense of both land and the physical body.[26] Should we follow the argument about cultural difference proposed in the new cultural racism (which is actually an old, modernist idea) to its logical conclusion, we might suggest that the mutual existence of different cultures leads necessarily in just one of two directions: ethnic conflict, or a process in which migrant cultures are subsumed into dominant Italian or European cultures.[27] Indeed, Sniderman found that the wave of prejudice and group conflicts washing over Western Europe was extremely menacing because so many people were indiscriminately ready to categorize others as belonging to a group other than one's own (Sniderman et al. 2000). And this eruption of resentment over immigrants strengthens the hand of the political right and exposes the vulnerability of the left.

Critics of "multiculturalism" are often assumed to subscribe to the rhetoric of the Italian political right. But intolerance of cultural difference is not the exclusive domain of the political right. One member of the PDS, the Partito Democratico della Sinistra (Democratic Party of the Left),[28] whose bicycle was stolen by a migrant, is quoted saying that "they" have to follow "our" norms instead of behaving as though they are living in Marrakech: "For years there has been a north-south festival and during the Unità festival,[29] there was even a Moroccan restaurant. But we also have to be able to say that those who stay in this country have to live according to *our* rules, *our* objectives. We follow our own rules, but the way they live, they seem to be in Marrakech!!"[30]

A series of "cultural misunderstandings" between various Italians and migrants are appearing in Turin (Maher 1996; IRES 1992). The idea of cultural mediation, first imagined by participants in the IRES research group on immigration and later developed by members of Alma Mater and Harambe, was conceived as a method for bridging misrepresentations and misrecognitions between newcomers and Italians. One effect of the new cultural racism is the manner in which the idea of cultural difference is employed to justify the construction of symbolic boundaries between migrants and Europeans. Culturally different practices among non-Europeans are frequently reduced to incomprehensible examples of barbarism, expressions of "unmodern" society. There is very little effort to recognize the workings of what are, in fact, numerous and diverse cultural codes, which are continually changing in the course of daily practices. As in San Salvario, a closed and exclusive sense of a truly "Italian," somehow monolithic and territorially bounded cultural identity has been portrayed as natural and real, in distinction from a homogenized vision of the neri. The reification of culture as bounded, fixed, or finished makes it difficult for many people to see beyond cultural stereotypes in which assumed cultural differences are considered unbridgeable (Pred 2000).

Faced with new and diverse cultural actors, the neighborhood of San Salvario has suddenly been reborn as an exclusively "Italian" rather than a socially heterogeneous place. History is inscribed in lived places, and some residents express nostalgia while recalling memories of the way the quarter once was (supposedly), when the trams did not yet have doors: "Under the porticoes of via Nizza, imagine this, there was the Montiglio: a bar with a small orchestra. . . . I took my husband by the arm, and we went to listen to the philharmonic. Now, it doesn't have to be the evening. You risk your life even in the daytime."[31] Images of the past are contrasted with what is regarded as a current moment of social illness. Another resident reflects: "It was a beautiful place, livable, happy. Now, if you look around yourself, you don't see anything but drug-addicts looking for stuff, and

A Nigerian takeout restaurant specializing in West African styles of cooking, 2001

lowered shutters."[32] Some residents desire return to an unforgettable time instead of embracing the changing world that many Italians living in San Salvario find threatening and anxiety-provoking (Pred 2000).

When a group of urban residents proposed the building of another intercultural center in an old school building near Don Gallo's church in San Salvario, there was strong popular reaction. The intercultural center would have been located in the western or working-class section of the neighborhood. Six hundred local residents signed a petition opposing the launching of a multicultural center, arguing that, instead of building a new multiethnic center, the city ought to relocate the police station in the same space.

An example of social conflict in San Salvario is illustrated in the story of a middle-aged Turinese painter, who, early one morning, sat in a local restaurant eating a pizza where several young North Africans were also consuming a meal. The local Italian claimed that the Africans were drunk and disorderly, speaking with loud, rude, and inappropriate voices. Turning in their direction, he instructed them to keep quiet, to which one of the young men allegedly responded by hitting the painter over the head with a bottle, and then abandoning the injured man, who lay flat on the floor. Once the Turinese man had regained control of himself, he ran to his nearby apartment, gathered a couple of loaded pistols, and began his "search for Moroccans" through the streets of San Salvario. Just as he was about to shoot an innocent North African who had completed his shift as a dishwasher at the Pizzeria, a police officer approached and arrested the Turin man. As it turned out, the arms were unregistered, and the man had a criminal record as an ex-terrorist from the extreme left group called Nucleo Comunista Territoriale. Here, as in other instances, former members of terrorist groups once assumed to be allied with the political left appear to have migrated to the political right. The Italian assailant was arrested for attempted murder and possession of illegal arms.

There are several significant dimensions to this story. From the middle-aged Italian man's point of view, the North African youth were behaving in a culturally inappropriate manner because they were loud and noisy. Furthermore, as an older Italian man with the authority of age, he was culturally justified in admonishing and putting the young men in their places. The fact that the North African youth did not accept this censorship may have something to do with the fact that "noise" is defined differently in their cultures of origin. The overreaction on the part of at least one of the North Africans—hitting the man with a bottle—may have been the expression of anger and frustration among youth and migrants who feel put down by local Italians and alienated in Italian society. Expressions of anger about noise and inappropriate behavior were common in San Salvario during the mid-1990s. At that time, many elderly residents complained that the loud noise coming from several neighborhood nightclubs frequented by Africans kept them awake at night. Some of the clubs have since closed, while other, equally loud nightclubs located throughout the residential zones of Turin have remained open.

Newspaper reports quoted people complaining, "We cannot live in this quarter." This lament was frequently instantiated by crime and noise. One news article described a night of conflict between "whites" and "immigrants":

> Again a night of disorder in San Salvario. Of furious fighting between whites and immigrants. Of wounds and denunciations. A night of deafening noise: screams, alarms set off, police sirens . . . there are youth who scream out songs, listening to music at all volumes: they are Moroccans, Nigerians, and Italians. The light goes on in three or four apartments, someone stands out on the balcony and yells: "BE QUIET." Another one hides behind his closed curtains and threatens to call the police. From a window a basin of water is thrown, from another a vase of geraniums.[33]

As the story continued, the contest disintegrated when a woman was hit with a bottle after she pleaded for silence. In another instance several Italian youth beat a migrant after they saw him urinating on a public wall—an image that was once captured in the Italian film *Bread and Chocolate* to depict the cultural displacement of southern Italian immigrants struggling to make ends meet in postwar Switzerland. In the film, Swiss police arrest a southern Italian migrant for urinating in public, a practice not frowned on in his place of origin.

Migrants are often selectively perceived in negative terms as dangerous, uncivilized, criminal, poor and abandoned, and extremely needy (Marini 1996). Many an Italian prejudice is produced through assumptions that migrants are "competing" with Italians for scarce resources, including jobs and housing (ibid.). Such fears are fueled by a conjunction of market uncertainty and a tendency to view foreigners as Martians or creatures from the deep, without any historical relationship to Italian society. As it was put in an article in *L'Espresso,* Italy is being "invaded" by strangers. This statement represents a ritual reversal or projection of danger, in which the migrant—threatened by expulsion, violence, and subtle prejudices—is instead perceived as the threat. This pattern, which Judith

Butler refers to as "white paranoia," operates in a historical-racist episteme through which the world is interpreted. Butler describes the black body as the identifiable site where racist violence both fears and protects itself against the specter of its own rage (1993). As Fanon suggests, white Europeans and Americans popularly characterize black bodies as essentially threatening, dangerous, and potentially violent; hence, white society has a continual compulsion to construct a physical distance to protect the sanctity of what is posited as "pure" space, namely, white bodies (1968). The white "community," as it is constructed, needs police protection against a threat signified by the black body. Feelings of anger, fear, and frustration among Europeans are projected onto the violence, which is envisioned as intrinsic to blacks.

Confronted by diverse international migrants from developing countries, some of Italian society turns inward, constructing itself in an imagined territory characterized by a common cultural identity (Delle Donne 1993). The many structural forms of distinction that preceded the current phase of international migration seem to have been forgotten (Goldberg 1993; Gilroy 2000; Gilmore 2002; Wieviorka 1993). But even in Italy, the present was not born from nothing, and the sediments of racial prejudice are not hidden very deeply beneath the surface.

Racialized Accretions of the Past: The South, and the South of the South

Paola Tabet likens the racial system in Italy to an engine that has been part of Italian culture for hundreds of years but began to be openly recognized and expressed only in the mid-1980s with the arrival of African migrants (1997). In everyday discourse one often hears Italians say, "We Italians are not racists, this is the first time we've had contact with them! So we don't know them, and it's only for a little bit of time that we've seen them . . . what do you expect, we don't know them."[34] This idea that Italian society has only recently been exposed to Africans and other people from developing countries is simply a myth that belies historical fact (Tabet 1997; Del Boca 1992; Labanca 1992). Africans and people from Oceania, America, and Asia became part of the Italian imagination when Europeans began invading their territories in the seventeenth century and forced on them a European concept of production and cultural values. Racialized images founded on ideas about natural differences between human groups and hierarchies based on the notion of unalterable domination of some and the subjection of others were constructed as part of specific historical and economic relations, including slavery and colonialism (Guillaumin 1995). Italian and other European missionaries, geographers and anthropologists, criminologists, Italian military, colonial administrators, architects, and settlers constructed "race" over hundreds of years (Del Boca 1992; Labanca 1992; Fuller 1988).

At least two historical moments most directly structure contemporary processes of racialization and racialized conflicts in Turin. One is the postwar internal migration of southern Italians, and the other is Italian nineteenth- and twentieth-century colonialism in Africa. As instruments in the organization of power relations and modes of insertion into social hierarchies, racialization and ethnocentrism are expressed in ideological constructions of difference embedded in colonialism and in northern Italian prejudices toward southern Italians (Tabet 1997; Dickie 1999). John Dickie points out that, since the end of the nineteenth century, southern Italy has been represented as a dangerous, primitive, magical, criminal, backward cradle of Italian and European civilization that is alluringly African or Oriental (1999). The repertoire of images and stereotypes of the Italian south is used to define Italy as a civilized nation, in contrast to the sense of where that civilization fades into barbarity. The "strange territory" of the south has been one of Italy's most important funds of images of alterity.

Regarding the presence of southern Italians in Turin, a former mayor, Diego Novelli, recently noted:

> There is all of this surprise about an immigrant emergency. This astonishes people. To me, the same film was shown thirty or thirty-five years ago. The same aggravation of the people, the discomfort, the intolerance, the dirt, the noise.[35]

Novelli recalls another instance of "emergency," another moment with episodes of intolerance when three hundred thousand to four hundred thousand southern Italians migrated to Turin to work for Fiat. During the 1950s and 1960s, the number of migrants that moved to Turin was equivalent to the size of the local population. Arriving at the Porto Nuovo train station, most were able to locate jobs but had considerable difficulty finding housing and maintaining their families. The signs attached to many apartment buildings read, "We don't rent to southerners" (Non affittiamo ai meridionali).

Many southern migrants, or *meridionali,* as they are popularly called, slept on benches in the small piazza across from the train station. Others stayed in crowded rooms with ten or fifteen of their compatriots (Fofi

1964). Few were happy about the way they were treated by Piedmontese, with whom most social interactions were limited to the work context. Outside the factory, most Piedmontese preferred to maintain superficial rapport with southerners that may have lived next door or in the same neighborhood.[36] Fofi documents the displeasure that many meridionali felt when northerners treated them with an absence of trust. Most reported that Piedmontese

> don't want meridionali to live next to them, don't want to be friends, keep us at a distance, they hate us, they exploit us, they cannot "see" us, they consider us like beasts, or they treat us with disinterest, and they don't miss an opportunity to make us feel inferior. (Fofi 1964, 251)

Many southern Italians believed the southerners and Piedmontese followed different models of comportment, the latter tending toward coolness and detachment, and the former showing boisterousness and warmth: "They can't deal with us because it is true that we are different from them" (Fofi 1964, 253). Southerners complained that any true effort to understand the other's culture was one-sided; only the meridionali tried to see and to understand the northern, Piedmontese worldview.[37] Southern migrants endured painful discrimination in employment and housing, and were socially ostracized: "In some places in Turin it was as offensive to be a southerner as to be poor" (Sabel 1985, 150; Fofi 1964). A northern epithet for the southerners was *marocchino*, a derogatory term northern Italians used to describe southern Italians, which came into vogue in the early 1990s to describe North African migrants.

During the postwar migration, Piedmontese described southern Italian migrants in Turin in the following ways: they don't want to work or are lazy, they are all "delinquents"; they are out to do something horrible to the Piedmontese; they use the knife too much; they are barbaric toward their wives and treat women poorly in general; they have too many children and do not use birth control; they are ignorant and stupid (Fofi 1964; Campani and Palidda 1990). These popular stereotypes served to classify meridionali as essentially inferior to and intrinsically different from northern Italians.

By the time southern Italians migrated north to work in the factories, popular codes of alterity had already been incorporated into modern European social science and state legislation. Employing a medical model of health and deterioration, the physical bodies of various classes, races, and genders were scientifically mapped along a scale of "normalcy" and "pathology" (Gilman 1985, 1986; Foucault 1978). On the basis of the empirical gathering of observable bodies, Italian social scientists such as Lombroso and Niceforo classified southern Italians as a separate and distinct "race" of people (Niceforo 1898; Lombroso 1923; Carter 1997). After national unification in 1861, stereotypes of southern Italians became entrenched in Italian regionalism (Levy 1996; Cento Bull 1996). Established stereotypes informed practices that relegated southern Italians to the lowest forms of skilled or unskilled labor.

The emergence of modern European social science and its rigid, hierarchical classifications by race, class, and gender corresponded to an epoch of exploration as well as imperialist expansion. The desire to discover the "mysteries" of Africa began at the end of the eighteenth century (Del Boca 1992). Italians, like other Europeans, had a passion for voyage and exploration in Africa that was often supported by Le Société Géografique. Italian explorers and travelers went all over the continent, but most were drawn to the area around the Nile Valley in the east. Italy declared part of Eritrea a colony in 1882 and they soon expanded into the Ethiopian highlands, where they began a two-decade war that they ultimately lost to the Abyssinians (Negash 1987). Humiliated, Italians nevertheless began a second war in Africa when they entered Libya in 1911 with one hundred thousand troops. Their interest was in seizing the best agricultural land for Italian settlers, and they hoped that through emigration the colonial empire could be transformed into an extension of the mother country (C. Segre 1974). Italian authorities hoped that colonial expansion would help ease national pressures of severe surplus population and unemployment, particularly in southern Italy (Hess 1966; Pankhurst 1964). Many were led to believe that they were traveling to Ethiopia, Somalia, and Libya to get "their" land—that is, land that belonged to Italians.[38] Italy first entered Africa in 1869 and remained there until 1943, when it was chased out of Libya. In this arch of time, a little less than seventy-five years, Italy conquered a colonial empire of some millions of kilometers.

The colonial war that involved a great deal of consent among Italian citizens was the campaign against Ethiopia. Del Boca suggests that Italians thought of Ethiopia as a mysterious planet, capable of igniting fantasies and of stimulating every variety of appetite (1992). When Mussolini's army invaded Ethiopia from the north and south with five hundred thousand troops in 1935, Italian colonialism took on new tones of racism and violence (Fuller 1988). For months, hundreds of ships embarked from Naples, carrying hundreds of soldiers and thousands of cannons and missiles. During the seven-month war and in successive operations of the "great colonial police," thousands of books were written, most of them autobiographies. Most soldiers, as well as cartographers, merchants, government functionaries, and "experts," went to Africa in search of adventure and glory, seeing their presence in East Africa as an expansion of the Italian empire. After the war, the masses of Ethiopians revolted permanently in small wars, which placed Italians on the defensive and, argues Del Boca, brought terror and genocide to Ethiopia (1992; Pankhurst 1998).[39]

When the Italian empire was proclaimed in 1936, Mussolini instituted a policy of direct rule and wrote colonial ideologies of the racial superiority of Italians into racial legislation and residence (Sbacchi 1985). Laws were issued to offset the Italian proclivity to fraternize with the Ethiopians, and to encourage in Italians a colonial consciousness and sense of Italian nationalism: "Fascist officials complained that the racial superiority of the Italian conqueror did not exist in Ethiopia because Italian colonial policy indulged in elevating the Ethiopians, according them clemency, and tolerating equality between Italians and Ethiopians" (Sbacchi, quoted in Carter 1997, 179). The politics of racial segregation, of the guardianship of the purity of the dominant "race," and the defense of the prestige of the race were imposed in ever more drastic ways by Fascist Italy. Claudio Segre suggests that Italians were as preoccupied as any other colonial power with maintaining their prestige and dominance over Africans (1974). Force tended to be applied arbitrarily, there was no justice system yet a great deal of abuse in military tribunals, and there was a general contempt for Africans, which was associated with the will to segregate them (Tabet 1997).

The madame system, or *madamism*—illegal or temporary marriage between Italian men and Ethiopian women—was diffuse among all social ranks in Ethiopia, Somalia, and Eritrea beginning in the nineteenth century (Pankhurst 1964, 1969; Sbacchi 1985; Carter 1997). Mussolini believed that madamism contradicted the rigid segregation of the colonized from the colonizer and detracted from Italian authority and prestige. Italian authorities took all sorts of measures to undermine this practice—for instance, by forbidding Italian bachelors to have female servants and preventing Ethiopian women from entering government offices alone (Sbacchi 1985). Racial laws prohibited the legal recognition of mixed unions and instituted a legal system of discrimination against the "half caste" children of these unions. In 1933, the Organic Law for Eritrea and Italian Somaliland introduced the idea of "physical characteristics" for making distinctions between persons. Children of unknown parentage, assumed through the reading of their physical characteristics to have at least one white parent, were entitled to petition for Italian citizenship. Under Mussolini in 1936, racist articles began to appear in Italian newspapers: "Fascism protects the race and tries to keep it pure. The Italian nation possesses qualities which should not be allowed to become general property" (Carter 1997, 181). By 1937, Fascist legislation assigned the children of Ethiopian women and Italian men to the status of the mother instead of the father. Africa, or the "south of the south," as it is commonly referred to, had become an imaginary territory inhabited by people whose racial and, by extension, cultural, inferiority was below that of southern Italians.

There is a myth in Italian society that even if Italians did engage in colonial endeavors, Italian colonialism was more humane, tolerant, and different from other colonialisms (Del Boca 1992; Tabet 1997; Dickie 1999). However, even if Italian colonialism was different from that of the English or French, for instance, Italy was in Africa for almost three-quarters of a century. The myth that Italians were kind colonists is supported by the commonsense self-representation that *Noi italiani non siamo razzisti* (We Italians are not racist). But as Paola Tabet suggests, racial ideology was active not only in Africa itself but in the colonizer's country and it was diffused in a variety of ways. Among the avenues of transmission were colonial novels that exoticized Africans, and daily local and national stories and images of black servants, or of blacks as savages and cannibals (Di Carmine 2004; Labanca 1992). Between 1935 and 1941, more than a million Italians went to East Africa, and through their stories and photographs the colonial imaginary entered directly into the historical familial and collective memory (Tabet 1997). Representations of Africa and Africans live on today in stories about experiences told in families and in colonial artifacts that one in ten Italians currently possesses (Del Boca 1992; Tabet 1997).

Criminalization and Policing

After *La Stampa* published Don Gallo's letter, rising tensions in San Salvario were escalated by intense and prolonged media attention. The neighborhood was gripped by a sense of panic over the increasing residential proximity of Italians to non-European *stranieri*. Many residents expressed fear of growing criminal activity, particularly in the form of prostitution, and the related practices of drug-trafficking, petty theft, and violent conflict between rival criminal groups. Although San Salvario had long been a site of Italian prostitutes and young Italian drug addicts, such criminal behaviors were incarnated in the figures of the foreign African woman prostitute and male North African drug dealer.

Neri were being criminalized, one of several processes of racialization that contribute to the social production and reproduction of subordination in contemporary capitalist societies. Criminalization is anchored in practices mediated by major social institutions, including the criminal justice system—the police, the courts, and the prison services. The criminalization and "Othering" of migrants operates as a representational field of practices that reinforces and reproduces labor market segmentation, providing a ready-made exploitable labor force, a reserve army of laborers, and a scapegoat for urban unemployment, housing degradation, and the expansion of poverty. As Michael Keith argues, "A criminalized section of the workforce, readily available for insertion into the morphology of postmodern urban capitalism, provides precisely the raw material necessary for the disciplined labor force so necessary to a city's strategies for survival in the newly competitive regimes of deregulated global economies" (1993, 207).

The racialization of space and the spatialization of race were crucial elements in this process. When large numbers of migrants settled in San Salvario and were classified as criminals, the material space of the neighborhood became racially constituted. Migrants were restricted to San Salvario and to other residential zones, and these spaces became synonymous with certain negative "racial" characteristics. As this process worked on itself, the stereotyping of migrants as criminals reinforced the notion of racial and cultural difference, which then became a further rationale for spatially confining them to marginal segments of the labor force. "Blackness" as a physical reference to phenotype and to national-spatial origin was discursively constructed as a synonym for crime, and the social identity of the migrant from developing countries was subsumed in a stigma that connoted disorder, degradation, and pathology (Goffman 1963; Cross and Keith 1993). The underprivileged outsider, or noncitizen, was an easy scapegoat for Turin's urban crisis.

Citizens and small shop owners in San Salvario were reportedly unanimous in their conviction that migrants needed to be severely regulated. Regulation meant a greatly intensified police presence and more severe state legislation against illegal migration. The mayor sent the city's councilor for commerce to investigate the issues that troubled residents. Some inhabitants complained about police negligence, arguing that not enough was being done to protect them from the criminal activity that gripped their streets. One resident who was part of a group planning to organize a private police force to patrol the quarter by night and day commented: "Yesterday a team of military police officers arrived. But what are they here for? After they leave everything goes back to the way it was before and they begin again to make things unclean and to aggravate. There's a need for more severe laws."[40] "They" referred indiscriminately to drug dealers and neri. Some people blamed Italian organized criminal networks, but the brunt of popular focus was directed toward the figure of the migrant.

Popular discussion focused primarily on illegal or clandestine migrants, and the need for stricter controls to prevent them from living in Italy. A growing public opinion supported by right-wing political parties favored the immediate deportation of immigrants without legal documents, particularly those involved in criminal activities. The mayor, however, publicly denounced the popular equation between illegal immigrants and criminals, and appeared on television to argue that immigration should not be construed as a problem of public order, even if delinquents had to be deported.[41] In the meantime, bands of young Italians gathered to fight "criminal immigrants" in Turin and acts of anti-immigrant violence became widespread.[42] Some representatives of political parties encouraged the growing anxieties, confirming popular fears that migrants threatened the social order.

The figure of the migrant provided a ready-made folk devil, an image of evil that could be easily employed to justify the intensified power accorded the urban police. As in other parts of Europe, "demands for a safer city were emotively tied to the realization that while the medieval fortress town had been a place of safe retreat against the external enemy, the enemy was now within the gates, in multi-racial European cities" (Keith 1993). A comparable process had occurred in Britain in the 1980s, when demands for "safer streets" became calls for increased police surveillance in predominantly black neighborhoods (Hall 1982).[43]

Employing images of social degradation in San Salvario, the Murazzi, and other "hot" zones, many Turinese claimed they needed stronger state regulation of social life in the form of strict police controls. The mayor sent a special police task force of *carabinieri* (military police) and *vigili* (police) to San Salvario, and it was not long before police surveillance was heightened in other known multicultural areas, including the Murazzi, where the Moroccan boy had drowned. A *numero verde,* a toll-free phone number, was established so that local residents might anonymously report criminal activity. After a couple of weeks, 335 calls had been made to report crime in San Salvario. The number of police arrests in San Salvario increased substantially: after just a couple of weeks there were sixty-three arrests, eighty-two denunciations, thirteen fines issued to landlords, and forty-three police calls; three public establishments were closed.[44] Relations of social control were relegitimated in this contemporary social and political climate. Many came to perceive the "fear of crime" as a legitimate social problem: "If the quarter was not presided over by police and carabinieri? There would be no one outside on the streets. I have almost no clients left, everyone has left here. I think, these are the worst years."[45]

If the semantic field has shifted to explicit emphasis on "cultural" racism, this has not affected preestablished patterns of racial subordination between Europe and its formerly colonized territories in Africa, Asia, and Latin America. The growing movement of people into new places may help us to understand why semantic shifts have taken place. The objects of difference are no longer limited to vulnerable social classes within national borders; the axes of symbolic power are instead concentrated on the far broader directions of north to south (Gupta and Ferguson 1992).

Racial Politics and the Debate about Legislation: The "San Salvario Decree"

In the wake of intensive media focus on the "immigrant problem" in San Salvario, political debate about immigration legislation was reawakened. Some political figures argued that social tensions surrounding the emergence of migrants and cultural diversity in Italy might be eased were the government to enact a new immigration law or to amend the existing legislation. San Salvario was appropriated as an icon of the type of public disorder and insecurity generated when immigrants concentrated in a particular location. Many argued that the most promising method available to repair the material sites of degradation in Italian cities was to strictly regulate the flow of movement between "real" members of the European community and the extracomunitari, or outsiders, from the southernmost parts of the globe. This, it was suggested, should involve more repressive state intervention, and eventually resulted in what the newspapers referred to as "the San Salvario Decree."[46]

From the perspective of many migrants, exclusion from Italian society and relegation to inferior social status were rendered most clearly apparent by the absence of legal permission to live and work in Italy. But prominent in the popular imagination was the idea that a tidal wave of illegal migrants was flooding Italian cities, and that they would eventually insinuate themselves into criminal networks. According to a national poll conducted by the magazine *L'Espresso* in September 1995, 62.7 percent of the Italian population believed that immigration of extracomunitari ought to be limited.[47] Political debates among the AN (Alleanza Nationale [National Alliance], formerly the MSI or Italian Fascist Party), the Lega Nord (the Northern League), the Verde (the Green Party),[48] and the PDS (Democratic Party of the Left)—some of the key political parties in power at the time—occupied a central role in the public discourse about immigration. "Expulsion" was the key term, while national-level debates centered on the various proposals that (1) illegal immigrants must immediately be deported; (2) only those immigrants who have committed crimes should be deported; and (3) there ought to be a new amnesty in which working but illegal immigrants should have the right to obtain legal work and residence documents, while those without employment would be deported.

The pressures of public opinion and the mandates of the Trevi and Schengan agreements placed heavy pressure on the Catholic and progressive principles of universalism and humanitarian kindness. Some right-wing political leaders openly proclaimed support for the protection of Italian citizens against "invasion" from the outside. There were no comprehensive joint European policies on migration and refugees, but the Trevi and Schengan agreements represented movement in such a direction. Both agreements emphasize restriction and exclusion (Castles 1993). Trevi and Schengan mandated a highly restrictive filter for new immigrants and refugees, as well as integration measures for immigrants who have already settled[49] (Balbo and Manconi 1992; Campani 1993).

In 1990, the Italian interest in following the dictates of the Schengan agreement led to formulation of the Martelli bill (Law 39). The Martelli Law was written at a historical juncture characterized by intense popular hostility toward migrants, the growing significance of immigration in political debate, and emergence of the right-wing Leagues.[50] At the same time, there was growing concern on the part of other European governments that Italy was becoming a third world entryway to the European Union. Under heightened pressure to follow the Schengan agreement, the Italian government concluded that it had to establish a comprehensive Italian immigration policy. The fundamental purpose of the Martelli bill was to close the borders definitively, commensurate with similar policies in the European Union nations. The Martelli bill temporarily lifted the requirement of producing documents as evidence of gainful employment, which made it possible for illegal immigrants working in the informal economy to regularize their status. To be granted residence documents, migrants had to provide proof that they had lived in Italy before December 31, 1989. As a consequence of Law 39, some 225,000 migrants obtained residence and work permits (Campani 1993). But the law further restricted future immigration by prohibiting the future entry of immigrant workers, apart from "programmed flows" (Vasta 1993).

The signing of Law 39 in 1990 did not stop the continual movement of foreign populations into Italy.[51] As Maria Viarengo, an Ethiopian Italian woman who lives in Turin, remarked to me in 1995, "Humanity knows no borders." Arguments against the Martelli bill in national politics helped to propagate the idea among the Italian public that the government was "doing too much" for immigrants (Campani 1993). The Catholic Church and its voluntary associations, as well as the political left parties, including the PDS, which claimed to favor the free circulation of people in the "global village" of the twentieth century, were blamed for the continual illegal entry of immigrants.

When Don Gallo and others called for "the return to legality," the cry struck a deep chord of frustration in many Italians who regarded the Italian state as apparently incompetent in its regulation of immigration.[52] In the early 1990s, the ongoing judicial battle against "illegal" transactions, including bribery and other forms of corruption among Italian politicians, corporate managers, and organized criminal networks, had shattered some of Italy's most powerful political parties and actors. By indirectly calling for more rigorous legislation, Don Gallo's forthright criticism of the illegal practices of Italian landlords evoked images of the immediate deportation of immigrant criminals as the only solution to what some perceived as an epidemic of urban social degradation: "There is nothing else left to do, certain immigrants will have to be deported."[53] Many blamed the police for failing to follow through with deportations that ought to have been more rigorously administered if the Martelli bill was respected. Others believed this legislation ought to be replaced by more stringent measures.[54]

A journalist for *L'Espresso* wrote that the myriad violations of "public order" by clandestine migrants ignited a bomb under leftist politicians and Catholic leaders.[55] With so much xenophobia in the air, the hiatus widened between the ethical principles of open borders for humanity and the daily troubles exemplified by the conditions in San Salvario. As tensions grew, a group of migrants living in San Salvario registered a protest against the way they were being treated in daily life and misrepresented by the press. Their banners compared Turin with Soweto, South Africa. The Center-Left Coalition, L'Ulivo, dominated by the PDS, was divided on the issue until leading members of the PDS announced clear support for the stricter control of illegal immigrants.[56] Some commentators, including political figures from the most traditional wing of the former Italian Communist Party, Rifondazione Comunista (Communist Refoundation),[57] and the Verde began to ask how "solidarity," a crucial principle in left-of-center political ideology, could be wed with police repression and the deportation of illegal immigrants.[58] A leader of the Verde, Luigi Manconi, rigorously debated this issue:

> Now we're participating in the expulsion of foreigners as a preventive measure. With this amendment the foreigner is officially registered as a category of dangerous persons, like members of the Mafia or drug-addicts. And in fact this introduces in my opinion something very similar to racial laws.

But with a popular electorate against immigrants, the PDS forged an agreement with the Northern League to design a new law, agreeing that immigrants who had committed crimes should be deported immediately. On October 15, the PDS participated in an anti-immigrant demonstration in San Salvario, along with the Northern League and the Alliance Nazionale.[59] The PDS did not wish the Northern League or the Alliance Nazionale to monopolize the protests and garner popular support. Intolerance, anti-immigrant sentiment, and a culture of legality could no longer be regarded as the property of the political right.

By November, the agreement between the PDS and the Northern League concerning an amended legislation had begun to collapse after certain League leaders proposed drastic actions against immigrants. Once again, an event in Turin catalyzed national alarm when a few migrants engaged in open conflict with police. In response to inflamed passions, the Northern League's Mario Borghezio proposed that Italian police should be armed with rubber bullets *(proiettili di gomma)* to protect them against dangerous, criminal migrants.[60] A few days later, a League leader, Ermino Boso, who months earlier had proposed to have footprints taken of all immigrants at the national borders, suggested that a national civil guard ought to be deposed in the "hot zones" noted for migrant criminal activity.[61] Boso also suggested that illegal immigrants be deported to their countries of origin on military planes, warning that should these migrants be transported on commercial planes, they might "rape the stewardesses" and make the other passengers uncomfortable from their "dirtiness and bad odor."[62] The League's suggestions did not rest easily with PDS leaders, and the temporary accord between the parties was ruptured. The Northern League criticized the final legislation for not including the sort of stringent expulsion measures against illegal immigrants that it had publicly endorsed.

The new decree on immigration was signed into legislation in November 1995. It facilitated the process of deportation and provided some illegal immigrants the opportunity to obtain legal work and residency documents. The article on expulsion provided the police and judges with additional power to deport "socially dangerous" immigrants believed to have committed serious crimes.[63] Deportation would be granted, provided "concrete evidence" was sustained to prove that the foreigner was a "dangerous element." If a foreigner did not possess permission to remain in Italy or her permission had expired, or she refused to show documents of identification to authorities, she would likewise be deported. Another article in the legislation implemented the formation of a centralized information system to better control the movement of foreigners around the Italian borders. This policy is consistent with a provision in the 1993 Maastricht Treaty, which established a European police agency known as Europol. The purpose of Europol is to command an advanced computer system to store all criminal records and through which such information can be speedily retrieved throughout the EU nations. Among the responsibilities of Europol is control of illegal immigration (see film series *Fortress Europe*).[64]

In the legislation, an article regarding another amnesty for illegal immigrants was directed toward migrants working in the informal sector. The government would grant work permits only to those migrants able to demonstrate that they were in possession of a work contract for a job that could not be filled by an Italian, had been employed for at least twelve months, and had somewhere to live. The employer was obligated to pay INPS (Istituto Nazionale della Previdenza Sociale [National Institute of Social Security])[65] six months of employee insurance coverage.[66] In practice, however, many migrants were obliged to pay the INPS sum themselves, under the employer's name. In some instances, the employer took the money from the migrant but never paid INPS.

Although the PDS broke its accord with the Northern League, the party retained a hard-line position on immigration, in some measure embracing the popular cry for law and order through intensified policing. Those who wanted someone to blame for the uncertainty of the present could rest assured that their privileges were being protected by the PDS, a party that would, as part of the Ulivo coalition, win majority power in parliament just a few months after the new decree was signed. The new, more stringent laws on deportation would reinforce the perception that migrants were competing with citizens for scarce resources—a popular anxiety throughout much of contemporary Western and Northern Europe (Pred 1998).

An issue that did not seem to have been seriously debated was the way in which more stringent measures against migrants might ultimately affect the rights of Italian citizens. The sociologist Emilio Reyneri noted:

> The leaders of the Left occupy themselves a great deal with television and very little with the effects of a politics of the right on the weakest levels of our society. The result: exasperated people unload their frustrations on the immigrants, without distinguishing between criminals and non-criminals. Certain discourses on solidarity are only another aspect of this disinterest.[67]

In Turin, some agreed with Reyneri's assessment, particularly leaders of the CGIL trade union, the Rifondazione Comunista, and a number of immigrants. To constitute the term "solidarity" as more than just empty rhetoric, and to dispel the representation of migrants as criminals, these various organizations staged a popular protest, marking the Turin streets with a new element in Italian history (Merrill and Carter 2002).

"Together We Construct Our City": Antiracist Protest and the Unification of Forgetfulness

The months of intense national debate surrounding the new decree on immigration were not ignored by various political organizations in Turin. The PDS, a party with close ties to the CGIL trade union, had alienated some of its humanist constituents and potential supporters, including a growing number of immigrants, by reaching an agreement with the right-wing and anti-immigrant Northern League, itself in a coalition with the AN, which represented the extreme right. Italians allied with the Rifondazione and Verde were particularly disappointed with an agreement that, in their view, would increase police power and legalize racial discrimination. There were also disagreements within the ranks of the PDS membership. Some members of the CGIL worried that the long struggle for worker solidarity and class struggle in Turin was being eroded by unnecessary attention to the alleged dangers of immigrants. These union members were convinced that a racialized category of persons within political debate would only provide an easier route for the political right to further slash hard-won welfare state benefits. They also feared that alienating migrants might further jeopardize the remaining power of the trade unions to negotiate with employers. Some union officials, aware of the dangers waiting in the wake of the anti-immigrant storm, were convinced that the negative representation of migrants as folk devils somehow needed to be dispelled (Pugliese 1993). To this end they began to take matters into their own hands, organizing one of the largest antiracist demonstrations in Italian history, which they called "Together We Construct Our City."

Barnor Hesse suggests that the geographical consequence of "black" settlement in Europe is to sustain a culture of black politics in European cities, marking out alternative local histories and re-inscribing cities as black culture's geographical expression: "The settlement is the movement" (Hesse 1993). In other words, settlement in spatial locations is more than just a moment in time; it is the basis for social movement, for identity politics among postcolonial populations and migrants confronted with contemporary European nativism and xenophobia. By living in Europe, migrants challenge the sense of a shared past, a shared identity (Hesse 1993; Hall 1991a). In Turin, it has become apparent that the presence of migrants has irrevocably transformed the identity of Italians.[68]

CGIL representatives were aware that certain social movements were gradually developing among some former colonial populations of migrants in Turin. The criminalization of migrants further encouraged the emergence of an immigrant subject position in Italy. The very construction of a stigmatized category of persons marked as culturally and racially different awakened a degree of political consciousness among some migrants labeled as black who were on the margins of established Italian political parties. The newly formulated group called the Comitato Spontaneo degli Immigrati expressed anger toward Italian political parties for using immigrants in national political debates, when migrant voices were seldom heard:

We don't want to be the roasted chickens of Italian politics any more! Enough with the politics of "Emergency"! Enough with the disinformation! Enough with the ceremony of public enemy number one![69]

The criminalization of migrants fed the adoption of a sort of cultural defensiveness among migrants, an effort to prove that they did not arrive from backward and ignorant cultural worlds. In other words, the culturalist racism and the criminalization of migrants in Turin triggered the desire to defend oneself by asserting real or imagined cultural differences on the part of migrants (Maher 1996).

At this time, the popular term *neri* captured all migrants in a single category, without distinction between the diverse ethnic groups that composed migrant populations. However, differences between migrants from one country—for example, Senegal—were often as extreme as differences between migrants from several countries. This presented some difficulty and what some have described as the false representation of, for example, Somali culture by so-called cultural representatives of Somalia. Some migrants used Euro-Italian stereotypes of certain cultures, and sometimes a strong similarity between dominant Italian stereotypes and migrant forms of self-representation began to appear.

Apart from support for the careful training of cultural mediators through associations such as Alma Mater, the Catholic Church and some of its voluntary organizations supported the idea that migrant cultural traditions ought to be protected and represented in Turin. In early November 1995, for instance, a Kurdish festival was organized in San Salvario, the first in a series of five cultural festivals, which were held in Don Gallo's church. Subsequent events featured the "cultures" of Senegal, the Maghreb, Peru, and Nigeria. The purpose of the festivals was to "understand the drama of a country and a people."[70] The Kurdish festival featured slides, music, dance, clothing, and Kurdish artisanship. During the summer months in Turin, zones such as the Murazzi had hosted a series of similar cultural events, often orchestrated by migrant ethnic associations.

The trade unions also defended the idea of tolerance for cultural differences. Struggle against the marginalization of migrants working in the informal economy would have to wait until the negative, racialized images of migrants were dispelled. The demonstration took place in this climate on Sunday, November 19, 1995. Class and racial-ethnic solidarity were fused in the path of unified antiracist protest. Explaining the motives for the manifestation, Gianpiero Carpo of the CGIL described:

> The reality of immigration is not only prostitution and drug trading, but work and the exploitation of work, exploitation by landlords at high prices. This is the reality that we would like remembered by the demonstration of November 19. . . . We would like a day of dialogue between Turinese and immigrants. A day in which it is remembered that criminality does not have a color.[71]

And the president of the Immigrant Consulta, Abdella Boutallaka, remarked, "We ask that the immigrants be treated exactly like Italians. And that dangerous aspersions cast on immigrants through information channels cease."[72]

Several anti-immigrant protests were organized before the day of the demonstration, including one by the Comitato Spontaneo of San Salvario, with the anti-immigrant slogan, "Pusher Go Home." One protester complained: "Stop it, you journalists who say that the Porta Nuova zone has always been this way. That's not true. We don't live anymore. And the mayor talks about a multiracial city, of solidarity. He should come here, and live here, and he wouldn't think this way anymore."[73]

In terms of its level of organization and the coordination between its participants, the November 19 demonstration in Turin was the first of its kind. Forty thousand people participated in a protest promoted by the CGIL, CISL, and UIL trade unions in collaboration with Turin's Immigrant Consulta. Also participating in the manifestation were the mayor of Turin, the Catholic Church, countless voluntary associations, the student union, and most of the major political parties, including the embattled Rifondazione and the PDS. The Italian Catholic Church named this day "the day of the migrant." The Northern League, the AN, and San Salvario's Comitato Spontaneo were conspicuously absent.

The trade unions and the Immigrant Consulta agreed to march in two processions that originated from different points in the city. Both groups were directed toward the same piazza. The group of marchers that departed from San Salvario was led by the Rifondazione, Verde, the antiracist Rete,[74] and some voluntary organizations. The other group—represented by the unions, the Immigrant Consulta, and the PDS—marched from Piazza Arbarello, a famous site of numerous youth movements during the

1970s. The forty thousand met in Piazza Castello, where they listened to political speeches, music, and prayer. Some of their slogans were:

We prefer unions dressed in blue to unity with racists.
The PDS did not understand. The immigrant is not a criminal.
We are black, we are white, and we are tired of racism.
We don't like this decree. Without justice there can be no peace.

All sorts of political-cultural positions were represented in a single, anti-racist demonstration. Moussa, from the Ivory Coast, held up his poem:

you're free, but without rights,
you're here, but you don't exist,
you're human, but different,
you're useful, but you don't count,
you want to die but you'd like to live
you'd like to go back but you don't know how,
you stay but without tranquillity,
you exist but you cannot be dignified[75]

In the name of solidarity between the unions and immigrants, the marchers argued that there was no difference between *neri* (blacks) and *bianchi* (whites).[76] They asked, "Where is the difference?" The demonstration seemed to heal some of the wounds inflicted during months of negative media coverage and the political discourse articulated around the criminalized portrait of the migrant.

The trade unions appeared to have succeeded in their efforts to ease tensions and restore some element of the worker struggle with a new migrant constituency. A year after the manifestation took place, many Turin residents to the political left and right reported that immigration was not a social problem in the city.[77] The marchers had tried to clean up Turin's image, to replace the idea of the "San Salvario Casbah" with images of multiculturalism and tolerance.[78] However, after examining the legislation that was signed in November 1995, it would be difficult to attribute total success to interracial unity. The call for legality, the promotion of increased policing of migrants, and the greater restrictions added to state-sanctioned legislation were sustained by power of state law. Immigrants were no more insiders than they had been before all of the conflict over crime in San Salvario had begun to unfold, and one was left to wonder, after all of the anxiety over immigration had been temporarily quieted, what had remained in the hearts and minds of Turinese?

CHAPTER 6

Turin Feminism: From Workerism to Interethnic Gender Alliance

In 2001, ALMA MATER HAD BECOME WELL KNOWN all over Italy as a site where immigrant women might receive advice, cultural representation, and work. It was one of the first places visited by migrant women after arriving in Turin via the Porta Nuova train station, where other newcomers often directed them to the organization. Many heard about Alma Mater through recommendations from various Italian civil servants and immigrant cultural mediators at the Officio Stranieri. Almost ten years after opening its doors, Alma Mater was a thriving site where immigrant women from all over the world hoped to improve their lives through contact with other migrant and Italian women. In June, I became member 3,108 of the organization. The Italian women who joined usually did so to help migrant women or to use the center's services—the Turkish bath, for instance, or the tailoring services. Migrant women became members as part of their effort to find housing and work.

In 2001, the third-floor rooms in Alma were usually noisy with the chatter of several women wearing jeans and jerseys, lengthy wraparound skirts and colorful head scarves from Africa, simple dresses and high heels, or various styles of Muslim dress and veils (hijab). The women showed various emotions and moods, from hurried and tense to anxious and upset, bored and distracted, and sometimes lighthearted and joking. On a typical day in the central office on the third floor, there was a woman from Argentina, a woman who called herself "half Italian and half Somalian," a Peruvian and an Italian woman who both studied herbal medicines and together taught a course on the topic at Alma Mater. On a couch in the large meeting room sat two Romanian women, and in the children's day care was a young Italian woman doing an internship as part of a university course she took in Milan. Another, older Italian woman took care of the migrant children as part of her training course in Turin.

The central office is a small, square room with a large, bright window and two walls of flyers and mailboxes. During one of my visits to the office, a woman older than most migrant women I'd seen in Turin sat behind the large, heavy desk covered with pieces of paper and a telephone. Fatuma, a tall, thin Somali woman of around fifty years of age, answered the office phone several days a week, a part-time job for which she was given a minimal allowance. She spoke fluent Somali, Arabic, Italian, and English. She had lively eyes, was friendly, and seemed especially tickled by the fact that I was American, which gave her the chance to speak English. When I asked about her journey to Italy, Fatuma emphasized family and work:

> I had two shops in Somalia, one selling food and one for electrical devices, especially lamps, because they were doing a lot of building in Mogadishu. Often for my business, I traveled to Kenya and to New Delhi, where I'd buy things to sell in Mogadishu. I speak English, and I love reading mystery and romance novels in English. Then came the war. I had seven children. So we left Somalia for Ethiopia, where we lived for six years. But there was nothing to do in Ethiopia, no work at all.

As she paused, Fatuma glanced behind me and waved at a woman passing by the office. When I asked about her husband, she sighed and continued:

> My husband was an engineer and army colonel in Somalia, but in Turin he works as a welder for a Fiat organization. This is better than construction. Construction is hard labor, but that's what he used to do here.

When I asked what she hoped for her life in Italy, she said she was in the process of applying for a bank job and really hoped she'd get it.

Fatuma was referring to an initiative orchestrated by several Italian feminists in Alma Mater, in which the Italian bank, Cariplo, had agreed to hire twelve immigrant women. Thirty-four women had applied for the positions, and when I spoke with Fatuma these women were in the process of taking written and oral examinations. Those selected from the group would be trained for six months, their training paid for by the municipal government. After the six months, the bank promised, it would assume the immigrant women as employees. This would be quite an accomplishment for migrant women because, in Italy, most women working at banks had university degrees, and until the 1980s, few Italian women held such public positions. Unfortunately for Fatuma, however, there was not much work to go around, and she was told she had not scored highly enough on the written exam to be offered a bank position.

Work is a central theme in Alma Mater. As I walked to meet a Nigerian informant for lunch one day, I overheard another Nigerian woman, Vivian, speaking in a loud and angry tone while walking down the stairs. Her round face wrinkled with a frown, her chin tight and constrained, she seemed to be caught between swelling anger and sadness. Plainly dressed in an inexpensive skirt and blouse and carrying an inexpensive purse, her hair pulled back in a ponytail without much care, Vivian was telling another Nigerian woman her problem while she held back tears:

> If not for you, I don't know. These people—I have been coming to this place for three years. I have been here. I would have thought that after this time they would be treating me better. They are treating me just like dirt, like nothing, like a piece of dirt to throw into the road, like nothing. For so long, I have been coming to this place. How could they do this to me? I don't have a home, a place to stay, nothing—they just threw me in the street like trash, like I'm just nothing. Anything could happen to me and they would not care. If not for you, I don't know. You helped me, and I appreciate that. When someone helps me, I never forget it. Please, continue to help me. Here, I will give you my phone number. And, here, if you want to know where I live, I live at Via X, number 9.

As the story was later explained to me, Vivian had been a member of the Alma Mater work cooperative, La Talea, through which she had held a contracted position at an elder care facility. According to the Brazilian director of La Talea, the people at the home did not like Vivian and did not think she was any good, so the cooperative had to let her go. By losing her job at the nursing home, however, Vivian lost the ability to renew her residence documents, for which proof of formal employment is required by the Italian state. She had, in fact, found a cleaning job, but in the informal economy.

While visiting Alma Mater, I frequently passed through a window into the growing cultural complexity in contemporary European societies and the migrant woman's struggle to locate herself and to be located. One day I met a young woman cooking in the kitchen on the basement floor where the tailoring service, La Talea office, and Turkish bath were also located. She was alone in the kitchen with several cookie-plate-sized combinations of eggs and onions, squash and eggs, and the like. Behind her were some beautifully displayed coconut-filled dates. She told me she was from Morocco and invited me to eat one of the dates, which I did with pleasure. She said she was cooking a meal for an Italian woman who was having a party at the Valentino Park and for which she had ordered an African meal. The plates represented not only Moroccan cuisine, but also foods from Tunisia, Egypt, and other parts of the continent. This young woman seemed nice but annoyed, not with me, but with the job or with the fact that she was left to do all of this cooking alone. She said that she didn't come much to Alma Mater, only every so often. When I told her that I was from the United States, she asked why I would come to Italy when I'm from America, explaining that she would love to live in America. I told her that I was in Italy for a two-month research visit, and that although America wasn't perfect, it was my home, the place where I was born. She responded by stating, "Yes, you're like me. I don't like my country either. Morocco, I don't like it."

In Alma Mater, a place filled with people from many different countries, it was common for women to make connections, to discover similarities between their positions and the ground on which they stood. In this place, differences were acknowledged and hierarchy was emphatically denied in philosophical discourse, framed by Italian feminists. One of my ethnographic informants was a warm, intelligent, articulate woman from Brazil who, like me, was trying to conceive a child. Roberta was president of La Talea, for which she was paid a minimum monthly salary but not a living wage. Her income was supplemented by that of her husband, an Italian man from the eastern part of the country whom she had met at a tourist site on the outskirts of Turin. Her husband had a sort of mechanics business with his brother; they made replacement parts for Fiat automobiles. He didn't make much money, however, and even with the two salaries the couple was unable to go to the movies, to take a vacation, or to buy good-quality clothing. Roberta told me that her clothing was "cheap—bought from the market, low quality." In Brazil too she had been poor, but her mother was "a fabulous woman with a grand vision":

> My mother always encouraged her children to study, telling us that we had the right to get out of poverty. So I went to school and earned a bachelor's degree in law. While still in Brazil, I worked a lot. I worked in a factory, as a caretaker of children, in a bread store, in an office, and then in a higher capacity in the office. Then I decided that I wanted to see another part of the world. My sister was already here in Milan. I had also met many Italians in Brazil and I had thought they were very friendly and nice. I wanted to see the world, so I came to Turin, and then I got sort of stuck. I might have made a mistake. I have no money, and I have been

unable to conceive a child. But I also realize that I have achieved a great deal, to have traveled to Italy as I have.

Roberta had begun school again, this time at the University of Turin. She wanted to obtain a law degree so that she could practice in Italy. She would be required to take twelve exams to do this. In the morning she studied, but at night she found it too difficult, and this meant that she didn't have enough time. But, she told me, she was hoping that her plan would end well, that she would one day be able to bear a child and make a good living. But she was homesick, missing her family and her country a great deal.

Another day, Roberta led me into the Turkish bath, hammam, to speak with members of La Talea employed there. The hammam occupies half of Alma Mater's basement, a rather dark underground area where in the course of a day there may be little if any contact with people on the upper floors. A Tunisian woman who worked in the bath told me that her life had been very difficult. In Tunisia, she had worked in a factory for eleven years. It was a large factory, and the work was unionized, yet it wasn't fixed work; she'd have three months on and three months off. Her boss was American and all the workers were Tunisian. After her husband died and her children were grown, she decided to come to Italy, where she had Tunisian and Moroccan friends. For a year, she lived with an Italian family, taking care of a boy. Then she worked cleaning at a hotel near Rimini, a popular Italian coastal vacation town. When she arrived in Turin, she had a lot of trouble finding a place to live. Of Italians she said, "All these Italian women are racist. All of them, they treat us like slaves, only for cleaning."

Another woman and former president of La Talea directed the Turkish bath, where she also did massages. Paula was a Filipina who played a prominent role in many Alma Mater events, including the popular theater company, Almateatro, and some of the ethnic dinners. She did not speak openly about her feelings, but readily described her struggle to make a living before and after her arrival in Italy. Her family lived in Manila as squatters. Her mother had seven children, and her father died when she was eleven years old, so she went to work to earn money for her family—in a supermarket, in a hotel, in many other places. Paula was an actress for three years and appeared in two or three films. "I was a good actress—I won an award for a stage play—but my friend told me I should leave, the money wasn't enough for my family. And this is not consistent work. So I went away and sent money back home for my family." In 1975, she applied for a contract with a Filipino agency to work as a domestic in one of several foreign countries and was offered a job in Italy. She explained:

> I didn't know how to do domestic work. I lived with a family. I had two hours off on Thursday and two on Sunday. My employer spoke English. Her husband had an import-export business, with three secretaries. He traveled a lot as a liquor distributor. The wife did not work. She checked on the babies, went shopping. They had a house outside of Turin, to swim, golf. I was not well paid, underpaid—told I'd be paid 120,000 lira then, but I was paid only 84,000. The children were six and seven. I did cooking and cleaning from 6:30 a.m. to 11:30 p.m., for four-and-a-half years. I had ten days' holiday. I suffered a lot with this family. I didn't get any rest. The second job was much better.
>
> After working for the family, I went to work as a cook in a Jewish family in Turin. I was assumed on a trial, for one week. I cooked French, Italian, and curry.
>
> Seven people competed for the job and I was the only *straniera*. There were only three people in the family. And I won the job. I had to cook for dogs and cats. I had to make three types of spaghetti for each family member—tomato sauce for the father, for the mother another kind of tomato sauce, oil and Parmesan for the child. I got there at 10 a.m. and worked seven hours a day, five days a week. I asked for much more than normal pay, and they paid it. They were Russian Jews. Had a tire factory.

Paula has two children and is married to an Italian man. She speaks not only Italian, but also the local dialect, Piedmontese.

It is not uncommon for migrant women to marry Italian men, although not a general norm. I met the Yoruba woman, Valencia, in the hallway of Alma Mater's third floor when she was preparing to visit Nigeria for a two-month stay to see her mother. She was a tall, large-framed woman who wore a lot of makeup and who was later described as beautiful by several other migrant women. She was very friendly and happy to speak with me. Valencia lived outside of Turin with her family, a thirteen-year-old son and an Italian spouse whom she had met while in Holland and who later brought her to Turin. She told me that she had received certification from the EU to work as a cultural mediator, and that she was employed as one of Alma Mater's cultural mediators. She worked for a woman's facility run by Catholic nuns, a place that housed migrant prostitutes (primarily Nigerian, in this case) for a period of six months after they had divulged the names of their sponsors to an Italian judge. The women were moved from one place to another, and at that time they were living at a church in the Turin hills. Valencia would mediate their relationship with the Italian nuns by helping them to understand that they had to follow strict church rules, which many found very difficult. For example, they were not permitted to go out alone and had to be accompanied at all times, which many had trouble with because "they were normally free to move around." So to the migrant women Valencia explained the cultural understandings of the nuns, and to the nuns she explained the cultural expectations of the migrant women. For instance, she told the women that the nuns were very bureaucratic, and the migrants didn't understand this. When asked about her relationship with Alma Mater and Turin feminists, Valencia explained:

> I'm not a feminist in general, but sometimes I am a feminist in Italy. Depending on the cause, I might sympathize. But at home in Nigeria, women rule, while here, men are the heads of households. And at home, women have lots of freedom that women in Europe don't have. So they don't have the same need for feminism, and yet here people assume that in Africa, women are at the bottom, but they're not. They assume that women there are so oppressed, when it's just a prejudice.

Valencia was depicting gender relationships in Yoruba culture as unproblematic for women, a view shared by other migrant women in Turin, yet not always agreed on, even among members of the same ethnic population. This is an argument that exasperates many Turin feminists, who have heard a great deal of criticism of Western feminism from migrant women, especially in recent years as newcomers have felt increasingly comfortable expressing their views. Whatever the status of migrant women in their various countries and ethnic groups of origin may have been, in Italy and more generally in Europe, they are identified not only as non-European extracomunitari and therefore out of place, but as women and often racialized Others, vulnerable to double or triple forms of discriminatory practice (Morokvasic 1991; Phizacklea 1983). In the statement above, Valencia was referring to what she viewed as a common misconception among Italian and other Western women and feminists who may assume that gender inequalities and other forms of discrimination such as silencing are even worse in economically underdeveloped regions than in the advanced capitalist world. Migrant women experience gender discrimination, but many of my informants described such treatment as a consequence of their outsider status exacerbated by Italian gender practices.

Migrant women like Valencia belong to Alma Mater and visit the organization in recognition of their uneven social position in Europe and, more specifically, in Turin. In the process, Italian feminism is opening to and even embracing a new, far more socially and culturally diverse world. It is, in fact, the history and character of Turin feminism in its integral relationship with other Italian social movements that, in part, explains the appearance of this interethnic migrant and Italian women's organization. The feminism that emerged in Turin in the early 1970s was influenced considerably by both the labor and student movements, and to the present day has retained a central emphasis on work. Turin feminism is in many ways different from Milan feminism, which is centered on sexual difference and with which Italian feminism has become associated in the United States (the Milan Women's Bookstore Collective 1990; Bono and Kemp 1991; Parati and West 2002). To understand how Alma Mater, with its flaws as well as its innovative expressions of feminist politics, came to exist at all, it is necessary to understand something about the specific form that feminism took in this industrial, workerist city, and what led Italian women to have any interest at all in migrant women. When Alma Mater appeared, most institutional support for migrants was located in Catholic charitable and voluntary organizations; but Alma Mater led the representation of migrants in a different direction, one linked far more directly with the political left.

Turin feminism is not a static social movement, and when significant numbers of migrant women appeared in the late 1980s, it began to experience a set of dramatic shifts that moved it into the orbit of postcolonial and antiracist feminisms. Today's newcomers bring diverse political-cultural beliefs and practices, and they have begun to influence the texture of Turin political culture. Southern Italian migrants of the 1960s and 1970s had also influenced the Turin labor movement as they brought their own cultural forms of resistance and social concerns to the local scene. We will examine the rootedness of Turin feminism in the worker, student, and extraparliamentary party movements, and its more recent expansion and engagement with postcolonial and international feminism.

Unione Donne Italiane (UDI)

Feminism is shaped in part by the peculiar cultural and political geography from which it emerges. Early Turin feminists struggled to redefine the issues raised by women in other parts of the peninsula in terms that would fit within the limited framework of Turin workerist politics. These feminists were forced to operate within the constraints of a political culture in which the working class was seen as the central political subject and agent. Judith Hellman suggests that it was a feminism highly conditioned by local politics: "In the most working-class of Italian cities, a new social movement, feminism, was conditioned by the workerism . . . (the Operaismo) that shapes all activities on the Turinese Left" (1987b, 113).

Shortly after World War II, the Unione Donne Italiane (UDI) emerged as the first national women's organization in Italy, established as a flanking organization of the Italian Communist Party (PCI) to promote its party politics. UDI developed out of the Resistance units in which women had been active (J. Hellman 1987b; Bravo and Bruzzone 1995). Italy had the largest communist party in the West, and Marxist philosophies influenced the early Italian women's movement in general, but particularly in Turin. Marx's insistence that a distinctive characteristic of the human species lies in the capacity for personal fulfillment through labor was emphasized by Palmiro Togliatti, leader of the PCI who was instrumental in establishing a place for women—at least, theoretically—in the PCI, beginning in 1944 (Caldwell 1991).

Immediately after the war, Turin was hit hard by economic dislocation and became the site of a number of bread riots, in which many women participated. For this apparent reason, numerous women joined the newly formed UDI, including Catholic and other noncommunist women. But by the mid-1950s, most Catholic women had left the organization, and even the socialist women had withdrawn. This meant that throughout the 1950s, communist women gained uncontested hegemony over the base, and UDI pursued activities in agreement with PCI policies and philosophies. The organization struggled to redefine issues important to women within the restrictive workerist discourse of the PCI, but until the late 1970s the PCI—the most powerful force within the progressive wing of the trade union movement—would not engage in any serious debate with feminists for fear of alienating the Catholic masses (Frogett and Torchi 1981). The emancipation tradition in Italian leftist politics stressed political activity and social relations outside the home and equal political and legal rights between the sexes. But there was major emphasis on the importance of family and a woman's role in the domestic sphere. The status of woman as mother and wife was virtually unquestioned until the 1970s, as were the implications of a gendered division of labor and occupational segregation outside the home.

In its early years, UDI operated within the limited PCI parameters of "women's politics," struggling to extend the familial, nurturing role of women into the public domain. According to this perspective, the obstacle for female "emancipation" was the primary responsibility that women had to the family, so that women needed only to engage in productive work in the public domain to become "equal" to men. The PCI saw women's productive capacities primarily in areas of help and support, considered suitably female domains of *assistenziale* (assistance). In the 1950s and 1960s, UDI sought recognition of motherhood as a social responsibility, against cultural expectations of motherhood as part of the "private" domain, and struggled with male-dominated Italian institutions to relinquish control over reproduction to women—for example, in the abortion struggles (Buttafuoco 1980). In Turin, as in other parts of Italy, UDI women agitated for day care, schools, laundries, and other social services connected with women's traditional activities, and participated in PCI mobilizations for peace and against NATO and the nuclear bomb (J. Hellman 1987b).

Turin's UDI women were particularly concerned to establish an organizational presence among women working in factories. However, in the 1950s, CGIL, the trade union most strongly linked with the PCI, was not particularly receptive to women's specific workplace demands, arguing that such "particularistic" concerns would serve only to undermine the solidarity of the workers' movement (J. Hellman 1984, 1987a). The Italian Communist Party and Socialist Party supported a limited conception of "women's politics" in which female liberation and economic independence would arise naturally from women's incorporation into the workplace. Although during the 1950s and 1960s UDI struggled to carve out a female space of activity, it was difficult for the organization to direct party or union attention to women's issues—for example, to the need to regulate the growing system of domestic piecework—and their efforts were virtually ignored (J. Hellman 1987b). Elsewhere in Italy, UDI women campaigned for the regulation of domestic piecework, but in Turin the heavy stress on the factory and the predominance of trade union imperatives overrode the issue. UDI stressed women's work and, within an emancipationist framework, struggled to promote equal wages for women, equal employment opportunities, equal access to civil service and teaching jobs, protection for working mothers, prohibition of the layoff of women when they married, and regulation of domestic piecework manufacturing. But even in the greatest industrial city in Italy, UDI had very little space to influence factory women. The unions held the position that male employment was more important than female and defended the male role as head of family (Beccalli 1985). Occupational segregation was ignored, even as most women labored in the lowest work categories. Even after equal-salary legislation was established in Italy, well before most other industrialized countries, discrimination legislation came very late. The trade unions supported legislation to protect and broaden the rights of the "worker mother," but the problem of equality of women and men in the workplace was not addressed (Beccalli 1985).

In the 1960s, UDI struggled for greater autonomy from the PCI and entered a period of self-criticism. The national leadership began to embrace feminism and was somewhat receptive to the feminist critique of the traditional parties and unions. Evidence that UDI embraced some feminist positions is found in the writings of their weekly magazine, *Noi Donne*. The periodical engaged in little discussion of personal feelings about the relationship of men to women typically labeled as part of feminist "consciousness raising," but some stories addressed issues of domestic violence and rape (Birnbaum 1986). In the context of a culture of work in Turin, however, UDI was at odds with both the traditional left and the new feminist organizations that began to develop toward the end of the decade. The organization was caught between the tensions of being too feminist to be taken seriously by the PCI and too workerist and communist-dominated to be taken seriously by new feminists. In the 1970s, the group failed to attract young Turin women who felt that spontaneous discussion was cut off by sectarian communist and male-identified women, as well as centralized hierarchical forms of organization quite similar to those of the PCI. There were conflicts between philosophies and political styles influenced by the radically antidisciplinist approach of the student movement and New Left, and a more orderly, traditional approach to discussion in which designated persons were allowed to speak in a more or less sequential and hierarchical manner. Many new feminists self-consciously independent of governmental institutions were driven away by hard-liners, although not before exerting some influence on UDI's organizational practices (J. Hellman 1987b). For instance, new feminists challenged the old-style format of the general meeting, which opened with a long address by a leader, followed by a series of speeches from the floor. During the Hot Autumn of 1969,[1] this style of meeting was displaced by a more open, somewhat looser, more informal, and democratic format, which gave a greater range of people an opportunity to speak.

UDI membership remained quite small throughout the 1970s, but maintained some political weight in local politics in cities such as Turin, where it was sustained financially by the national organization. The feminist movement came into conflict with the workers' movement because it challenged workers' hegemony within those forces committed to transforming the existing order, thus raising questions about some of the deepest beliefs of the working-class movement itself (Buttafuoco 1980). Ultimately, the old organizational style in UDI prevailed, for the old guard was particularly reticent to endorse criticism of the PCI as a sexist institution. The women of UDI posed themselves as true political leftists, arguing against the new feminist organizations that they believed spoke only self-referentially or for particular interests, while UDI articulated the interests of "all women" workers. Many Italian feminists came to distrust the UDI, whose history was closely bound with the PCI's, and which was considered timid, employing a political tactic reminiscent of male-dominated practices (Buttafuoco 1980).

New Left Extraparliamentary Groups and Turin Feminism

At the end of the 1950s, both left political parties—the Italian Communists and Socialists—were internally in conflict at the levels of both the rank and file and leadership. At this time, Italy was being vaulted into position as a leading nation in the global economy, and the Italian left was not prepared for this transformation (S. Hellman 1976).[2] The economic changes led to debates over Italian capitalism, including the need for a nonbureaucratic, broad-based "revolution from below," with the goal of the worker's direct control over the means of production. As they criticized the party, some prominent members of the PCI's left wing began to be called "the New Left." By the late 1960s, a number of student and extraparliamentary groups critical of the PCI had emerged, and these groups were often quite workerist. Many women who were involved in struggles at the universities entered New Left extraparliamentary groups, which eventually led to the emergence of Italian feminism (Pitch 1979). Appearing out of a highly politicized social context, the Italian women's movement was characterized by an emphasis on politics as opposed to career. Tamar Pitch suggested of Italian feminists, "Our real emancipation was to be found in politics, in the great dream of emancipation for all" (1979, 3). However, as I will discuss further below, there were two lines of feminist thinking and practice in Turin: the political and the psychoanalytic (Damilano 1996).

It is often pointed out that disappointed women activists in the student and workers' movements created Italian feminism.[3] Males had dispatched women students to distribute leaflets in front of factories, believing that workers would better accept them from women. But through these and other experiences, women activists became aware that the working class was a historically male actor. While women held up picket signs protesting hierarchies within factories and schools, they found themselves in supportive roles, almost always secondary to their male counterparts (J. Hellman 1987a; Birnbaum 1986). The trade unions and political parties ignored gender inequality for a long time, and it was absent from public debate even in the sociology of work until the 1980s (Beccalli 1985). This was true because even within the trade unions and some extraparliamentary groups, the conception of the family and of the sexual division of labor differed little from that of the conservative vision in which women had responsibility for family work, and men for earning wages.

Melucci (1981) suggests that the first major break with Marxism in Italy came with the women's movement, which introduced language and categories relatively new to the traditional left. Employing a Marxist idiom, students had criticized the separation between politics and society and the professionalization of politics, but women went beyond this by denouncing the conflict between the private and public or sociopolitical spheres. Students practiced their critique by occupying universities, interrupting classes, and introducing countercourses. Women instead used small group meetings to struggle against the separation of the private. Their analysis of everyday life was tied with the analysis of women's historical subordination and with the ideology that this subordination was natural. Early feminists argued that the left participated in this ideology by forgetting about it, thereby reinforcing the invisibility of invidious gender distinctions.

While women began to object to persistent subordination to men within activist organizations, in Turin they were not (as in other parts of Italy) catalyzed by a discourse of antipatriarchy and the assertion of female differences. The feminism that emerged in Turin was deeply embedded in the left political culture of the city and its existing political organizations. As stated by Maria Teresa Battaglino, an Italian feminist active in the creation of Alma Mater:

> Even if I agree that much of neo-feminism was born from the position
> of inferiority that women had within left groups, it's also true that in left
> groups you found a convergence of women who already had a feminist

sensibility and that wished to rouse things at the social level. There was a need to avoid closing oneself off at the point of consciousness, in order to change life for the better. (In Zumaglino 1996, 57)

The wellspring of feminist discontent in Turin flowed from within women's practical engagement in PCI, and in student and extraparliamentary struggles against dehumanizing work conditions, particularly in the factory. But by the early 1970s, women activists had begun to turn a corner by examining the relationship between authoritarianism and patriarchy.

The importance of left-wing extraparliamentary groups for the development of Turin feminism should not be underestimated. Some 90 percent of Turin feminists in the mid-1980s participated at one time or another in far left organizations (Zumaglino 1996). The majority of extraparliamentary groups were radically anti-institutional and antiauthoritarian; they advocated opposition to established organizations such as political parties and trade unions. The first women's extraparliamentary group to influence Turin feminism was Demau (Demistificazione Autoritarismo, or Demystification of Authoritarianism), founded in Milan in 1966 to explain the relationship between authoritarianism and patriarchy and highly critical of the "masculinity of the state and market" (Zumaglino 1996). Demau scrutinized authoritarianism and the concept of the psychological internalization of oppression by examining writers from the Frankfurt school, such as Hannah Arendt, as well as scholars within the classical Marxist tradition. Turin feminists were concerned about the failure of postwar democratic legislation that had not broken up Fascist norms of the *difesa della razza* (defense of the race), including an arsenal of civil and penal codes that conserved rigid sexual and social roles and that contrasted with the needs of a society undergoing major social transformation (Zumaglino 1996).

Other extraparliamentary groups with a more direct significance in the Turin scene included Lotta Continua and especially Avanguardia Operaia (Zumaglino 1996). Lotta Continua held its first convention in Turin, where it sought to form a women's section that integrated feminist consciousness-raising practices with political activism. And a considerable proportion of Turin feminists were members of Avanguardia Operaia (AO), a major protagonist in the student movement. AO adhered to a Leninist philosophy that advocated bringing consciousness to workers who would otherwise be stuck in old-fashioned trade unionism, and encouraged women and men to join the unions to influence change. While some women tried to integrate feminist issues into discussions among members of extraparliamentary groups such as AO, there were those who objected to incorporating the theme of women into struggles surrounding factory work. Even some female members of extraparliamentary groups mistrusted feminism:

> When I talk about a small group of women in Avanguardia Operaia, I don't wish to suggest that all women of AO were feminist. At the beginning those that frequented the groups of women were seen as marginal to politics, those who didn't understand well or how they did these things. Many women of Avanguardia Operaia, militants, women who had gone to the door or who had more experience than me in political organizations, regarded the women's organizations with a critical eye. There was an enormous separation.[4]

Within circles of traditional as well as New Left politics, it was not easy for women to find a place to voice their concerns about women's lives, and Turin's first feminists did not prioritize the women's struggle.

Although not as strongly as in other cities such as Milan, feminist collectives appeared in the 1970s in Turin and played a significant role in circulating critical appraisals of the differential social treatment of men and women in Italian society. Feminist collectives sought to create an alternative reality based on exchanges between women. The collectives usually concentrated on autonomy issues, women's health, abortion, and unequal power relations within the family expressed in control over the female body. An assortment of women's collectives appeared, primarily among veterans of the student movement and extraparliamentary left. But many women within extraparliamentary groups and unions criticized them for ignoring global political issues and emphasizing critique of the male-female dyadic relationship.

The Turin collectives were also subjected to internal criticism for the prominent role played in them by middle-class women (students, teachers, white-collar employees), for whom "consciousness" came more easily because of high levels of schooling and the relatively comfortable material conditions of their daily lives. Women who joined the collectives discussed the need to be sensitive to the specific concerns of working-class women and housewives, while at the same time helping to furnish them with the instruments with which to raise their consciousness about areas of oppression within the family (Zumaglino 1996, 84–85). To bridge the gap between middle- and working-class women, some sought to reach the base of women and construct a mass movement. The collective Lotta Femminista held to the philosophy that they could not teach oppressed women, but they could *discover with* other women and act collectively. These women tried to adopt an antiauthoritarian approach to the masses without any specific persons or members of hegemonic social classes accorded special authority to speak for others. They tried to combine universal principles of solidarity between the exploited and oppressed with goals of equality between men and women. Their critique of capitalism was marked by the conviction that women suffered most of all from the predominant forms of capitalist production, their bodies and minds invaded and consumed by the mechanics of the drive for profit.

The first feminist group in Turin was the Collettivo delle Compagne, which gave birth to a feminist collective commune in Via Petrarca called Alternativa Femminista (AF) and the Collettivo Femministe Torinese of Via Lombroso in the middle 1970s. Initially, the Collettivo delle Compagne did not favor the centrality of the women's struggle, but continued to give priority to the class struggle, or at least oscillated between the two (Zumaglino 1996). The women who formed the Collettivo delle Compagne in the 1970s had experience with UDI and had read about the feminist movement in the United States. American feminist literature, sent principally by Boston women's liberationists, was translated into Italian by a group, principally wives of prominent members of the left who had been involved in the student movement but who were never awarded leadership positions. Several members were also part of CR (Comunicazioni Rivoluzionarie), a New Left group that exchanged and translated information about cultural revolutions in the United States, including the Black Panthers and anti–Vietnam War struggles. The members of the Collettivo and CR translated underground literature from the New American Left, through which they acquired knowledge of the American women's liberation movement and the appearance of a new, female political subject (Zumaglino 1996, 62).[5] They began to see women as members of a special caste, yet their focus remained primarily within the orbit of traditional worker politics, and they tried to reach out to proletarians to lead them to a higher level of consciousness.

Alternativa Femminista (AF), the first Turin collective to adopt the word "feminist," disagreed with the Collettivo vanguard model with which women struggled on behalf of others. AF women argued that this philosophy pushed women into activities that were an extension of traditional nurturing roles, or that imitated the traditional left's pattern of mediation

(J. Hellman 1987b). Instead, AF demanded more of state institutions and laws—for instance, legal abortion and prostitute rights. The theme of the sexual division of labor was present in many of the group's writings, considered one of the "many forms of exploitation" that the family helped to sustain (Zumaglino 1996, 178). AF considered itself part of the left, arguing that the "contradictions between the genders can be resolved only with the radical transformation of the society in which we live and the values that this society inspires" (Zumaglino 1996, 178).

The CLD (Collettivo Liberazione della Donna) was the first Turin feminist group to adopt a model of "double militancy," in both politics and feminism. The participants struggled to politically change women's inferior position in society by attacking bourgeois class hegemony. The CLD agreed that the common worker *(operaia comune)* possessed the solution to class and sexual oppression, suggesting that feminists should adopt an analogous figure of the woman to that of the common worker. But the CLD never had a great deal of success. Other feminist collectives such as Alternativa Femminista played a more significant role in circulating feminist ideas. They distributed flyers in neighborhoods, sent letters criticizing patriarchy to the local newspapers, and participated in open debates.

Early Turin feminism was somewhat influenced by Milan and Rome women's collectives, which understood female sexuality as the organizing force of relationships between women in feminism, and for whom the nature of the dynamic between women was a critical question of exploration. But in Turin there tended to be ideological division between women interested in questions of female subjectivity and consciousness, and women more concerned about politics and work and involved with more traditional left issues. Some argued that it was necessary for women to develop an analysis of class, while others emphasized creating spaces in which women could explore their differences and distinctiveness from men. They debated whether they should "save only the workers, or all the women" (Zumaglino 1996, 113). Both strands of Turin feminists tended to reject intellectual and political language they thought abstract and removed from women's experiences. They also increasingly held the view that solidarity and sisterhood were ideals, while in practice, personal conflicts tended to dominate, often expressed in ideological terms (118). In 1979, they opened the Casa delle Donne in a site once occupied by a mental asylum. In 1980 more suitable quarters were provided by the municipal government (J. Hellman 1987b; Zumaglino 1996). Turin feminism has been described as somewhat anti-intellectual; as local feminist Patricia

Celotto remarked, "Turin feminism is very much linked up with politics" (legata alla politica). It is highly practical; it chooses to take action on issues, ideally with direct control as opposed to state control.

In Milan and other Italian cities with less prominent labor unions and politics, consciousness-raising through the reading of feminist literature was more pronounced. Turin feminists considered themselves activists, influenced by an Italian feminist theory of difference, but not particularly interested in theoretical debate. This theory is based on Milan feminist engagement with practices of sexual difference. In their view, freedom for women is engendered by taking a position in a symbolic community and through feminist practices discovering or inventing a "genealogy of women" (de Lauretis 1989; Cavarero 1987; Bono and Kemp 1991; Parati and West 2002; Milan Women's Bookstore Collective 1990). They suggest that a conceptual and discursive space of a female genealogy can facilitate a woman's relationship to a symbolic world constructed by men, allowing her to define herself as a female being, a female-gendered speaking subject. Influenced by Luce Irigaray's discussion of women's denied and unauthorized relationship to the symbolic order in Western philosophy, these Italian feminists argue against American and other feminist struggles for equality. In this view, equality only reproduces male-created discursive practices, so that what is needed is a radical separatism, where women are different not only biologically from men, but as historical-material subjects, or a different production of reference and meaning from an embodied knowledge that continually emerges but that reaches back to realize the past. Milan feminists stress the importance of recognizing female interlocutors, instead of struggling for women's rights, because "neither laws nor rights can give a woman the self-confidence she lacks." And "a woman can acquire inviolability by creating a life which has its starting point in herself and is guaranteed by female solidarity" (Milan Women's Bookstore Collective 1990, 31).

This perspective stresses the role of the symbolic mother, drawing from Irigaray's discussion of the mother-daughter relationship as missing in representations of Western society, in which the mother is always seen carrying her son (Zumaglino 1996). In Turin, a concern with the mother is apparent, but not theorized. It should be noted that cultural accounts of mothers and their importance were also historically bolstered by Catholic ideology. As Caldwell suggests, "Both in its statements and in the institutional support it has given to welfare networks directed toward the family,

Catholicism has insisted on the central role of women in the family as mothers" (Caldwell 1991, 104).

The theory of sexual difference has had a great deal of influence on progressive Italian political thought, insisting that communist women must also be feminists. Italian women may grant sexual difference political status, but they have also criticized the Milan group's theory and method as individualist and elitist. De Lauretis suggests that this theory of feminist social-symbolic practices leaves little space for differences between and especially within women (1989).

Women's health was a major issue for feminist activists of the 1970s, and discussions of abortion increased the challenge to the frequently rhetorical celebration of motherhood as posed by statistics on illegal abortions. Feminist collectives stressed that health care in Italy manifests in material form the tremendous contradiction between the symbolically elevated status of the mother and her power in the domestic and familial sphere, and the social deprivation and ignorance in which the psychological and physical implications of motherhood are lived. These issues found practical expression in the development of Consultori Autogestiti Torinesi, or self-directed neighborhood health clinics. Women occupied vacant public buildings, forming health clinics where some themes from the feminist collectives were reproduced, for instance, consciousness-raising, external community-outreach activities, affirmation of the autonomy of the women's movement, and class-conflict. Consultori were established in various working-class neighborhoods and served as outreach centers for local women invited to participate in meetings, speeches, and discussion groups about female sexuality. The Consultori developed out of the feminist struggle for free contraception, abortion, and good gynecological care. Health professionals volunteered their services for public information sessions as well as for direct medical examinations. Consultori were often the only means for working-class women to procure a badly needed physical examination (J. Hellman 1987a).[6]

Factory and Social Space:
Intercategoriale Donne CGIL-CISL-UIL

In 1975, a group of women trade union delegates in Turin formed a multipartisan interunion organization called Intercategoriale Delegate Donne CGIL-CISL-UIL (Intercategory Delegates). Intercategoriale represented the two hearts of Turin feminism: the drive for women's autonomy and workerism (Zumaglino 1996, 101). The gesture to unify the three trade unions with their diverse political allegiances was not unprecedented, but it was unusual within a history of interunion relationships fraught with competition and conflict. Trade union victories of the late 1960s and early 1970s, including the right to hold collective assemblies during work hours, to post union notices, and to participate in 150-hour courses,[7] encouraged collaborative action among women. When the labor unions had won greater bargaining power than ever before, women delegates wished to expand the potential of union strength to encompass recognition of gendered occupational segregation and other discriminatory practices. The factory remained the site where the largest number of women aggregated, and where solidarity between women with workplace concerns might be most easily consolidated.

Women delegates decided to join ranks after participating in a 150-hours course at the University of Turin between 1974 and 1975.[8] The course employed feminist language to examine the relationship between women and work, and the contradiction "man-woman." Members of Intercategoriale did not necessarily believe that their organization approached women workers from a feminist perspective, but instead as a specific component of a particular global labor problem in which the working class was exploited in a variety of ways. They explained, "We think that these problems must not be understood or set apart as 'feminist' issues, but rather as specific components with their own particularities, of a global problem that clothes the entire class movement" (La Spina 1979, 35). They stressed the "female component" within the labor movement as a priority because of the growing number of proletarianized women workers around the world.

The Intercategoriale leadership was composed primarily of metal and mechanical-factory office workers[9] increasingly frustrated about the sexual division of labor. A wide range of women were drawn to the organization, including members of feminist collectives, political activists from extraparliamentary groups, blue- and white-collar workers, unemployed women, housewives, women working in the informal economy, activists, students, and university professors. Many had experience in the worker and student movements and were dedicated to the ideal of constructing autonomous, antihierarchical and decentralized spaces for women workers. Intercategoriale sent out flyers to raise consciousness about specific issues, held meetings among delegates, organized open assemblies, designed and taught 150-hours courses, organized protests, and held assemblies on topics specific to women workers.

Among the goals of Intercategoriale was to transform union organization by influencing the democratization of its structure and expanding base participation. Participants were frustrated with traditional male-centered authoritarian union structures, in which very few women held leadership positions. They argued that women could not have a significant role in transforming society unless they were awarded positions in union management and allowed wider participation in union activities.

Intercategoriale challenged official union ideology, which denied the existence of sexually differentiated labor practices, and struggled to incorporate women-specific issues into union discourse (Marcellino 1975). It also challenged unions to remain open to their base, avoiding pressure by conservative political forces to push them back into traditionally staid and rigid forms of institutionalization (Il Sindacato di Eva 1981). Intercategoriale struggled against a very strong front of male leadership that did not think women's issues were significant, and that often accused union women of representing individual interests instead of acting as part of a collective effort to promote working-class interests in general (Il Sindacato di Eva 1981).

Although Intercategoriale stated formally that it was "not feminist," the feminist collectives, UDI, and feminist arteries of the extraparliamentary left increasingly influenced it. When it was formed, the organization was against any form of consciousness-raising (autocoscienza), a position that turned away many women from the feminist collectives. Others rejected the group because they were highly critical of the trade unions: "La Firma CGIL-CISL-UIL = Satana!" ("The name CGIL-CISL-UIL = The Devil!") (La Spina 1979, 303). However, the anti-institutional philosophy of Turin feminism ultimately exerted an influence on the evolution of Intercategoriale, which over the course of the 1970s became ever more cognizant of the limits of working within traditional and patriarchal organizational structures. Nevertheless, there continued to be an effort to work for change within unions instead of rejecting them. For instance, Intercategoriale interpreted consciousness-raising to mean improving social and institutional conditions by becoming aware of oneself as a woman (Zumaglino 1996).

Intercategoriale focused primary attention on issues surrounding women and work, arguing that females were particularly vulnerable to the effects of industrial restructuring, including increasing mechanization, de-skilling, downsizing, and the consequent layoff of workers. The organization was acutely aware that the numbers of women wage workers was on the rise globally, but that there was a contradictory tendency to eliminate women from factory employment in advanced industrial zones like Turin as part of a process of industrial downsizing. Between 1973 and 1975, the number of employed women fell by 1.2 million (La Spina 1979). Intercategoriale argued that the expulsion of female workers opened the door for employers to attack workers in general, and that the unions would ultimately pay a high price for not sufficiently defending women workers. Intercategoriale urged the unions to recognize that women workers had global problems that concerned the working-class movement in general (La Spina 1979, 35). The defense of work, they implored, had to address the attack on the most vulnerable category of workers: women.

Within Turin's segmented labor market, women's jobs were more vulnerable than those of men, and females were generally in the lowest skilled, most repetitive, and least prestigious sectors (La Spina 1979, 49). Intercategoriale suggested, "In the general attack on work we see that women are affected in a dramatic way, inasmuch as we find them employed in the weakest and most backward sectors that require a more or less unskilled labor force, and in sectors where production is fragmented in small firms and thus where workers are less organized" (La Spina 1979, 49). The organization suggested that the vulnerability of women workers was linked with the manner in which women were socially naturalized in families as mothers and housewives and held responsible for the reproduction of male workers. As a consequence, women were not professionally trained. Apart from generating problems such as low salaries, this lower status rendered women workers extremely vulnerable in the face of the attack on work. And because many women worked informally in small factories or in home/cottage industries where they lacked union representation, it was very difficult to organize them to defend themselves.

The growing feminist influence on Intercategoriale was reflected in their argument that the precarious position in which women were situated in the Italian labor market had to be confronted as a gender problem, not easily generalized across the working class, and that a broad lens was necessary to understand and confront the peculiar difficulties experienced by women workers. Gender relations within the family, they suggested, were mirrored in factory hierarchies where women were the most exploited and least represented workers:

The condition of the working woman is always a condition of super-exploitation derived not only from the fact of being a worker like other workers; but above all the fact of being a WOMAN, and therefore with a series of specific problems.

To arrive at these specific problems it is necessary to avoid falling into the error of seeing the Woman only as a worker, thus only when she's inserted into the factory. It is instead necessary—also as a method of inquiry, of analysis and of debate (in discussions, meetings, etc.)—to see the woman as a worker also outside of the factory, individuating the first moment of exploitation in the family, which the capitalist society uses to burden her with a very specific socially subordinate role, and from which the Woman is not released once she enters the factory! (La Spina 1979, 46)

Intercategoriale called on the labor unions to press the government to implement a parity law to provide equal pay and equal access to jobs for women, reserve a fixed percentage of new jobs for women, and guarantee their admission into courses designed to upgrade skills. The organization also demanded that laid-off women be rehired strictly according to the date they were let go. They pressed the trade unions to become more committed to the protection of women employed in piecework at home, and argued that the recent entry of thousands of women into the factories had led to certain problems, contradictions, and prejudices about a woman's "place in the home." There was a great deal of sexual harassment toward women in the workplace, and Intercategoriale urged the unions to consider women in relation to the "humanity" of work organization in factories and offices. Improved state controls on health conditions were also needed in the factories where dangerous work conditions affected women in particular ways (La Spina 1979).

Further expanding the labor and New Left struggles of the late 1960s and early 1970s, Intercategoriale pressed the trade unions to integrate into their contractual demands issues designed to transform the lives of women, both inside and outside the factory—in the areas of family and reproduction, education, and health, for instance. Employing a feminist argument that the "personal is political," the organization argued that the problems of women workers must be approached by adopting a holistic lens to encompass the whole of women's daily lives:

Today it's essential that the union movement take up the challenge of a global intervention, one that in the light of restructuring, and the reconversion of investments, might find a way of welding together the struggles and initiatives on the problems in the factory (employment . . .) with that of the problems beyond the factory, that is, the realization of social and health services. (La Spina 1979, 79)

For instance, they demanded forty hours of paid leave for one working parent to care for sick children, employer-supported day care facilities, flexible working hours, and after-school supervision for the children of working parents. They also pressed the unions to participate in the struggle for safe and legal abortion. Intercategoriale tried to persuade trade unions to address issues of permission for a designated number of hours in which men and women could leave work to care for sick children, for improved health conditions in the factories, and for expanded maternity leave. They also urged the government to establish a greater number of state-funded day care centers *(asili)* and elementary schools *(scuole elementari),* which they argued would help create new jobs outside of the factory. They suggested that schools concerned not individual but collective interests because of the nature of these sites as crucial loci of socialization where consciousness develops (Il Sindacato di Eva 1981).

Aside from merely pressuring the trade unions to innovate their organizational structures, Intercategoriale took their own initiatives to press for change within Turin society by seeking contact with the rank-and-file worker bases from which, they argued, the trade unions were alienated. Intercategoriale women were key participants in the movement for the Consultori, or women's health clinics, for which they pressed for public funding. Located in working-class neighborhoods, the Consultori became important sites of interaction between feminist activists, housewives, and unemployed women (J. Hellman 1987b). Overall, through the neighborhood health clinics and the 150-hours courses, Intercategoriale moved beyond the exclusive domain of highly educated middle-class women toward a more decentralized feminism, developing links with working-class women as women (La Spina 1979).

They also organized and taught several courses designed for women in the 150-hours program under the rubric of "women's condition" (Caldwell 1983). The courses dealt with issues of health, family relations, sexuality, body language, women's literature, women and work, and women and union militancy. The group organized an intensive course on the female condition in the factory and in society, designed to raise consciousness about women's doubly exploited position as both factory worker and homemaker. The course treated the issue of the socialization of women in the family, at work, and in personal and social relations, while reconstructing women's histories from stories told and written by women themselves. All of the 150-hours courses operated by Intercategoriale included a time for the exchange of experience and opinion between women toward the construction of women's solidarity (Il Sindacato di Eva 1981).

Another Intercategoriale course was directed toward women's health *(salute della donna)*. The course trained women to better understand the functions of their bodies to empower themselves vis-à-vis the family and local hospitals and in dealings with doctors who had a hand in controlling female reproduction. Employing feminist literature, the course explored the power relations involved in the appropriation of women's bodies by the medical profession and familial institutions. The course was developed around the belief that women could obtain knowledge outside the domain of medical or other experts to better equip themselves should they have to enter a hospital to give birth or for other purposes (Il Sindacato di Eva 1981). They made an effort to encourage a specifically woman's point of view of the female body and to raise levels of knowledge, consciousness, and control over reproduction. The 150-hours courses brought more workers and housewives into the feminist movement because the courses were taught during hours convenient for these women. Intercategoriale published a periodical on the 150-hours programs for women, which was called *Riprendiamoci la Vita* (Let's Take Back Our Lives).

It is important to remember that this women's organization was formed within the seat of established trade union institutions, which provided Intercategoriale with a socially recognized base they would not otherwise have had. The only other public spaces occupied by women at this time were the feminist collectives, but these lacked a formal relationship with Italian state entities and political parties. The downside to the formal institutional basis of the Intercategoriale was that women were forced to operate within the parameters of a union structure that they did not construct, and that was reluctant to expand its ideological parameters beyond the scope of the protection of factory workers. By the early 1970s, the women's movement in Italy had begun to elaborate a practical politics derived from the argument that, in regard to women's roles in society, "the personal is political." However, Intercategoriale would find itself limited by the expectations and philosophies of a union structure that had developed in response to the needs of male manufacturing workers, and that was not yet prepared to incorporate the demands of an increasingly complex population (S. Hellman 1988). Through the Intercategoriale, Turin union women accomplished more than they did through UDI, but their concerns were not taken seriously enough by the unions and they tended to remain on the margins of Turin political culture.

Beyond the Gates: The International Feminism of Produrre e Riprodurre

The Turin feminism with the most direct genealogical link to Alma Mater is Produrre e Riprodurre (P&R, Production and Reproduction). Formed in 1983, the organization dominated Turin feminism, at least until the early 1990s. P&R's philosophy unites themes of class conflict expressed in the worker struggles of the 1960s and 1970s with a distinctive feminist approach to issues of work and society.[10]

P&R was initiated by former members of UDI, Intercategoriale, and Turin feminist collectives, many of whom operated under the umbrella of the Casa delle Donne (Women's House). The women organized an international convention in Turin for the purpose of addressing problems of women and work as well as the interconnected domains of family, social services, and culture as experienced by women in industrialized countries. Supported by local political figures and state functionaries, some six hundred women from various organizations from throughout the peninsula, France, Spain, Belgium, Greece, Holland, Germany, Luxembourg, Switzerland, England, Australia, and the United States met in 1983 at the Palazzo del Lavoro in Turin to celebrate the formation of an international organization of women from capitalist, industrialized countries (P&R 1984). P&R coordinated efforts with the Center for Research on European Women in Brussels and the Bureau of Women of the EEC (the European Economic Community). These women wished to form P&R to expand their networks with women's organizations connected with politically left parties and labor unions in industrialized countries, and with women independent of institutional allegiances. More than half the conference participants came from women's groups without formal institutional connections, a quarter from women in trade unions, and the remainder from political parties and the news media. Perceiving the advantages of an official organizational structure, the members of P&R, many of whom had been active in the Italian trade unions, constituted their group as a juridically recognized association, with a president, secretary, and treasurer. The basic features of P&R were formed during the course of the three-day conference.

P&R represents the "second phase" of Turin feminism beginning in the 1980s, prompted in part by profound transformation in the organization of work, family, and society (Zumaglino 1990). Participants sought to investigate what women could do to improve work and social conditions in post-Fordist economic and political circumstances, and they were interested in work/production as well as the reproductive domain of the household, family, sexuality, and the body. Consistent with long-standing emphases on work within UDI and the Intercategoriale, the new organization focused much of its energy on how women fit within a transforming labor market. Participants suggested that, although the women's movement had made significant strides in helping to raise the percentage of employed women in Italy, millions remained unemployed or employed in the most precarious and low-status occupations of an expanding tertiary sector. The development of information technologies that raised the demand for highly skilled workers and cuts to government expenditures, they argued, had the most deleterious impact on women workers. The women who formed P&R asked how the increasing restrictions on work outlets within a late twentieth-century economy would influence feminism, and how feminists would react to significant mutations in the labor market. They suggested that feminism found itself confronted by the stubborn walls of strategic institutional opposition just when significant numbers of women had finally obtained factory positions traditionally reserved for men.

P&R interpreted the backlash against female employment as an international issue, particularly for women in similar industrialized contexts where reductions of women's jobs and pay scales were occurring. They realized that the issues would be different for women from diverse countries, but wished to find common ground. They also suggested the need to better incorporate feminist philosophies of equality and difference into the organization of work under capitalism. P&R sought to reexamine the interconnection between productive and reproductive practices, validating the central role of gender differences that emanate from practices within the reproductive sphere.[11] Intercategoriale had criticized the hierarchical organization of the workplace, as well as the capitalist values of competitiveness, speed, and aggression, which the organization interpreted as dehumanizing. P&R sought to take these concerns to an international arena, creating a more geographically far-reaching solidarity between women concerned about the contradiction between the cooperative interpersonal exchanges that took place within the sphere of reproduction and the rigid, abstract interpersonal environment of the capitalist workplace. They argued that because the two domains of production and reproduction were interdependent, society should be prepared to respond constructively to the needs of working parents who required more flexible work schedules and greater respect for the part of life lived at home.

A major theme of the 1983 conference was to find a solution to the contraction of jobs in the current phase of capitalist economic restructuring, processes that negatively affected the number of women employed and the categories of work they obtained. Many suggested that women create jobs in "autonomous" forms of labor (*lavoro autonomo,* or self-employment), which in Turin were dominated by men who had lost jobs at Fiat or other firms. Women wished to break into lavoro autonomo and to expand their skills in the form of women's cooperatives. P&R saw autonomous, cooperative work as a medium through which to create women's spaces, where women's distinct identities might be expressed in forums untainted by the dominant work rhythms of capitalist production regimes. Often when women entered a traditional workplace dominated by men, it was argued, they were forced to assimilate to pregiven arrangements. P&R believed that through cooperative organizations and self-employment women might become professionals without reproducing typically masculinized forms of conflict, power relations, role divisions, and competition. Although the issue was debated, many believed that women's practices in caretaking or positions of help and nurturing in the household and as childbearers provided women with an approach to the world that was not easily translatable into the work styles generally adopted within modern capitalist firms. They advocated several cooperative forms to express women's differences, including those specializing in social services, cultural production (libraries and research), and artisanal production. Participants suggested that within co-ops, women might discover how to direct themselves autonomously, without scattering and fragmenting themselves within formal institutions. P&R adopted the co-op as a model for dealing with economic crisis, suggesting that both the women's movement and the Italian cooperative movement operated according to a similar logic: the refusal to be mediated by external institutions.

Clearly, the most important component of P&R was the redefinition of "work." Drawing on the kind of idealist-humanist philosophy exalted by Marx in his early writings, these women defined work as the practice of free and necessary self-expression through which one created oneself and society. They defined work against a dominant model of efficiency and productivity that did not in their view correspond to basic humanity (P&R 1984). They therefore adopted forms of self- and cooperative employment as a way to avoid dependent forms of labor not only difficult for women to secure, but seen as routes to fragmenting the self without ever realizing a finished product. Autonomous and cooperative work would theoretically permit a degree of creative expression, even pleasure.

P&R also addressed issues of reproduction—for example, sexuality, maternity, and self-perception. The organization seemed to have adopted a developmental model of gender relations within families, in which women from nonindustrialized southern Italy and other parts of Europe were deemed more oppressed by patriarchal structures than their northern Italian and European counterparts. P&R seemed to accept the stereotype that southern Italian women were not permitted to leave their homes without the express permission of a husband or someone from the extended family. Such a view was adopted from a developmentalist model, in which gender relations in precapitalist societies were interpreted as more patriarchal than in the advanced industrialized world.

P&R did not advocate a wholly negative perspective on household practices, but wished to incorporate some of the positive aspects of familial life into a new understanding of women and work. They interpreted a certain intrinsic value to the household as a space in which social relations were less abstract than in the "public" domain of dependent employment. However, the monotonous aspects of household responsibilities such as cooking, cleaning, and shopping were believed to lend themselves to feelings of isolation and anxiety among women not engaged in extra-domestic wage earning. P&R viewed domestic work as a highly undervalued form of activity that frequently led women to feel socially inferior and peripheral. The women who were considered the most socially marginal were paid domestic workers who experienced feelings of inferiority derived from the undervaluation of women's work and magnified by their low-class status. Domestic workers "are to an extent the quintessence of the horrors of femaleness; they are at the center of our history and our conditions." Emancipation was seen as impossible for women who were confined entirely to the home, whether as housewives or domestic workers.

Emancipation was not, however, assumed to flow broadly from the simple procurement of wage employment. Members of P&R asserted that, for instance, when southern Italian housewives began to work at Fiat, they were crushed under tedious work conditions. Yet waged work was believed to provide opportunity for women to be socialized in shared spaces, whereas housework offered little possibility for the development of solidarity between women operating within highly restricted and fractured spaces. When confined to the home, they suggested, women were encouraged to compete with each other over men and sexuality (P&R 1984).

P&R sought to discover ways to unify wage-earning women with unemployed women, domestic workers, and housewives. Their goal was to open new spaces for female solidarity and to challenge dominant social and economic values. They aimed to encourage recognition of female differences and to struggle for equality with men in the image of a world with a more equal distribution of wealth.

In the late 1980s and 1990s, P&R further expanded the goal of international solidarity between women to include women from nonindustrialized and economically developing parts of the world. Donne in Sviluppo (Women in Development) was a splinter group of women in P&R who became interested in what one member referred to as the "colonization of third world women's work," in which the products produced by these women were exported, yet secured little profit for them. Participants in Donne in Sviluppo, some of them having spent time in West Africa, were impressed with cooperative ventures initiated by women in Africa, and they wanted to better understand the similarities and differences between what appeared to be common conditions faced by women in industrialized and nonindustrialized contexts. They were impressed with the role of African women in the development of small and medium firms. Their concerns were framed within an understanding of Africa as underdeveloped, yet they wished to understand the meaning of "underdevelopment" in unorthodox ways. In the words of one of the key early Turin feminist participants in Alma Mater:

> My desire to grasp what the women of the south were beginning to say about their economy was born when, finding myself in one or two voyages in Africa as part of an Italian cooperation, I had realized that it was true that there existed an underdevelopment that had serious repercussions on the conditions of people's lives . . . very poor conditions of health, extremely low incomes . . . there also existed a functioning economy that did not function in relation to the model of development/underdevelopment. In 1987 there were the first embryonic analyses . . . above all relative to the area of the Sahel . . . that this economy of survival in which the language of survival assumed connotations different from the usual . . . analyzed by us as survival is that which is below "living" . . . internal zones of African countries live, or lived, at this level of "living"

without having major disasters either from the point of view of health, or from the point of view of the conditions of life.

The most salient fact for me was the realization that this was about an economy substantially directed by women . . . the income circulated between women was used by women. . . . In other words, in these countries, the informal sector of the economy . . . played a fundamental role and was a central part of the survival strategy. (Zumaglino and Garelli 1995, 26)

In 1989, P&R was involved in a two-year formation course to promote women's entrepreneurship in Africa. Nineteen women from eleven Francophone countries in Africa participated. The goal was to create what was later called La Nuova Africa (The New Africa), a laboratory of feminine solidarity in the spirit of female entrepreneurship through the role of the female protagonist (Zumaglino and Garelli 1995). Their goals, later echoed in some of Alma Mater's initiatives, were to promote economic and cultural orientations favorable to the commercialization of products made by African women. As the project went on, the goals were modified with a predominant cultural valence, and included women from English-speaking parts of Africa as well as Asia and Latin America. In the words of Turin feminists Piera Zumaglino and Annamaria Garelli: "We hope that this . . . will be a reference for others who wish to promote a multicultural dialogue among women" (1995, 9). An ideal that became quite pronounced during the 1990s and that was expressed by one of Alma Mater's most active Italian participants, Laura Scagliotti: "I wanted to discover this new world, and understanding it through the women who came from other countries intrigued me a great deal" (in Zumaglino and Garelli 1995, 27). To this end, they sought to meet women immigrants in Turin and to join with them in their struggle against racism: "We met for a week to discuss the valorization of the African woman, her entrepreneurial spirit, her products, her culture. This valorization was particularly important at a time when, following the growth of African immigration, Italy was discovering racism until then hidden" (31).

The members of Donne in Sviluppo were among those who developed the first ties to immigrant women, and they were approached with the idea of creating a large intercultural women's center of cultural and entrepreneurial activity. Through the project La Nuova Africa, they established relationships with some of the ethnic associations in Turin and with migrant women in the associations Shabel and AIDA.[12] In 1990, for instance, they helped to create an initiative called Tamtamtavola, in which African meals would be made and distributed on request (Zumaglino and Garelli

1995, 125–26). It was through these efforts that they began to participate in the Alma Mater project.

Turin Feminism and Alma Mater

It would be unfair to associate all Turin feminists with Alma Mater, for in 1996 more than a few had never set foot in the intercultural building. However, by that time Alma Mater dominated Donne in Sviluppo and P&R meetings held at the Casa delle Donne. A member of P&R and Donne in Sviluppo, a long-term participant in the feminist movement and a member of CGIL in 1996, worried about the effects Alma Mater was having on local feminism:

> Alma Mater has ruptured the previous equilibrium of Produrre e Riprodurre. All of the association's money goes to the functioning of Alma Mater. All of the meetings end in discussions of Alma Mater. Until recently, Produrre e Riprodurre handled the money given Alma Mater by the comune, and this created a lot of problems because they didn't know how to administer the funds. Then there is the fact that the women in Alma Mater, the immigrants, are not interested in issues of concern to Italian feminists, such as the problem of women's rights, reproduction, and so on. They say that Italians and white women in general are more attached to men than they are, so that for them feminism makes little sense. But they come from polygamous societies! They don't have a head for creating a different society . . . they just want to be equal to Italians. (interview by author)

In 2001, several Turin feminists told me that they thought feminism in Turin was as dead as it was in Italy at large, and that they rarely if ever had P&R meetings anymore. Some special events, they explained, were still organized at the Casa delle Donne, but the majority of feminist activity in Turin, or what remained of it, took place in or around Alma Mater. One Turin feminist in her sixties, who was more involved with the Casa delle Donne than with Alma Mater, expressed her disappointment about the death of Italian feminism. With resignation she remarked, "Young women don't consider themselves unequal to men, so they don't see the need for feminism."

In 2001, I traveled with a group of women from Alma Mater to attend a Global Feminist Forum that preceded the G8 summit in Genoa. While aboard the train, I asked two Turin feminists in their middle fifties about contemporary Italian feminism, and they told me that feminism had

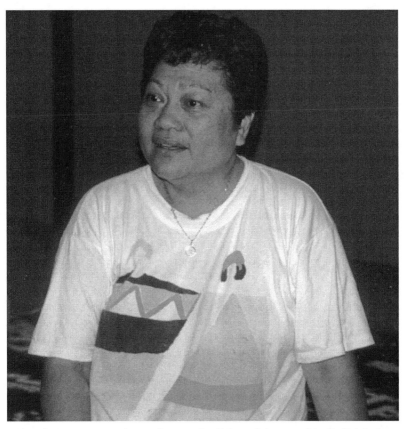

Pas, a Filipina immigrant, former director of La Talea and director of the Turkish bath

changed a lot during the past decade, since the immigrant women began to arrive. Marianna said, "Because young women don't come to the meetings at the Casa delle Donne, there really is no feminism." Disagreeing, her friend, Maria Lucia, suggested that feminism still existed, but was weak. She showed me a feminist newspaper to which she subscribed, and explained that she had been part of the 1970s feminist movement, which made her an "old feminist."

While having dinner with the group associated with Alma Mater after a long day of forum presentations and meetings, a formerly prominent member of P&R told me, "Feminism in Turin is now *all* Donne in Nero (Women in Black)[13] or Alma Mater." She added that she was at first reluctant to participate in Alma Mater, but that she had gradually warmed to the place. She and another member of P&R expressed their feeling that, because there were only "old" women like themselves who went to Casa delle Donne, they were really no longer interested in the place. They said that without the younger women there they felt like a bunch of old ladies rehashing the past. We all commented on the sizable number of young women in attendance at the Global Feminist Forum, and one Turin feminist expressed her excitement about this. She said that she thought it was because of the recent governmental offensive against abortion, which had given young women something to be angry about.

When Alma Mater was in the process of becoming an intercultural women's site, several members of P&R and Donne in Sviluppo drew on old friendships and political alliances with government officials in the PDS, as well as the CGIL and CISL trade unions. It was apparent that, while I attended Casa delle Donne meetings that were still active in 1996 and while I spoke with these women at their homes or during the trip to Genoa in 2001, Turin feminists had a great deal of knowledge about each other. Most of these women shared a history of activism as part of extraparliamentary left organizations, Intercategoriale, or the feminist collectives. To Alma Mater, they brought extensive experience and knowledge of local political culture.

One of the former directors of Alma Mater, Laura Scagliotti, was a founding member of P&R. A small, rather shy, but energetic woman in her early sixties, she rapidly resolved immediate problems as they arose in the interethnic women's center, speaking quickly, always in a hurry, always busy and pressed for time. During interviews she was frequently interrupted to answer phone calls. When she was finally able to sit down and express her thoughts in some detail, I found Laura Scagliotti to be a woman with an enormous depth of experience and knowledge about local politics. Laura, then retired, had worked as a secretary in a metal mechanic factory beginning in the late 1950s. She joined CISL in 1970 and was elected a delegate shortly afterward. She was introduced to the labor union by a group of workers who met clandestinely after work at a bar next to the factory. The workers talked about their situation, expressing opposition to hierarchy and arguing for autonomy. They did not talk about women, but about human dignity, and their discussions centered on worker rights, including the right to be treated with respect (Zumaglino 1996, 30). Laura was enthusiastic about working in a factory, a form of work she believed highly dignified. Among the first wave of delegates following the struggles of workers and unions that won this right in the late 1960s, Laura was ostracized in her workplace. None of the offices wanted to hire her, for

Laura Scagliotti, 2001

she was considered a "spy for the enemy." Finally, she was assigned to the company's legal office, where a powerful manager scrutinized her closely. Her fellow workers were instructed not to speak, sit, or eat with her. If not for the other delegates in the firm, she'd have always eaten alone (Zumaglino 1996, 48). Her exposure to feminism came from her membership in Intercategoriale, which broke up in 1985, and through her exchanges with women who had been part of the feminist collectives.

Maria Teresa Battaglino, a founding member of Alma Mater, was a social worker and active Turin feminist. A cordial woman in her early fifties, she was easily at home in new surroundings. She wore loose-fitting clothing with colorful sixties and seventies designs. Maria Teresa had lengthy experience in various feminist collectives, both extraparliamentary and student groups. She had been a member of Demau, as well as a Leninist collective of the student movement Lotta Continua and Avanguardia Operaia. She lived in a commune during the 1970s and was involved with the activities of the Intercategoriale, including the movement to create self-managed health clinics, or Consultori. An original member of both P&R and Donne in Sviluppo, she traveled extensively in West Africa. Maria Teresa, before helping to establish Alma Mater, participated in at least one

Mariateresa Calloni, speaking at the Gender and Globalization Conference in Genoa, 2001

global conference on women, held in Nairobi. With a passion for African cultures and societies, she led the original feminist effort to make contact with immigrant women and to help insert them into local society.

Marite Calloni remained active in the direction of Alma Mater. An attractive woman in her fifties, she wore her hair in a stylish shoulder-length cut, which made her appear younger than her years. Marite was focused on the task at hand, avoiding contact with newcomers unless pressed. In 1996 she was an appointed member of the Piedmont Regional Commission for Equal Opportunity (Commissione per le Pari Opportunita della Regione Piemonte), an organization that she helped put into place and over which Laura Scagliotti had previously presided. This organization provided financial support to the Alma Mater theater group, designed, as it was, to allocate regional funds that promoted women's equal opportunity. A member of both P&R and Donne in Sviluppo, Marite was a retired white-collar factory employee delegate for the CGIL. She described the gender dynamics of her work and union experience:

> Workers were almost all men, because of the idea that "only men have careers," and those women who worked in the factories were mostly

in white-collar jobs. It was difficult to be a delegate because most men thought that they could represent women in the unions, but that women could not represent men. This hasn't changed much. Even if on the surface they say that they accept you, in fact they never had any consciousness . . . they forget to invite you . . . and you get really tired of it . . . tired of arguing. Between women it's different.

Marite also participated in Intercategoriale. Formerly a member of the PCI and later the DS, she had a close friend in the municipal social service administration that was instrumental in gaining political support for Alma Mater.

The Turin feminists who contributed most prominently to the production of Alma Mater were identified as members of particular political organizations, a requirement for anyone wishing access to the local government. These women contributed to one of the world's largest and most passionate labor movements, in a city where certain neighborhoods, piazzas, and cafés have come to be associated with specific political histories, and where it is expected that anyone involved with worker politics will claim membership in one or more recognizable group or political entity. The depth of these women's social knowledge and commitment to local political culture has been bred over many years of activity.

In her beautifully written book on workerism and fascism, Luisa Passerini (1984) describes Turin as a city where cultural primacy is given to the political, by which she means that political responsibility, burden, and entitlement lay claim to political gains passed on from one generation to another. But without the participation of Italian youth in Turin feminism and in the political activism that has characterized this city for almost a century, how will local political culture be reproduced? The absence of young Italians described by Turin feminists, their lack of interest in and commitment to political struggle, is echoed by many Turinese over the age of forty-five, who express all sorts of complaints about a young generation "spoiled by overconsumption," unwilling to work hard or to sacrifice for a greater social good.[14] The relative absence of young women in Alma Mater events and meetings, with the occasional exception of theatrical performances and ethnic dinners, is significant both for Italians and for immigrant women. The passage of political knowledge from one generation to the next that Passerini described is, in fact, taking place in Turin, but more in relation to a newcomer population than to a younger generation of Italians. Migrants have become the inheritors of an incredible Italian tradition of engagement and activism, the agents through which political traditions are reproduced at a complex level.

Women dancing in the Alma Mater meeting room as part of an antiracist exercise, 2001

It seems that the older generation of Turin feminists, active in trade unions and New Left organizations, see themselves as having more in common with immigrants than with many younger Italians. With the newcomers, they share a history that is uncertain, when they did not live in a society with a significant middle class, a "consumerist" society where goods are available for those who can afford them (Ginsborg 2003). Immigrant women are becoming the agents of the reproduction of Turin feminism, and in the future these newcomers will transmit local political culture to others, migrants and Italians alike.

CHAPTER 7

Making Alma Mater:
Gender, Race, and Other Differences

> It is through the effort to recapture the self and to scrutinize
> the self, it is through the lasting tension of their freedom
> that men *(and women)* [my italics] will be able to create
> the ideal conditions of existence for a human world.
> —*Frantz Fanon*, Black Skin, White Masks

Globalization and the Empowerment of Civil Society

Alma Mater appeared at a historical moment when the "third sector" of nongovernmental organizations commonly equated with the interests of civil society took on increasing spatial significance in Italy and around the world. Some have suggested that the third sector embodies a means of dealing with global economic crises, when the states' weakening capacity to provide social services for its citizens could be resolved by empowering civil society (Korten 1990; Rifkin 1995). From both sides of the political spectrum, scholars contend that democracy can be fully achieved only through the agency of civil society, that is, the nonprofit sector as a site of innovation, alternative vision, community values, and tolerance for social and cultural difference. From the United States to Mexico, Brazil, France, and Italy, many nongovernmental organizations (NGOs) are invested with the agency of popular social movements in the advanced capitalist world (Alvarez and Escobar 1992; Chalmers et al. 1995; Gill 1995). However, some commentators suggest that to attribute a major social and economic role to organizations outside the government and business sector is to merely shift the burden of social resource provision from public agencies to local communities (Craig and Mayo 1995). Intrinsic to this debate about the function of civil society is a tension between the neoliberal philosophy of self-help and a Marxist concept of the creative construction of the self and collectivity through practice (Marx 1987).[1] This tension is reflected in Alma Mater, a nongovernmental organization at the crossroads of an increasingly culturally diverse Europe, constituted by new forms of alliance, interethnicity, and feminist politics.

Alma Mater's appearance is linked with recent changes in global capitalism, including shifts in the international division of labor, intensified economic interdependencies between societies all over the world, and widening economic disparities within and between countries. Despite an explosion in discourse about the increasing ease of financial, commodity, informational, and cultural exchanges across national borders and a world of global flows between equal partners, shifts within capitalism during the past thirty years have led to incredible polarization between wealthy nations, where most trade occurs, and the vast majority of people, who live in poor areas. In 1992, 91.5 percent of foreign direct investment went to parts of the world that contained 28 percent of the world's population.[2] In developing countries, debt crises, currency devaluations, falling commodity rates on such products as cocoa and ground nuts, the shrinkage in government, and the failure of schemes to capitalize agriculture have contributed to a growing pressure to migrate.

Alma Mater emerged at a time when many Italians were looking toward nongovernmental organizations to meet the challenges of growing cultural racism and persistent high unemployment, especially among youth. As an alliance between migrants and Turin feminists, Alma Mater is an example of a postcolonial grassroots politics that represents myriad differences. Whether or not the organization succeeds in constructing an enduring form of antiracist and interethnic grassroots politics in Turin, its emergence is a sign of the ambiguous cityscapes of today's Europe and a signal of the future present:

> It is the city administration that is at fault, not the women. It does not support, invest enough money in the place. Alma Mater is an association and there are others in Turin. The city cannot give all the money to one association, OK, yet they do give loads to SERMIG,[3] where there are many beds for immigrants. Alma Mater is a flower in the lapel of the city government; it is known all over Italy and throughout Europe. But the municipality doesn't give it any money. It begs them not to close it down because it is known all over Europe and because they are doing something, providing a space for these women—where the state is not doing so. (Maria Viarengo 1995)

Between Oppositional Politics and Reform:
Alma Mater and the Third Sector

Waldemar Nielsen first used "third sector" in 1979 as a catchall term for the sector that operates between the government and market economy. Nielsen described the third sector in the United States as a sphere of not-for-profit, frequently socially alternative activities devoted to the general welfare. These "operate in that large sphere of life which does not center on power and authority or on the production and acquisition of material goods and money. They embody the counter-values and complementary beliefs of our competitive, capitalistic, materialistic, egalitarian culture" (Nielsen 1979, 4). The term *third sector* (Terzo Settore) has been widely adopted in Italy, employed loosely to refer broadly to nonprofit nongovernmental organizations, voluntary organizations, cooperatives, and associations. In practice, this third sector has expanded considerably since the mid-1980s, particularly in urban industrial centers and developing economies, and in Turin popularly through the form of the cooperative.

The recent popularity of nongovernmental organizations is frequently viewed as a consequence of drastic reductions in state social-welfare expenditures that have been underway around the globe since the 1980s (Waterman 1998; Conroy 1995; Kramer 1992; Wolch 1989). With a huge public debt, the Italian state has been in a fiscal crisis for years, forced to roll back public spending to qualify for the Euro currency (Ascoli 1992; Ginsborg 2003; Agnew 2002). At the same time, poverty has expanded, and basic needs are growing among the elderly, immigrants, youth, the mentally ill, and the drug dependent.[4] These social categories of people are frequently lumped together as "problems" threatening the well-being of society if not repaired. However, with continual contractions in public spending and the privatization of public services, the responsibility for social welfare has shifted to an ever-greater extent from the public sector to local communities, families, and the private commercial sector (Mingione 1993). Italian political scientists often use the concept "mixed economy of welfare" to describe, in ideal terms, a collaborative relationship between the state and the nongovernmental sector, popularly referred to in Italian as the *volontariato,* or voluntary sector (Ascoli 1992; Ranci 1992).

Italian scholars on the political right and left debate the appropriateness of further advancing the Italian third sector as a solution to persistent unemployment and spiraling poverty. When the American journalist-scholar Jeremy Rifkin proclaimed that the third sector of voluntary activism was the answer to the inevitable obsolescence of thousands of jobs as a direct consequence of advancing technology, many Italian intellectuals seemed to agree (1995). They also suggested that the expansion of nongovernmental activities, particularly social cooperatives, could create many needed jobs and social services in an era of reduced public spending. Those who advocated this citizen's approach to social services argued that the welfare state of today could not resolve worsening social inequalities. Advocates described the mixed economy of welfare as a series of contractual relationships between the state and civil society, leading to the greater independence of citizen groups from a rigid and labyrinthian Italian state bureaucratic system (Ascoli 1992).

Many on the political left have supported the increasing involvement of non-Catholics in voluntary or nonprofit activities. For most of the twentieth century, Catholic voluntary organizations such as Caritas dominated the social field of community help in a privileged relationship to public and private sources of funding. Catholic organizations continue to dominate almost the entire world of Italian benefit societies, and even those not directly identified with the church are often in the arch of Catholic influence. By contrast, the Italian left has limited itself to trade union activities or to work-cooperative ventures. The popular form of the cooperative first appeared in nineteenth-century Italian society among peasants and artisans in the form of mutual-aid societies inspired by socialists. Popularly associated with the political left, many co-ops were seats for the Resistance during Fascism, and until the 1960s they were more or less designated as the domain of the Italian working class (Holmström 1989). The cooperatives formed in Alma Mater are part of this older left tradition, but Alma Mater has expanded the practices of cooperatives to include areas of service and cultural-artistic expression, normally the restricted domain of Catholic voluntary associations.

In the past two decades, nongovernmental organizations have come to be associated with social activism or social movements designed to challenge relationships of power between citizens and the state or between citizens and a profit-driven market. As discussed in the last chapter, some Turin feminists wished to promote an international women's space as a means of empowering women. Voluntarism in Italian society is often equated with the highest of human values and sentiments, altruism, hope, cooperation, and solidarity. Among politically left youth of the upper or middle classes, there is a way of viewing voluntary activity in Italian society as an expression of anticapitalism or anticonsumption practices to which one ought, at some point, to contribute. Some have equated the explosion of social cooperatives and voluntary associations since the mid-1980s with social protest in the previous decade, characterized by the intensified individualism and greed that marked a neoliberal political era (Ascoli 1992). In certain parts of the world, NGOs are frequently viewed as sites of feminist social activism (Korten 1990; Fisher 1997). Sonia Alvarez describes the discourses of feminist NGOs in Brazil as an expression of advancement toward a new concept of the "democratic citizen" and as a challenge to the rigid hierarchies of gender, race, and class that traditional institutions have helped reproduce (1996, 1997). Alvarez and Escobar suggest that Latin American social movements today, many operative as NGOs, involve a more diverse group of participants than have participated historically, a "multiplicity of social actors that establish spheres of autonomy in a fragmented social and political space" (Alvarez and Escobar 1992, 3). Contemporary forms of social activism may include participants from diverse social classes and ethnic or religious backgrounds who struggle as members of civil society—a concept borrowed from Gramsci, linked with contemporary social activism, and employed as a dynamic tool for forging more democratic and less socially stratified societies.

A word of caution is necessary, however, for as much as the third sector might be an ideal domain in an empowered civil society in partnership with state and private organizations, it can also be a sphere where social inequities are reproduced (Bryant 2002; Fisher 1997; Mohan 2002). Some Italian feminists and migrant women have expressed concern that Alma Mater is becoming a help organization similar to traditional Catholic organizations, rather than a site for social activism and oppositional politics as in left discourse. Migrant women also complain that voluntarism and "help" contribute to enduring dependencies and a colonizing, paternalistic relationship between migrant and Italian women. Some Turin feminists argue that ideas and practices of assistance and voluntarism belong to Catholic charities in which women's unpaid labor has long been exploited not to feminist politics (Donini 1996). Some critics have also argued that because many NGOs are drawn in the direction of incorporation into official bureaucratic structures, and into operating according to a market-driven logic, they cannot be genuinely empowering to the disempowered (Craig and Mayo 1995; Conroy 1995). Many NGOs, like development organizations, accept the prevailing economic order, seeking to "modernize" the poor by setting an example of diligent work habits (Galjart 1995).

NGOs can reproduce existing inequalities when they become overly formalized as institutions (Alvarez 1996). Third-sector organizations tend to exist within a tense contradiction between reformism and opposition or radical transformation.

A Politics of Space and Scale

As discussed in the previous chapter, Alma Mater is situated in the local history of Italian social movements of the 1960s and 1970s. The labor, student, and feminist movements permanently marked the political identities of Turin feminists who, together with local political figures and migrant women, helped bring Alma Mater to life. Like the Casa delle Donne, which Turin feminists established as a space for women, the interethnic coalition was intended to be rooted in a site where women could gather to safely promote their cultural and economic visions, express their personal concerns, and seek support for their social troubles.[5] By responding to the current historical context of unprecedented international migration, the organization opened a far wider net, linking itself with postcolonial and global feminist concerns.

The organizational structure of Alma Mater reflects emphases in the Italian labor, student, and feminist movements on work and autonomy and against hierarchy. Work, a central pillar of Turin feminism, became a critical building block in the interethnic coalition. Alma Mater put together two work cooperatives to expand the nature of employment for migrant women in the city. They stressed lavoro autonomo and sought to create work spaces for migrant women in Turin's private and public sector. Ideally, autonomous, small-scale entrepreneurial activities would express the diverse cultures of migrant women—for instance, in handmade clothing, theatrical performances, and ethnic dinners. Donne in Sviluppo was interested in helping migrant women from developing countries to promote indigenous forms of small business enterprises in Europe.[6] The interest of Turin feminist groups, such as Intercategoriale and P&R, in promoting self-employment for women converged with migrant women's desire to make a living in the European context while using the skills they had acquired in their countries and ethnic groups of origin.

Postcolonial women and feminist Italians designed Alma Mater as an alternative space for migrant women whose lives in Turin are restricted to private Italian homes and work sites where they often feel alienated from other migrants and have limited access to Italian society. By providing

From left to right, the children of a Moroccan activist couple and our two children, Nicolas and Eliana, in front of Alma Mater in 2001, after spending the day in the Alma Mater day care *(nido)*

a place where they could rework daily practices and media representations, the coalition sought to challenge racialized and Italian hegemonic discourses that constructed metaphorical boundaries around migrants as dangerous, criminal, socially and culturally strange and out of place, or from entirely unknowable spaces at the national and community scales. By constituting a place of convergence, Alma Mater sought to help mold a tolerant society of empowered women.[7] They did this by seizing a municipal space and expanding the boundaries of their social practices to the scales of the urban and national administration, economy, and field of representation (N. Smith 1992). As in Neil Smith's discussion of New York's homeless expanding the boundaries of the home through mobile shelter vehicles, postcolonial migrants and Italian women stretched their ascribed boundaries in private Italian homes, or on marginal and illegitimate streets, to the scale of urban politics and ultimately national politics.

Alma Mater is an exceptionally diverse interethnic place, representing women of various social classes and religious and ethnic backgrounds. The differences between the many participants in Alma Mater are inscribed in the public and private spaces of Turin, marking the daily practices of walking, looking, touching, and breathing. When migrant women leave the Alma Mater building, they enter a world in the shadows of Italian familial, friendship, and political networks. The local cartography that migrants follow in the course of their daily pursuits leads them in separate directions from the social geography inhabited by the Turinese majority. Many migrant women and men work in precarious, dangerous jobs with long hours—for instance, as domestic servants or in construction lifting heavy objects or using heavy equipment. At night, a number of North and West African men and women sell various objects such as watches, CDs, artwork, or jewelry along the dimly lit routes of Turin's commercial district, scrambling to make enough money to survive and send to their families as remittances. Many live in apartment rooms with floors covered by makeshift beds or in minuscule spaces stuffed with portable stoves, beds, and baggage and lacking toilet or shower facilities. There are exceptions, for a few migrants live in airy, furnished apartments or houses and even some of their fanciful desires may be regularly met.

Within Alma Mater, there are tensions between the small number of migrant women who live in comfort and the majority that struggle to make a living—tensions about access to material and symbolic resources. But most often these tensions are expressed in a binary language of racialized differences between migrant and Italian women, so that migrant women living in relatively comfortable conditions are generally not resented by other migrants. However, relatively well-off migrant women are frequently the objects of blame for practicing ethnic partisanship; that is, preferential treatment toward women from their ethnic or national origins. A highly articulate, university-educated, and politically active Moroccan woman, for instance, who was instrumental in putting Alma Mater into place, later resigned from the organization when she was continually accused of "helping only other Moroccans." Participants may also express tension about access to resources by ascribing to each other privileges based on differences in educational training, ethnic origin, or skin color. Between women with various degrees of schooling, there are often conflicts over administrative positions within the organization and jobs as cultural mediators. In 2001, there was a widening belief among migrant participants that preferential treatment was given to lighter-skinned migrants in Turin and sometimes in Alma Mater. "Lighter-skinned" was located at the continental, ethnic, and national scales, where women with relatively light skin tones—for example, from Peru, Ecuador, Morocco, Tunisia, and the Philippines—were believed to be preferred as employees.

Maria Afonso, president of La Talea, 2001

Regardless of material standing, the majority of migrants are excluded from Italian leisure activities and social-political networks. The experience of being an outsider within one's local environment can lead to considerable stress and feelings of alienation. When migrants travel on public transport, enter grocery or clothing stores, and visit public offices, coffee shops, or open markets, they may experience forms of hostility and feelings of vulnerability that few Italians understand. Migrant women's bodies are marked as sexually loose, undeserving, lacking the positive attributes of modern society, and potentially criminal. They may be treated with disrespect or disregard.

These material-ideological conditions are part of the landscape of meaningful practices in which the identities of migrant women unfold. In challenging living conditions, as a form of self-protection, some migrants who may never have practiced their religions in their countries of origin have begun to assert religious beliefs and the right to express them in Italy. Others insist that integrity of their cultural beliefs and practices be honored in Europe, including particular birthing and marriage practices, certain rituals, clothing styles, and artistic expressions in painting, craft work, music, theater, and dance. Many cultural-artistic practices have

taken on new meaning in Italy, becoming a medium for the defense of migrant dignity. The notion of female empowerment is generally based on an
Italian model of what an ideal Euro-Italian woman's life ought to be like,
derived from an Italian meaning of democracy. Conceptual models and
symbolic classifications of the proper Italian exist alongside other notions
of the African, Muslim, and person from the third world, which project
expectations that affect the way lives are lived on a daily basis.

Alma Mater expands Turin feminist struggles to create respect for and
protection of women's differences, at least in principle. The center was established to encompass a wide range of intersecting power relations, including cultural racism and European hegemony. Recognizing a broad matrix
of power relations is of crucial significance to postcolonial migrants. Many
women migrants arrive from former European colonies, where, through
colonial and postcolonial struggles, they cultivated ideas of cultural pride
and difference from European cultures. Instead of seeking assimilation
into Italian society, many migrants express the desire to be incorporated
as equals, but at the same time to have their own cultural-political practices represented and respected in local neighborhoods, the media, work,
and local and national politics. Critical about Europe's relationship to developing countries, migrants from former European colonies express the
need for their cultures and social and religious practices to be respected by
Italians in the face of what they view as a kind of Western cultural imperialism that effaces their own past in the name of Western interpretations of
modernity and progress. Many, while living in Italy, remain circumspect
about their relationship with Europeans.

The People and Place of Alma Mater

Alma Mater is situated in a long, three-story, white-and-brown-colored
former elementary school building in Reggio Parco, an old working-class
quarter on Turin's northern perimeter. At a distance from the historical
center, it is located near the city's cemetery in a factory zone with working-
class housing complexes. Alma Mater is not far from Via Milano, the
major road that leads out of Turin toward Milan. Some members and
visitors reach the center by car and, after entering a high iron gate, park
in a wide graveled lot flanked by patches of grass, bushes, and tall trees
that face the building's entrance. Most Alma Mater participants arrive
via a lengthy trip from the urban center on several buses or trams, which

are normally crowded until they reach the commercial district of Porta Palazzo. The building is surrounded by a Catholic church, several abandoned factories, a park, a few small shops, and a small open market that, like the other markets in the city, is open every morning except Sunday. Unlike in the urban center, a sense of meditative quiet fills the air, almost as if a huge parade has just passed through the streets, leaving everyone with a sense of waiting for another exciting event to lighten the day.

Entering the building, one's feet touch heavy, old gray iron floors. Stairs lead down toward the office of the cooperative La Talea and the laundromat, the kitchen, the sewing room, and the Turkish bath. The first room one sees is that of La Talea, which handles the finances of the Turkish bath, a highly popular site among Italian women who pay to have a luxurious experience, perhaps a massage. It is located at the far end of the floor, past the kitchen and sewing room, until the turn-of-the-century laundromat and a series of bathrooms and showers. Italian women frequent the Turkish bath almost exclusively because migrant women are unable to afford the fees. Italian women who visit the Turkish bath often become regular customers and may order dinner parties around certain ethnic themes arranged and orchestrated by members of La Talea. Italian customers typically enter only a few rooms in the Alma Mater building, descending to the basement upon their arrival and unaware of goings-on at the upper levels.

The Alma Mater building stairway is wide, gray concrete that seems to project light. The concrete walls are cool to the touch as the visitor is drawn slowly upward, walking several short flights of stairs past light walls and some shaded windowpanes with flyers representing upcoming or past cultural events. Moving past a second-floor administrative room, whose door is almost always closed, to the third-floor entrance and center of activity, one passes the office of cultural mediation, where there are often several Italian and one or two migrant woman in a meeting or on the telephone. The library is open several days per week, operated by a scholarly Italian woman interested in creating a carefully documented history of the organization and in shelving the stacks with books representative of the cultures and societies from which the participants have arrived. The day care room, to the left, was sometimes empty in 1995 and 1996, but in 2001 it was always full and staffed with one or more Italian women watching some fifteen migrant children. There is a small central administrative office to the right, followed by a large, well-lit room for gathering and a long meeting room where seminars on such issues as the adoption of Somali children, dance classes, and ethnic dinners are held, and where the Almateatro practices.

In the morning, when there are no special events or meetings planned, the building is almost silent except for the rapid clip-clopping of a woman's shoes along the hallway, the sound of a ringing telephone, or a voice. In the afternoons and some evenings, Alma Mater is pulsating with activity, several people crowded around the central office desk, people milling about in the hallways, women seated in pairs or in larger groups on couches in the gathering room or in the meeting room that is filled to capacity. The long meeting room is decorated with framed posters of African textiles and photos of African or Latin American women in groups and of children's faces. Many tables and chairs furnish the space of the meeting room, ready to be used for the next event. In the gathering room, several couches, two small tables, and a chair are surrounded by walls covered with announcements about language courses for immigrants, elections held for immigrant representatives, services for battered wives and children, ethnic cultural events such as Senegalese dances and Moroccan dinners, conferences on intercultural exchange or racism, and newspaper clippings that cite Alma Mater initiatives in the struggle against acts of racial and gender discrimination.

Second-floor hallway, Alma Mater, 2001

Although the diverse women in Alma Mater ally on the basis of gender, their conflicting ideologies, histories, and social positions inflect this basic similarity. The women who constitute the Alma Mater membership are from widely diverse cultural, religious, and class and caste backgrounds that reflect differences both between and within countries of origin. Their differences also span generations and political orientations.

We may begin to understand differences in Alma Mater by observing the manner in which the respective participants experience the spaces and places of daily life in Turin. Turin feminists live in comfortable conditions, such as apartments that they own, where they either live alone or with a partner and children.[8] Turin feminists retired from full-time jobs are able and willing to devote much of their time to Alma Mater, working as volunteers.[9] Most of these women were born in Turin or migrated to the city from a rural hinterland at an early age. As discussed in the previous chapter, the seminal members of Alma Mater participated in political organizations and are embedded in local political culture. Several women scholars from the University of Turin have played an active role in Alma Mater. Most of the Turin feminists participate in shared forms of leisure activity and are connected to diverse networks of friends, family, and political allies. They have acquired a vast insider knowledge of Turin's social and political landscape, which is perhaps more crucial in Italy than in other parts of the world (Ginsborg 2003). Until migrant women began to appear in Turin in large numbers at the end of the 1980s, Italian feminists operated within a small, relatively closed circle of women activists. Some have commented that it was then easy for them to understand each other and to negotiate disagreements because they had a sense of each other's personal idiosyncrasies, interests, and political orientations. The presence of migrant women and the operation of Alma Mater has created a new set of challenges for Turin feminists.

Some of the migrant women who initiated the Alma Mater project have lived in Turin for a number of years and speak Italian fluently, sometimes impeccably. They are formally educated women from North, East, and West Africa, the Philippines, and South America. Some are married to Italian men and live in spacious, safe homes with their conjugal families. These homes may be modest in value or costly. Their husbands are either employed professionals or work in white-collar forms of industrial labor. Many of these migrant women have degrees from Italian universities. They were trained as lawyers, social scientists, or office administrators, and may have held or continue to hold full-time jobs in Turin, but are more often unable to procure gainful employment reflective of their skills and training. Some with extensive transnational networks are politically active in their countries of origin. More than a few readily identify with the parties of the Italian political left, such as the Italian Communist Party, now the DS (Democratic Left) or Rifondazione. Others are religious, preferring church-related activities to political activism. Most of these women travel to Alma Mater in vehicles that they own and, if they do not have young children, are able to easily attend evening meetings or special events. Several have held top-ranking administrative positions in Alma Mater, and others have held lesser administrative positions within the organization, such as administrator at the front visitor desk or operator of the Turkish bath. Their common experiences of social and cultural exclusion in Turin, and the peculiar political culture of Turin, led these women to take action in support of newly arrived women migrants.

Other migrant women are relatively new to Turin, having arrived during the late 1980s or early 1990s. Most of these women did not attend university, but many began or completed high school. Some are skilled in special areas such as hairstyling or seamstress work. Many traveled alone, seeking friendships with conationals after they moved to Turin, while others had friends or family members already living in Italy. A few were able to bring their children to Europe. For example, one East African woman, Felicity, is from a family ostracized by the government in her country of origin for its political beliefs. Felicity traveled to Italy to escape what she considered oppressive conditions for women in her country of origin and to discover the world of Europe, which she had heard and read a great deal about. She wanted to make a decent living for herself and for her daughter in Europe and eventually to return to her country of origin with enough money to build a home and perhaps open a business. In Turin, Felicity struggles daily to survive with some sense of dignity and takes great pride in her African heritage. She speaks Italian fluently, but not flawlessly. Felicity moves frequently from one overpriced apartment to another and has been evicted on more than one occasion. Her daughter was schooled in an elite private school in Turin, from which she frequently ran away. Felicity has felt estranged from her daughter, whom she describes as an "exotic object" in the eyes of many Italians. To make a living, Felicity crafts or buys African objets d'art from other traders to sell in Turin markets; she dances, acts, and paints. She wishes to be more fully incorporated as a leader within Alma Mater. Other migrant women with backgrounds similar to Felicity's have held low-ranking leadership positions in the women's coalition. Many work as in-home aides to the elderly or in other forms of domestic service.

There is another category of migrant woman participant in Alma Mater that experiences daily life in Turin as a constant struggle to survive. Such women, and they are numerous, often live in crowded housing arrangements, where they share small apartment spaces with several other people. They may or may not have access to a shower in their building. Most work in temporary, low-paying informal jobs as cleaners in restaurants or households, and earn some income selling African or South American goods such as textiles and lotions in their homes or along city sidewalks. A few work as cleaners in small textile plants or in market stalls. Berthe, a Senegalese woman in her thirties, lived in Turin with her husband and young child. While working as a housecleaner, she left her son to be cared for by a Tunisian woman at Alma Mater's day care center. During the summer vacation months for Europeans, Berthe would travel to Italian seaside resorts to sell African products and style hair on the roadside. She spoke a bit of Italian, but was more comfortable conversing in French or in her native language, Wolof. She had extensive networks among other Senegalese living in Turin and in other parts of Italy (see Carter 1997). Other women similar to Berthe have been forced to leave children behind in Africa or the Middle East to be fostered by family or friends. These women often seem to carry a great deal of weight on their shoulders, sending back remittances as much as they can and hoping that one day they may be in a position to bring their growing children to Italy. Such migrant women are often in Europe to earn enough money to feed and clothe the children they left behind in their countries of origin.

The women of the Alma Mater membership span a wide range of class and ethnonational backgrounds. Although migrants may share a similar positioning in relation to Turinese, there are considerable differences among them. With no known exceptions, all migrant women experience frustration about the manner in which they are stigmatized as sexually and racially different in Turin, regularly treated as potential sexual targets by Italian men. A stereotype, a kind of generic portrait of the migrant, has been drawn from local knowledge. However, there are vast ethnic, national, and religious differences between migrants, mediated by social class or educational variations. Class also mediates gender in the relationship between Italian women and the majority of migrant women. Gender seems to intersect ethnonational and racial identity, observable in differences in social status, material well-being, and degree of cultural comfort experienced in Turin. But generalizations about gender or sexual difference are also fraught with tension and sometimes conflict.

Hegemony and Difference

Feminist politics in Alma Mater is achieved by means of the building of affinities across myriad differences. Some of the routes used to express mutual understanding and common purpose are straightforward; others are replete with obstacles. Gender identity, the common thread binding the various members of Alma Mater, frequently comes into conflict with other forms of identity such as race, ethnicity, and class.

As an organization of women unified on the basis of gender but whose members experience different social positioning in relationship to the state, economy, and local society, Alma Mater struggles to create alternatives to dominant racial and gender images. However, some of the same contested assumptions about essential differences appear in the ongoing relationships between participants. Although migrants and Italians established the coalition against stereotypical and racialized representations of foreigners that contribute to exclusionary labor practices, participants have not yet escaped the insidious power of dominant racial and modernist ideologies. Without intending to, the women of Alma Mater engage in practices peculiar to Turin political culture and Euro-American visions of modernity that exclude other members and keep in place historical boundaries between Europeans and non-Europeans.

Gender identity binds Alma Mater participants in an identifiable women's organization, but daily practices are mediated by local Italian evaluations of social and political affinity and by the much broader Western hierarchical and essentialist assumptions about people from different parts of the world (Young 1995; Castles 2000; Gilmore 2002). Taken-for-granted cultural practices sometimes lead to conflict and undermine trust. Just as southern Italians were popularly perceived in Turinese society as racially distinct, a notion of racial distance between Italians and international migrants has reemerged in response to migration, and migrants are popularly equated with their spatial and national origins. Today, Eastern European migrants are popularly lumped together with Africans and Latin Americans as essentially poor and less "developed," but this has not always happened. Racial classifications that stigmatize certain populations are constructed with elastic boundaries, always allowing for the isolation of a category of people according to a specific historical circumstance (Trouillot 1994). At some historical intersections, people of certain national origins—for instance, Albania—have been considered similar to Italians, while most recently Albanians are stigmatized as distant outsiders. When Muslim Albanians began to arrive on the southern Italian coast in the early 1990s, they were not welcomed as fellow Europeans. Migrants from such Latin American countries as Chile, Argentina, and Brazil, where there are large Italian settler populations, are in an ambiguous category; in some ways they are viewed as linked with Italians, and in others as unwanted migrants from poverty-ridden nations.

When interviewed, migrants from economically underdeveloped countries as far apart as Romania, Brazil, Morocco, the Ivory Coast, Cameroon, and Senegal described themselves as outsiders in Italian society to the extent that they believed Italian society perceived them as somehow racially different. A Romanian migrant explained that as an Eastern European, she is, like other migrants, assumed to arrive from the "'third world'. . . which is a terribly racist, derogatory term, meaning to be vermin, to come from an inferior race." In fact, Romanians in Italian society are popularly equated with the much-maligned category of "gypsy" or "Rom." Some migrant women openly express their anger over a sense of being dismissed as essentially inferior in Italy because they are from poor countries. Others are afraid to make their feelings known to Italian feminists, not wishing to risk angering women whom they believe to be in a powerful position to help them improve their situation. For example, an East African migrant woman speaking of Alma Mater in 2001 told me that there is a hierarchy within Alma Mater:

> The Italians pretend to allow Africans to run the place, but there are really three Italians who run it. They and other people in Italy have profited from the idea of "immigrant," but they are people who know nothing about immigrants, but only rally around the idea for self-gain. They see immigrants as needy, dependent people who go to Alma Mater with problems, and they take them on because they're weak and vulnerable, while others, well, the Italians want to help people with problems. The Africans who are supposed to have run Alma Mater, or to be running it, are in fact puppets of the Italians, when, in fact, only Italians have ever run Alma Mater. A lot of the older migrant women look down on the Africans as if they have learned how to overcome problems, while the others have yet to learn how to overcome problems.

Despite the possible failings in Alma Mater, the organization is unique in that it encourages the formation of interethnic bonds between migrant women from diverse countries; in most other Italian contexts the acknowledgment of similarities between migrant experiences is undermined. The Ufficio Stranieri, for instance, classifies newcomers according to their ethnonational origin. Members of national groups with the highest numbers of persons registered as resident in Turin qualify for a cultural mediator, who is hired by the municipal government to act as a linguistic and cultural translator on their behalf. The ethnic associations among Nigerians, Moroccans, Senegalese, and Filipinos, for instance, are also divided according to ethnogeographical origin. The Italian state has permitted migrant populations to organize only according to national origin, in ethnic associations that tend to divide migrants and contribute to interest politics that pit migrant population against migrant population, undermining the potential unity of a grassroots politics derived from a common cross-national position (Mouffe 1992; Hall 1996a).[10] Alma Mater is the only organization in Turin in which migrant women from diverse ethnic backgrounds, together with Italian women, meet in the same location and in the process learn something about one another on a daily basis. Nevertheless, even within Alma Mater, conceptions of essential differences produce a certain degree of distance between migrant women from diverse ethnic backgrounds and between migrants and Italian feminists as a whole.

Color has rapidly emerged as an axis of difference and division. In the process of forming Alma Mater, there were several training classes sponsored by the municipal government and the Commission for the European Union. The courses were organized in conjunction with the International Labor Organization and various public offices in Turin, including the Ufficio Stranieri. There was a course dealing with women's small enterprises and another on cultural mediation. Two migrant work cooperatives were constituted out of the courses, La Talea and Mediazione. Both cooperatives were initially part of Alma Mater, with offices located in the Alma Mater building. Each cooperative included between twenty and thirty female members from all over the world who sought work contracts and operated the small enterprises within Alma Mater, such as the Turkish bath, ethnic dinners, and laundromat. La Talea, handling the Turkish bath, was more fortunate than Mediazione, which directed the laundromat, a business that has produced little profit. After a year or two, members of Mediazione decided to attenuate their relationship with Alma Mater, choosing to publicize their cooperative in the building but to hold meetings in private homes. Mediazione decided to include within

Zahra, a Somali immigrant, with a guest at an Alma Mater ethnic dinner and fund-raiser for her family, 2001

their membership only persons with very dark skin. Their cooperative was to be based not on national or ethnic origin, but on skin color alone, which meant that the grouping would include only black Moroccans, Nigerians, Somalis, and Brazilians and not those from the same countries with lighter skin tones. This form of grouping that migrants are in the process of constructing represents a system of color identity or classification that crosses forms of ethnonational identity. This is an example of the way that racial and gender configurations, never fixed, are always historically and geographically contingent (Gramsci 1989; Hall 1991b; Gilroy 1991).

The impression that dark-skinned migrants are treated differently from the lighter-skinned has, unfortunately, taken hold among migrants within Alma Mater. "The Italians treat the blacks worse, like slaves," said a migrant woman in 1996. Another complained, "Alma Mater is run by Italians. . . . The next tier is the Moroccans, who are the ones who get the jobs. The blacks only clean." A migrant woman working in the Turkish bath told me in 2001, "The Italian women are racist, very racist. They all act so nice, squeeze your cheeks, say 'How are you?' in their sweet voices, but they are liars, fake. They think the straniere are incapable—are not capable, are not good, are from the bottom of the world—that they are fit for the basement." Another woman added, "The straniere cook for them, but the Italians have never cooked for the immigrants. And when they have a *festa* upstairs, they never invite La Talea."

A so-called North and sub-Saharan African divide is reflected in language employed by Italians who, by the mid-1990s, had come to describe North Africans as Arabs *(Arabi)* and sub-Saharan Africans as Africans *(Africani)*. Migrants too have begun to employ this discourse in their own struggles over access to political and economic resources in Italy, dividing themselves along religious and ethnonational lines or according to skin color. One woman remarked, "There is also racism among the foreigners. People are always heard saying, 'I don't want to talk to that one with white skin, that one with yellow skin, that one from Morocco.'" As a Somali woman told me, "Arabs are the most racist people in the world. These people who clean car windows won't even ask to clean mine, because they consider people with black skin inferior."

It seems to have become easy for some migrants to forget, while living in Italy, that there are vast differences among Africans. It is impossible, for example, to accurately characterize all Moroccans in relation to a monolithic culture because there are considerable differences between Moroccans based on religious practices, political allegiances, levels of education, and historical constructions of class. Some migrants have argued in more detached contexts that there simply are no Arabs and no Africans because there are so many differences between people described by such homogenizing categories (IRES 1992). Among Somali migrants inside and outside Alma Mater, there are historical conflicts between members of diverse, sometimes warring groups that are expressed in argument or distance between various Somalis in Italy. General categories delineating difference are frequently deployed to construct imaginary and artificial divisions between individuals.

Although porous, the division between Italian feminists and migrants in Alma Mater is fairly wide and has not been fully confronted by participants. Italian women possess considerable local knowledge and operate within local social and political networks. Their access to local knowledge and political figures within the municipal government made the creation of Alma Mater possible. Even migrant women married to Italians and with high levels of formal education do not have access to the local geography of knowledge and power available to many Turin feminists. The desire among Turin feminists to take action on behalf of migrant women led them to seek alliances with migrant women in AIDA already struggling to obtain the necessary space and funding for Alma Mater. If this alliance had not been formed, the Alma Mater school building probably would have gone to another group competing for use of the property. Following the opening of the center, the local power and knowledge held by members of P&R was translated into a right and obligation to direct Alma Mater. The municipal government gave the Turin feminist association P&R responsibility for the financial management of the coalition, and Italian feminists consequently became the legally recognized Alma Mater leadership. P&R's virtual control over the workings of the organization triggered immediate tension, for Alma Mater was originally conceived by migrant women intending to maintain full directorship of the center.

Although the first Alma Mater director was a Somali woman, Giovanna Zaldini,[11] migrant women eventually voted to replace her with an Italian woman with the social and political connections they believed were needed to run the organization. In 1994 Giovanna was replaced by Turin feminist Laura Scagliotti,[12] assisted by several other Italian and migrant women. In 1995 and 1996, the most visible figures in the Alma Mater building were Italian women operating the office of cultural mediation, the library, and the front reception office. Front-desk operations were, however, rotated on a daily basis to include a combination of Italian and migrant women. Migrant men directed the two cooperatives, La Talea and Mediazione, including the laundromat, Turkish bath, seamstress shop, Almateatro, and the catering operation of "cultural dinners."

Turin feminists stress equality in decision making and in the delegation of authority between women, and they have sought increasingly to include migrant women. But the ideal of equality can become an empty discourse if it shields relationships built on real power differences. The tensions between migrant and Italian women are based not only on the status of Italians as insiders and citizens with relative rights, but may also be attributed to the significant age differences between feminist Italians and many of the migrant women. Differences grounded on access to knowledge and power within the spaces inside and outside Alma Mater also promote tension and the deepening of symbolic boundaries. Many migrant women interviewed expressed the belief that Italian women were running the organization, and that they did not care to include migrant women within the decision-making processes. A South American woman complained: "Italian women want to be in the position of delegating help, of creating dependencies, and they do not want any of the immigrant women to have their own initiative, or ideas." Some migrants seem to equate anyone who directs Alma Mater with "the Italians," where Italians are understood as enemies that dominate people from former European colonies.

Heads of local organizations are uniformly Italian, leaving migrants to believe that there is no place for them. Some migrants complain that if Italians hadn't been directing things, a given initiative or organization would have worked. Sometimes this blaming of Italians is employed as a way of mobilizing people around a migrant's own interests. But in practice it is accurate that most migrant interaction with Europeans is mediated through institutions controlled by Europeans. Italians mediate economic and political resources, and the common perception among migrants that Italians direct and control everything is confirmed in structured practices. Italians not only possess the citizenship rights that most migrants lack, but they have a certain cultural citizenship that gives them considerable symbolic capital, which ought to be contrasted with the absence of cultural citizenship among migrants.

The issue of the migrant woman's dependency on feminist Italians within Alma Mater was echoed by numerous migrant women in 1996, when Alma Mater had been in operation for almost four years. Several women referred to the problem as an example of a "colonization of the mind of the straniere," or migrant women, in which they believe themselves incompetent in relationship to Italians (Fanon 1968). The dependency is assumed to be unintentional, for there is an emerging diasporic culture among migrants in which one struggles to be seen as equal to any Western European. This is a highly complex relationship; it can be characterized neither as simply colonization/submission nor as resistance to European societies. We might begin to understand what is happening between migrants and Italians as the formation of a postcolonial diasporic subjectivity, in which migrants from former European colonies critical of Europe's relationship to developing countries express a desire for their cultural practices to be respected by Europeans in the face of a kind of Western cultural imperialism. There remains, however, a basic inequality in access to knowledge, power, and resources that is sometimes reflected in the way decisions are made and authority delegated.

Before the arrival of large numbers of international migrants to Turin beginning in the late 1980s, Italian women had little actual contact with people from developing parts of the world. A few feminists in Donne in Sviluppo had participated in international conferences on women, and a handful had traveled in Africa, Southeast Asia, and parts of Latin America.

However, the mission of Donne in Sviluppo, as its name indicates, is "development," a term that lacks meaning except in relationship to its opposite, that is, underdevelopment. In their desire to encourage women's production in poor or underdeveloped countries, the women of Donne in Sviluppo inadvertently assumed the role of helpers of the less fortunate, not only in their own country, but in other parts of the world. This model has created certain structural and philosophical problems for Alma Mater as an interethnic organization constituted to contest racialized forms of exclusion. Italian help or assistance organizations have generally not been designed to contest ideologies and exclusionary practices, although Turin feminism combined a bit of both roles by assuming advocacy and activism on behalf of women. In 1996, an East African woman complained that Alma Mater was "nothing but a help organization, not a front, not a place that is innovative in that it would open up new work avenues for women. Instead it is an organization of assistance, of voluntarism." Another migrant woman said:

> The Italian women look upon the Africans and the others, but especially the dark-skinned and Moroccans, like the poor Africans [povere Africaine], so it's a kind of colonialism in which the Italians can continue to look upon the straniere as incompetent, poor, in need of help, in need of leadership, etc., instead of helping the newcomers to have autonomy through knowledge.

The question of Alma Mater's role as a help organization and as part of the third sector is debated among Turin feminists. Those who object strongly to the assistance model equated with reformist church activities favor the oppositional and transformative politics that characterized much of 1970s feminism. However, it is clear that Alma Mater has become a magnet for recent migrant women without a place to stay and lacking work. A number of Italian and first-generation migrant women reason that until newcomers can locate stable places of living and work, they will be unable to become involved in political and oppositional activity. On one occasion, two Romanian women sat anxiously in Alma Mater's sitting room. The Romanians had arrived at the Porto Nuova train station the previous afternoon and had spent a cool October night sleeping on park benches in the adjacent piazza. Having been referred to Alma Mater by the Ufficio Stranieri, a Romanian cultural mediator was translating for them. Alma Mater's Italian director responded to the plight of these women with considerable concern, running back and forth, speaking with an anxious tone as she sought to find a place for them to sleep in a Catholic charity organization. In this, as in so many other instances, Alma Mater serves as a mediator in locating sleeping arrangements and jobs for migrants. The problem is that most of the work available to migrant women is in the very same category of work that Alma Mater was designed to help migrant women avoid, namely, domestic service.

Many migrant women complain that the only work Alma Mater finds for straniere is in domestic service, elder care, or cleaning. As a Somali woman told me in 1996:

In Alma Mater, all they do for straniere is refer them to jobs as COLF [domestics] or help for the elderly, or cleaning. An original goal of Alma Mater was to help women obtain legal and other recognition for the training they received in their countries of origin, but this goal has not been met, this has not happened. So you still have this dependency.

In part, the tension over this issue stems from an absence of class consciousness among migrant women, in contrast with an acute sense of workerism among a generation of Turin feminists who, as part of local political culture, came to value the rights of all workers to be protected from exploitation. The issue of class mobility is for them of secondary importance at best. By contrast, for the many migrants who were part of a post-independence would-be middle class in their countries of origin, the idea of being identified with and of defending working-class rights has not become a critical issue. Never having had experiences resembling involvement in the labor struggles that occurred in Italy during the 1960s and 1970s, some young migrant women have interpreted the attitudes and behavior of Turin feminists as condescending and paternalistic, reminiscent of the Western colonial domination they have heard so much about. Furthermore, to refer to oneself in some countries as a communist could result in being thrown into jail. For these reasons, there is considerable division and conflict surrounding issues such as the omnipresence of migrant women in domestic work. Turin feminists who have struggled to convince the trade unions to recognize the importance of this category of principally female workers do not approach the question of domestic employment as necessarily a problem of being relegated to an inferior, marginal status. The term "empowerment" may have different meaning for Italians and for migrants because of their distinct experiences in Europe.

There is some degree of tension in Alma Mater about the common-sense identification of participants as feminists. Although most migrant women would agree that, in Europe, there is considerable gender inequality, many shy away from identifying themselves with the term *feminist*. A Somali woman commented:

> There is no feminism in Somalia, because women are taught to be strong. It is the women who decide who their children are to marry. My mother beat me if I did not receive the highest marks in school. My mother believed that my success was more important than that of my brothers.

Another migrant woman said that, in Somalia, a woman might be the head of a clan, a position of considerable prestige that obliges all siblings to report to her.[13] And with irritation, a Romanian woman argued, "In Romania there has been an equality law since 1922. A king instituted it. That's why I don't understand feminism."

Migrant women did not participate in monthly feminist meetings at least until the late 1990s at the Casa delle Donne. Some Italian feminists complained that migrant women did not show any interest in learning about Italian feminism: "Few of the straniere are interested in feminism. For them, feminism equals imperialism." Some complained that they would like to share their feminist experiences and insights with migrant women, but that these women were interested only in improving their own situations, not in learning anything about Italian feminists or Italian feminism. One Turin feminist told me, "Their attitude is always, 'Give me, give me, give me.'"

By 2001, a few migrant women in Alma Mater had begun to identify themselves as feminists or, some might argue, as postfeminists (Baumgardner and Richards 2000; Gamble 2001). A Turin feminist in Alma Mater told me that although foreign women had in the past expressed passionate disdain for the term "feminism," by 2000 or so they had stopped reacting so vehemently to the word, which indicated that their negative passions had subsided. When asked, a Peruvian woman in her fifties told me that she thought of herself as a feminist because "women are more sensitive, more intelligent than men, and so, yes, I feel a solidarity with women in general." Another Peruvian woman in her thirties who is active in Alma Mater told me emphatically and without hesitation, "Yes, I am a feminist." A Somali woman in her twenties explained that she did not consider herself a feminist if feminism meant what it did in the 1960s—"fighting on the streets, having manifestations, and all that against-men stuff." She added, however, that if feminism meant fighting for women's rights today, she was in fact a feminist. This expression was shared by several other young African women at Alma Mater who described themselves as feminists, not as in the 1970s, when Western women held posters and took to the streets, but in the sense that they were currently struggling for women's rights.

Despite an absence of consensus about feminism, gender is a binding force within Alma Mater. With the exception of special events, only women are permitted in the building, which many told me made it possible for Muslim women to enjoy Alma Mater. There is also a sense of gender solidarity that permeates many of the services and the central sitting room. This sense of gender identification cuts across religious, class, and ethnic identities. With a group of women from diverse countries, for example, one can on a given day prepare a lunch meal of pasta to eat in the sitting room while discussing common problems that each woman has come across in Italy and in other societies.

Turin feminists have self-consciously sought to help empower migrant women in Europe, but coming out of a history in which class power and patriarchy were the objects of struggle, they do not always meet on the same ideological terrain as the newcomer and especially younger immigrant women. Turin feminists seem to follow a logic based on a European model that promotes the empowerment of women in such areas as employment, health, and family. For an older generation of feminists, the protection and representation of women in the workplace, home, and health and children's services were central issues. Turin feminists integrated working class issues with issues of patriarchy. By contrast, and this should not be taken for granted, many postcolonial migrant women claim that their problems do not necessarily involve male hegemony, but rather European structures of hegemony that stereotype people from developing countries, exploit their labor power and resources, and relegate them (along with their male counterparts) to marginal forms of employment and social status. Migrant participants in Alma Mater agree that, at least in European society, women are treated as inferior to men; but many are convinced by their experiences that, as migrant women, they also share unequal power in relation to Italian women.

Conflicts and tensions in Alma Mater are in part based on an asymmetry in material conditions, or the manner in which migrants and Italian women experience space and place in Turin on a daily basis. To survive, migrant women may be forced to accept almost any kind of work. It therefore stands to reason that to have a successful politics, they must create alternatives to precarious forms of work. They have begun to attempt this—for example, with the 2001 bank initiative—but the issues have not yet been given adequate political attention. There is also the problem of how women from so many diverse backgrounds can meet on similar ideological and philosophical terrain, a question that members of Alma Mater do not seem to collectively interrogate.

Issues such as how feminism is to be defined, the ways that race and migrant status distinguish some women from others, or how woman is defined in different societies are not yet rigorously questioned by participants, who are usually preoccupied with immediate problems. In the process, an Italian model of essential womanness tends to be assumed as common sense.[14] Outside Alma Mater, many Italians assume that migrant women don't even understand such basic things as how to operate kitchen appliances, and consequently migrant women have been sent to training programs to learn these elementary skills. With some tension and a level of mistrust in everyday interactions, participants have not yet made enough effort to understand their cultural and historical differences, and especially the way such differences affect their positioning in Italy. The perception that migrants always ask, always demand, that Italians ought to give them something is (probably inadvertently) consistent with the Italian popular belief that the migrant has nothing to offer Italian society, no significant knowledge to bring to the modern Italian world. The contributions that women migrants may potentially make to Turin political culture have not yet been fully explored.

Making Common Place

Differences among members of Alma Mater negotiated in daily practices at the community and bodily scales are producing a more immediate interweaving of histories through time. A Turin feminist told me that face-to-face interactions with migrant women were forcing her to reflect on and change some of her long-held beliefs and assumptions. Choosing her words carefully, she talked about the way that practical exchanges between different women were, in effect, sites where the world unfolded and was made, where connections were formed that had not previously existed. During the 1990s, migrant women were beginning to more freely assert and express their ideas and objections to Italian women. However, few seemed to believe that they were capable of significantly affecting Italian political culture. A Somali migrant told me in 2001:

The migrant women have come here and upset the Italian women at Alma Mater. Straniere put them in crisis because they now question their cultural knowledge. They are accused of not understanding the straniere. In Alma Mater it's the immigrant women that challenge the Italians to change, to think about who they are, to admit that they don't understand others, which they have great difficulty admitting. Italians think they're not racist, and they think that they know all about "others." They don't think they have a lot to learn from foreigners—they think they know, and to challenge them to recognize that they don't know is very upsetting to them. So the immigrant women have this power of knowledge and the ability to put the Italians into a crisis about their knowledge and way of life. Immigrants know about immigration, the experience, what it feels like to immigrate, etc. All of this knowledge, also of difference, they bring to the table.

One evening in 1996, La Talea organized an ethnic dinner to raise money for a Zairean[15] woman and member of the cooperative to visit her natal country and retrieve her child. This migrant woman had waited four long years for the required government documents. To attend the dinner and festivities, guests were asked to pay twenty-five thousand lira per plate (depending on the exchange rate, between eighteen and twenty-five dollars). The dinner was an ethnic smorgasbord representing a sample of dishes from the Philippines, Tunisia, Morocco, and Zaire. Although at the time a Brazilian woman directed La Talea, the Filipina woman who ran the Turkish bath seemed to take the lead role in orchestrating the event. Assisting the event were another Filipina woman, a Nigerian, and the Zairean woman herself, while the Brazilian director remained downstairs in the kitchen. The food was prepared downstairs and then brought up and placed on a long buffet table. Next to the table there was a small African band, and in the rest of the long room were a series of tables and chairs. Most of the guests were Italian, but there were a few migrants present. The Filipina woman seemed to know a number of the Italian guests, greeting more than a few with the customary Italian kisses to each cheek. She and the several other women from La Talea named and ethnically located each dish for the guests before serving them to each table. There was little evidence of close affinity between the Italian guests and migrants; most of the latter sat at one of two tables near the front of the room, while Italian guests occupied the rest of the room.

After the food had been consumed, an East African woman read a poem she had written and she then began to dance for the guests. She wore no shoes, and African amulets embraced her wrists and ankles. She danced as if somewhat uncomfortable, but with skill. The Zairean woman for whose benefit the dinner had been arranged later joined her and danced to a much more rapid African rhythm. The two seemed to dance for hours, joined eventually by a Nigerian woman and, for a brief time, by the only Turin feminist attending the event. The Zairean woman, who would soon be reunited with her child, gave a brief, tearful speech thanking everyone and La Talea for the greatly needed support. For the hours-long duration of this ethnic dinner in this small Alma Mater room, migrants seemed to control the power to represent themselves. The spatially segregated worlds of a few Italians and migrants were brought just a little closer. The symbolism of the poem, the dances, the traditional clothing worn for the dances, and the various ethnic dishes brought together diverse worlds through food and clothing, two of Italy's most culturally significant products.

However, latent tensions between migrant women surfaced the following day when La Talea members argued over money. The Zairean woman accused others of not giving her a significant enough figure from the proceeds of the event, as she had expected much more. Resentment and competition over scarce resources are not uncommon in Alma Mater, which promises much but is unable to deliver suitable and well-paying jobs for everyone. The Zairean woman was particularly angry with the organization's director, a woman with a university degree, who was envied by some because her educational credentials seemed to help her obtain administrative positions in the organization. La Talea's director was visibly shaken and hurt when accused of being dishonest. While the disagreement between the two migrant women was eventually resolved, such conflicts are not unusual under conditions of limited access to resources.

One of the most widely circulated cultural-political artistic genres adopted by Alma Mater participants to project antiracism is the theater group Almateatro. The relationship between mother and daughter is the theme in one play that was written, directed, and performed by Italian and migrant women in 1994. The play, *Luna Nera*, opens with a birth scene, a woman in labor guided by a midwife and observed by four other women. In diverse languages, the six actresses express joy when they learn that the child is a boy. But then when a second child is born, a girl, there is an awkward silence, gestures of disappointment, and forced words of encouragement: "What's important is that it's healthy." Following this opening scene is the introduction of the characters, who each say something about their mothers and several grandmothers and aunts in their diverse languages—Spanish, Italian, an Italian dialect, Filipino, and Somali. They comment about their mothers' personalities, dispositions, and appearances: one mother is cold, calculating, and possessive, another is happy but obstinate, one has dark skin, while an aunt's skin is light. There is then a scene in which the characters observe themselves individually in a mirror and each describes the physical appearance of her mother in comparison with her own body weight, height, eye color, size of thighs, shape of nose and feet. Some of the migrant actresses reflect on the way that their geographical distance from home has led them to reach new perspectives about their mothers, sometimes accentuating the similarities across spatial and temporal distance. A Somali actress says that her connection to her mother is inscribed in her body, and to her mother she imagines herself saying, "Here I wear a covering over my head like all women in my country, and in this, we are the same." The point appears to illustrate that she is more like her mother from a distance than she was when living in the same household, because across worlds it becomes clear that they are united by body and culture.

In *Luna Nera*, cultural differences are symbolized by evoking diverse languages, yet actual differences in family and social practices are unexplored. Represented is a collective subjectivity based on what appears to be the biological and psychological experience of being born female. The story explores what is viewed as a vital and apparently global psychological experience of being at once merged and separated from one's mother as a daughter. Migrant and Italian women wrote the play to represent a common ground that unites all women, namely, being daughters and often becoming mothers themselves. At one point, a migrant woman mentions that not every woman *has* to become a mother, primarily because mothering is an experience that requires considerable self-sacrifice and is therefore not always desirable.

The central motif of *Luna Nera* is that women are united by sexual difference and led almost inevitably to play socially defined roles of woman and mother. Mothers, who have a crucial role in social reproduction through the cultural education of their children, are said to pass on to daughters the role of a lady, contributing to the feminization of women. A Filipina actress in *Luna Nera* describes being scolded by her mother for talking loudly, for becoming dirty while playing, and for running—all directives designed to make her daughter into a socially acceptable woman. The Somali woman is instructed by her mother not to go outside without a veil and not to be brazen. In this portrait, there is also rebellion against the constraints of the mother-daughter relationship—for instance, when a Peruvian actress tells of her refusal to apologize to a teacher who insulted her honor by accusing her of not properly completing a sewing assignment. The daughter-student is subsequently expelled from the school, forced to attend another school that separates her from the social class of her mother. From that day forward, her mother ignores and dismisses her because she has broken with her womanly role. The Peruvian actress becomes an "Other" in her natal family and town.

Luna Nera portrays the close physical and psychological bond between mother and daughter as integral to a woman's identity. Toward the end of the play, however, the actresses argue over whose life should take priority from the point of view of a daughter: the life of one's mother or one's own life. There is a tension between what the playwrights seem to suggest is a Western practice of placing one's own life above the life of one's mother when a daughter leaves her mother to create an autonomous life. A Somali actress remarks that if her mother should need her, she would turn her back on the life she has built on her own to live with and care for her mother. An Italian actress argues that it is *her* life that matters now: "I can't be a daughter forever! It's natural to separate—even though it's difficult." A Peruvian actress laments that mothers sacrifice too much for their children, that mothers cannot be egoists, while the actress who speaks in an Italian dialect suggests that womanly self-sacrifice and self-denial lead to resentment, self-hatred, and hatred of other women. As the story unfolds, there is an effort to heal the wounds expressed in different languages by uniting again as women. Somali, Italian, and South American women discuss the love and tensions inherent in relationships between mothers and daughters, and the loneliness in being a woman with the great weight of familial responsibility on one's back.

Finally in *Luna Nera*, there is the positing of a modern, Italian world as a place in which women may choose to live alone, without the responsibility of caring for their elderly mothers. This modern European culture is contrasted with that of a Somali woman, who suggests that were she to live alone she would lose her name, and that without a name there is no life. The Somali actress argues that Italians merely use things and people and then carelessly discard them.[16] Movement from attachment to the mother to separation corresponds to a developmental model of progress in which the choice to be independent from the mother, and therefore free, represents a socially advanced stage of progress. An Italian actress says:

In my country one can live alone—it may not be easy, but one can choose it. . . . My mother represented another culture—I can no longer find myself in her and she does not understand me—but I prefer solitude to a life under the strings of the family. Thus, if I have a child, I'll tell her not to be afraid to be alone.

The idea expressed here is that in Italian society, a daughter is able to exercise free will, to break from a previous generation, and to follow a nontraditional lifestyle. An Italian daughter may struggle to find her own way, but she is not, as in Somalia, constrained by the obligation to be like and to take care of her mother. So there is an implicit contrast between the modern and traditional mother-daughter dyad, reflected geographically in the spatial worlds of Somalia as opposed to Italy.

The Almateatro play seeks to represent the "general within the many particulars" that constitutes Alma Mater and the international migration to Italy. There is an effort to represent solidarity between women by underlining a common womanness in a world structured by constraining gender roles. Differences between women are represented as cultural, expressed in multiple voices and languages. Implicit is the Italian philosophy of a female subjectivity autonomous from male subjectivity, with its own values, models, and standards that correspond to a woman's historically lived reality (de Lauretis 1989; Parati and West 2002). Female subjectivity, viewed as cross-cutting differences of social position and ethnic and class backgrounds, is articulated in an Italian feminist philosophy of sexual difference. *Luna Nera* expresses an Italian feminist philosophy that women cannot claim subjectivity until women themselves, in their relationships with their mothers and other women, are able to address their own problems (Cavarero 1987).[17] The symbolic mother figures prominently in this feminist discourse; she is, for women, the figure of God, the father, the party, and the state. The symbolic mother has the capacity to recognize and affirm women as subjects in a female frame of reference that transcends individual women's differences. According to this feminist philosophy, a woman's symbolic debt to her mother is to be paid publicly and socially, before the eyes of both men and women.

Luna Nera portrays women's practices with more similarity than is observable according to the realities of everyday life. Like the theory of female social and symbolic practices and sexual difference, the story fails to explore the manner in which the experience of being a woman and daughter differs among women according to social position and classifications such as race, class, and religion. There is a sense in this story of woman being defined by her biological being, as if the body contained an intrinsic power to constrain action. The written text of *Luna Nera,* distributed to the audience, introduces the play as an instance of the confrontation between ethnic identities, an expression of multiple codes. But the story shows a marked absence of attention to problems of racialization, a crucial foundation of Alma Mater. The representation of women as universally united by their relationships with their mothers obscures the situated and lived differences between participants in Alma Mater. Putting forth the image of a common, intercultural woman, Almateatro contributes to the image of an ideal world, free of power differences between women. It is also the subjectivity of the European woman that is assumed to be more potent, because it is more "free" than any space constituted by women or mothers from developing countries. This way, the uneven relationships between Europe, Africa, South America, and the Philippines, and between the members of Alma Mater, are effaced by a dream world of harmony based on the alleged acceptance of differences according to shared experiences.

Social, Cultural Politics

If one could examine Alma Mater through a microscope, it would appear as a multilayered prism, its colorful contours separated by a long, open-ended, incandescent fissure. Close exploration of the prism would reveal the many social histories from which the coalition emerged during the early 1990s, histories of the Italian labor and student movements, Turin feminism, the aftermath of Italian and European colonialism, and the diverse untold struggles of the women who constitute Alma Mater's membership. Wending its way around the prism, the fissure is constituted by common experiences of economic and social struggle, racial and gender exclusion, and the continual negotiation of differences, however vast they may seem to be at any given moment.

There are considerable theoretical difficulties in treating an emergent interethnic alliance. There are so many differences within Alma Mater that studying the organization is almost like examining a whole city. Participants may or may not identify themselves as migrant sojourners in Italy with ties far beyond Europe's geographical boundaries. Many migrants are establishing a number of alliances not always easy to identify, at one moment speaking with a CGIL trade unionist, at another with an

Islamic sect or a Catholic church, at home in several languages and able to debate topics that require considerable knowledge and training. Migrants form alliances with diverse ethnic groups at one moment and turn inward to one's fellow Moroccans or Senegalese, Filipinos, or Nigerians the next. Some remain closely tied to political interests in their countries of origin, while others fear return to these places because of political repression or the common belief that, without success stories and the material possessions to substantiate them, they can never go back. Yet even migrants who feel there is no home to which they may return see themselves as outsiders in Italy, not only because of xenophobia and racism, but also because of their own postcolonial histories, the past that many carry like a safe place and source of pride. Many migrants today are neither desiring of nor able to assimilate into Italian society.

The intersecting identities within Alma Mater, based on class, gender, race, caste, ethnonational background, and age, cannot be subsumed within any simple model of feminist politics established on common experiences in relation to state and familial organizations. Nor can overlapping differences of position be understood through a model of locally constituted cultures, ethnic groups, neighborhoods, or organizations with particular class or other identities. Alma Mater is far more complex than this, requiring an accounting for vast and continually shifting differences in a world of broad and intersecting relations on multiple scales.

Speaking Subjects

Contemporary Europe is constituted not only by the unification of nation-states, but also by the growing presence of international migrants. These newcomers arrive at a moment of radical disjuncture and uncertainty, when post-Fordism is producing insecurity in the labor market, unemployment rates are relatively high, and jobs are often temporary, and when discourses of terrorism have instilled a state of fear that resonates through the popular imaginary. Despite tightened legal restrictions, labor, refugee, and other migrants continue to enter Europe, contributing to growing social heterogeneity and to shifts in daily practices that will in time produce new meanings. However, in the short term, and constrained by the weighty hegemonic constructs that inscribe migrant worlds as opposed to those of the West well before they ever arrive in Europe, how is it possible for the women of Alma Mater to push Turin political culture to become inclusive, tolerant, and open to the normally silenced?

Does Alma Mater's struggle translate into a migrant capacity to really speak, or does the hegemonic structure of everyday life at a number of scales, including the international division of labor and commonsense understandings of self and Other in Turin, prevent migrants from truly constituting an alternative space? Is it possible that Alma Mater's politics of difference might serve to silence as well as give voice to migrant women? These are important questions for any postcolonial and feminist politics seeking to reclaim identities from histories of multiple assimilations, and, in the words of de Lauretis, to represent "the conditions of existence of those subjects who are muted, elided, or unrepresentable in dominant discourses" (1986, 9).

Although Alma Mater struggles to construct a space alternative to those that silence, exclude, and often erase migrants and women in Italian society and to stretch the scale of their movements, the organization has little choice but to operate within established Turinese and Italian codes, expectations, beliefs, and practices. To a certain extent, immigrants may be unable to construct practices that entirely replace those that preceded their arrival in Turin, and they are more likely to influence the reform of Italian and Turinese institutional practices than to cause their dramatic alteration. The question is how newcomers fit into Turinese and Italian-European common sense at least as much as how common sense will change with the migrant presence. This is not to suggest that common sense is static or that it cannot be transformed, but rather that the weight of established cultural traditions is heavily embedded in daily practices that flexibly respond to gross contradictions and are relatively slow to change. Migrant interpretations are constrained by existing dominant local, national, and international spatial relations—the sum of the past interpretations of those spaces. Space is, however, a flexible medium of representation and communication, and elements may be used in various contexts to present different points of view and even to stretch boundaries, if only temporarily.

Not readily accepted as valuable additions to Italian society, migrants in Turin strive to create spaces where their "unspeakable" stories might be told. Postcolonial migrant subjectivities can therefore be understood in part as defensive collective identities constructed against racializing and other discriminatory beliefs and practices. The migrants who resist exclusion and who, in struggling to speak, emerge as subjects, constitute a counterpolitics, or a Gramscian "war of position." Asserting the value of their differences, the women in Alma Mater rework and strive to give positive valence to popular European stereotypes. They might not fully achieve an alternative space, but within a dominant framework they carve out a place where migrant and Italian women may value themselves together and as individuals. As they negotiate their various needs, desires, and points of view, these women employ the feminist method of speaking and listening to one another, which encourages self-reflection, and in so doing they continually re-create themselves. This is a fundamental expression of contemporary feminist philosophy and politics, described as follows by Teresa de Lauretis:

> The practice of self-consciousness, which, according to Catharine
> MacKinnon, is the "critical method" of feminism, its specific mode of
> knowledge as political apprehension of self in reality, continues to be
> essential to feminism. It continues to be essential, that is, if feminism
> is to continue to be a political critique of society. Even more important,
> or more to the immediate point, the practice of self-consciousness—of
> reading, speaking, and listening to one another—is the best way we have

precisely to resist horizontal violence without acquiescing to institutional recuperation, the best way we know to analyze our differences and contradictions even as we accept, as we must, the liberal allocation of a tiny amount of "equal" time in which to present our "opposing viewpoint." (1986, 8)

It is this critical approach to knowledge and to "reality" within Alma Mater, although not always fully operative, that makes possible the clarity needed to come to what Stuart Hall (1988) refers to as a "stop," or the necessary break that makes meaning possible. Hall suggests that the stop is contingent and a form of positioning, but that without stopping we'll never say anything at all. And because the point where we are saying something is reached through practices of speaking and hearing, it has the capacity to affect substantial alteration in ways of thinking and acting. Albeit limited in their ability to create dramatically new spaces, grassroots political groups, with patience, do effect social transformations within their own ranks that reverberate and even stretch spatial boundaries in other parts of the society. It is through the lived negotiations, contestations, and agreements of everyday life that culture is produced and reproduced, because cultural meanings are much more than epiphenomenal—they saturate our worlds.

Finally, how might a politics of difference such as Alma Mater ever truly challenge exclusionary practices rooted in modern, commonsense ideas and systems of classification when it seems to share the very ideas that constitute the hegemony in the first place? This is to suggest that by asserting the integrity of diverse cultures, Turin's feminist politics of difference appears to employ a language similar to the current wave of cultural racism that permeates much of European politics and common sense. Using a language of particularism or difference might undermine their efforts and at the end of the day reinforce the very ideas and practices that keep migrants symbolically, if not literally, at the social and political peripheries. I would suggest, however, that the apparent similarities are actually a bit more complex because, in practice, cultures in Alma Mater are neither stationary nor monolithic and rooted in a circumscribed local territory, but are instead connected through culture and history to other parts of the world at a number of scales. This means that there is really no such thing as a pure Cameroonian or Ethiopian, but that people, like places, are constituted by multiple and overlapping identities that stretch far beyond their immediate spatial context. Many contemporary migrants seek to retain their religious, familial beliefs and practices, but they also speak at least one European language, identify with a common European and colonial history, and subscribe to many Euro-American values and ideas. They may maintain transnational ties with countries of origin without fully identifying themselves with one country, one ethnic group, or even one culture. And as migrants they tend to create new cultural meanings rooted in their countries of origin, settlement, and frequently other parts of the world.

Some of my informants describe Alma Mater as a social politics in process, every day woven together by women who speak hundreds of different languages, practice a number of religions, and represent various social, economic, and symbolic statuses and ethnic backgrounds. Alma Mater seeks to assert the richly textured cultural practices that newcomers bring to an Italian context for the very purpose of transforming commonsense, stereotypical assumptions about migrants that help reproduce their class position in a racially segmented labor force and residentially segregated housing market and society (Cristaldi 2002). The problem of cultural differences frames their struggle to a considerable extent because they must operate within the constraints of given languages of cultural and "racial" differences or ethnicities—that is, because their differences are classified and treated by Italians in specific ways that neither migrants nor Italians can simply wish away. These women assert cultural differences as part of a war of position, in which the actors are postcolonial subjects and their allies representing third world peoples daily confronted with exclusionary practices in Europe. These migrants do not struggle simply for social recognition of their cultural integrity and value in relation to Italy and the West, but for fair treatment, both as human beings with basic rights and as people with histories deeply interconnected with Italy and Europe. That they do this, in part, by representing their cultural identities is entirely within reason given the vast chasm between their self-perceptions and the misconceptions and representations of them in dominant Italian and European society (Carter forthcoming). They must effect changes in dominant representations that inform perceptions of migrants in order to shift the field of practices beyond the exceptional. It might be helpful to approach the study of modern forms of politics and power relations as cultural, that is, as systems of meaning that give some the power to define, to decide, and to choose the way that life is lived by many.

Gender and Globalization at the G8 in Genoa, July 2001

IT WAS A HOT DAY IN JUNE 2001 when, with other members of Alma Mater, I boarded a train in Turin headed for Genoa to attend an international conference about gender and globalization. The conference was organized as a feminist response to the July meeting of G8 leaders scheduled to take place in the struggling port city of Genoa, and as the country was bracing for anticipated popular demonstrations, in which police later killed an Italian youth.

Several Turin feminists from Alma Mater invited me to accompany a group of some fifteen women, also from the organization. Six Italian women attended the conference, including two Turin feminists with recent ties to Alma Mater, among them a retired bank employee active in an Alma Mater initiative designed to insert migrant women into bank jobs. There were also a couple of Italian women peripheral to Alma Mater, one of whom worked with homeless women who wished to form an alliance with Alma Mater on the basis of common gender and class struggles. Among the migrants, there was a young Somali woman, a Cameroonian student, and three Peruvian women in their thirties, forties, and fifties.

The conference took place in an old administrative building, with the usual group of *carabinieri* (Italian military police) holding down the entrance by greeting guests with a stiff glance. More than a thousand participants, 95 percent women, filled a huge, high-ceilinged room decorated with large portraits of stately looking Caucasian men and filled with chairs and tables featuring books and flyers that addressed issues related to the conference theme. There was a long table and podium at the front of the room where invited guests were seated. During much of the conference there were not enough chairs to accommodate all of the participants; some were forced to find seats on the floor or to stand in the back of the room and against walls. As I scanned the huge meeting space, I noticed

193

there were a surprising number of young women in attendance—that is, women in their twenties whose generation, most Turin feminists asserted, has shown little interest in feminism. There were also a large number of women in their forties and fifties, elderly women in their seventies, and a fair number of non-European women or women of color (some 20 percent of the total). The ages of the women of color ranged from early twenties to late forties, with the majority in their twenties and thirties.

Numerous languages were spoken at the meeting. As is customary at European conferences, participants borrowed recording devices and ear-phones while translators made the words of various speakers more or less comprehensible. One could hear translations to and from Italian, French, Spanish, or English. During the second day, someone was called in to translate Arabic for various women from the Middle East and Afghanistan. Later, a Spanish speaker translated an indigenous Latin American Indian language that someone else translated into Italian, enabling the audience to understand an Ecuadorian woman's impassioned plea for women to unite globally against the oil pipeline that threatened her people, their sacred land, and their livelihood. She likened the Earth to the "Motherland," arguing that "development" and modernization through Texas Oil and the Italian firm Agip were polluting the Amazon and threatening the Galápagos and the coastal regions. "The Earth," she said, "is used in favor of the state. What about the communities?" She described toxic waste in rivers and the pain felt by women but not published in the press: "We marched, women, and submitted a proposal to stop this, but our voices were not heard. We were ignored. Why? Because we are women? Or be-cause we are native people? We all have the right to speak and be heard!" Her speech was met with grand applause from the audience.

The woman from Ecuador was not alone in speaking out against devel-opment and the need to protect natural resources, and this was one of the conference themes. A Turin physics professor, Elizabeth Donini, argued that we need to find alternative solutions to the increasing violence that characterizes the world and is made more egregious through the scarcity of resources, which is exacerbated by warfare. Donini blamed the U.S. gov-ernment for investing in oil ducts and military machines in order to con-trol more and more resources around the world and to exert the greatest influence on global economic and political policies. Production systems, suggested Donini, are increasingly agro-industrial, requiring investments in new technologies and oil produced principally by OPEC countries. She urged women to work together to refute the "aggressive and destructive" global politics of the United States and OPEC nations and to stop biotechnology from being patented as war. In a special session organized to discuss women, globalization, and technology in greater depth, participants criticized patriotism and nationalism as "patriarchal identity myths" that lead to warfare and that women have been compelled to identify with as citizens of particular nations or ethnic populations.

Many women pleaded for global feminist solidarity against the effects of globalization and the attendant racial and religious intolerance in their countries. An Algerian woman talked about the destructive effects of the World Bank's Structural Adjustment Programs in her country. A Kurdish woman from Turkey spoke of the anguish, rape, and torture experienced by Kurdish mothers:

> Our villages have been burned down, our children have disappeared. We've cried a lot. We've had nightmares every night. . . . Mothers have started a durable struggle for peace. We have struggled because we want to show the world that Kurdish people exist, but we also want peace. Stop the attack against the Kurds. . . . Once we came back to our village of Kurdistan, there were five women and Turkish forces arrested us. They did terrible things to us. We were women, so they thought they could do anything they wanted against us. I'm wearing a white veil because it is a very important symbol for the Turkish, but I'm wearing it for *all* people to live in brotherhood.

Her speech was met with a loud, long standing ovation.

An Afghani woman exiled in England also received enthusiastic response from the audience. As she ended her plea to free the women of Afghanistan from their imprisonment under the Taliban regime, she put on a blue burka to show the audience how women in Afghanistan live. A member of the organization Women in Black stood near her to represent female solidarity against war and violence. The two women held their hands high, their arms making a diamond shape while a tearful audience loudly clapped to three beats.

A few speakers directly criticized neoliberal capitalism and the increasing commodification of everyday life. They blamed neoliberal policies for deregulating labor markets, allowing companies to reduce labor costs at the expense of human health, informalizing local labor markets, and restructuring the nation-state to make it more attractive to foreign investors by disinvesting in social welfare. They blamed neoliberal policies for producing an uneven global playing field that created rather than

At the Gender and Globalization Conference in June 2001, a standing ovation for an Afghani woman, seen in the middle wearing her burka

eliminated poverty, thus fragmenting people along class and gender lines. An American woman called for global unity in the spirit of Seattle and against the authoritarianism of neoliberal capitalism and the dominant world organizations of the G8 and WTO. Many women urged the audience to continue to gather globally in support of each other's local struggles against global power structures and their destructive effects. They called on women to get out from the shadows and force those in power to listen to their pleas in the name of humanity.

Among the many themes that emerged during the conference, discussion of the global labor market and the attendant north-south divisions between women were central. Over and over, migrant and some Italian women voiced concerns about the way that women from developing parts of the world and migrants in Europe experienced the imposition of the World Bank in their daily lives. Their countries, some argued, were creditors and their resources stolen by business interests and governments of powerful nations. "Class, ethnic, and gender inequalities," insisted a woman from Colombia, constituted the framework in which global feminism must be built. Most migrant women from the south and east, they argued, work in the service sector or sex industry: "Why are only certain jobs available to migrant women?" Many women argued that inequalities between the social and labor positions available to European and migrant women were crucial issues that needed to be addressed by global feminists.

In a smaller group organized to discuss work, migration, and globalization, some suggested the formulation of a working definition of "woman" that was not singular, but multilayered. Several women suggested that the division between different generations of women was central. Older feminists complained that they were not respected by younger women and that they wished to forge more open, cross-generational ties. In addition to ageism, there were countless references to racism and the divisions between women, that is, woman-woman relationships cross-cut by racism/nationalism. With the vast majority of migrant women working in Italy for Italian women as domestic servants, how, it was asked, could women find a common basis for feminist alliance?

One of the most compelling speeches was the first, given by Christa Winterich of Germany, who discussed the strategic role of women in a globally gendered division of labor, arguing that in globalization, "gender is not neutral." Men and women, she suggested, are caught in the webs of globalization in different ways. Although the rate of female employment has grown substantially during the past two decades, she explained, the kind of work in which the majority of women are employed is low-paying, inflexible, dead-end, and unregulated. In workshops, factories, and homes, and in part-time, temporary, and increasingly informal labor, women are employed in the most menial and low-status forms of service, including domestic work, cleaning, and prostitution. The most underpaid and undervalued work is "female." New social classes are created out of globalizing economic processes, including the "dot-com class of men," with very few women at the top and with the bottom defined by a new class of the working poor that is increasingly female, as well as by a growing female global middle class. Competition among women is on the rise globally, with Asian or Latin American women, for example, competing with African women for jobs in Europe and the United States. Under current conditions, asked Winterich, are there common gender issues and concerns?

Connecting Women, Locally and Globally

One of the most important arguments presented at the Gender and Globalization Conference was that "globalization is not gender-neutral." Many women drawn to the conference were motivated to participate in the creation of a transnational feminist network against neoliberal capitalism and the large governmental organizations that support it, exemplified by the G8 and the World Trade Organization. The conference was followed by a peaceful demonstration in Genoa, but participants were encouraged to attend a series of demonstrations against the G8 meeting itself later that month. The latter demonstrations drew thousands of protesters who were called the "People of Seattle" to represent transnational objections to global economic and political destruction by the most powerful countries and their political and business leaders.

There was a lot of energy among the conference participants, but suggestions about how to organize and theorize a feminist alliance along diverse lines were not directly offered. How could Western feminists, Italian in particular, become motivated to struggle for fair labor practices among migrant women from the so-called third world? Or to struggle for improved wages, legal residence, an end to or regulation of the sex trade, the halting of oil pipelines in the south, an end to systematic, structural discrimination and racism? How was it possible to apply the legacies of Western feminist struggle to global campaigns against gender discrimination when, although globalization is not gender-neutral, it cannot be said to affect all women in proportionate ways? In fact, as one speaker mentioned, there is growing worldwide polarization between middle- and working- or lower-class women, a segmentation often reinforced by ethnic differentiation. Relatively few women have gained access to managerial positions with authority over male employees, but there is a steadily growing female middle class around the globe. This structural pattern affects women locally and nationally in specific ways.

Contemporary capitalist social and economic practices create a growing global segment of poor laborers, many of whom are women. No longer an excess or reserve labor force, millions of women work, yet they are often economically, socially, and politically marginalized. Migrant women from poor countries are often subjected to sexual abuse and violence and tend to occupy the most underpaid and undervalued forms of work. Included on this bottom rung are working poor women who live in parts of Africa, Asia, and Latin America, as well as poor migrant women in the United States, Canada, Hong Kong, and Europe. For many of these women, it is the social classification of their ethnicity or "race" as much as, if not more than, their gender that mediates their relationship with the rest of the world. In global capitalism, existing structures of inequality are further exploited to create a highly differentiated labor market in which there is growing polarization within and between societies and between women as well as men (Hall 1991a).

Global economic processes are not gender-neutral, but they do affect women in different ways. Gender informs the type of work and pay scale available to women, but not without other power relations based, perhaps above all, on racial or ethnic classification—international ranking of one's region and country of origin and social and economic class position. These are not static forms of classification and identity; they are dynamic, shifting along with ideas of belonging, in time as well as in space. For example, migrant women from former European colonies may identify themselves as both European and Ethiopian and come from high-status and university-educated African families. In Italy, however, they will be classified at a low social rank as dark-skinned women from underdeveloped parts of the world, presumably willing to accept the most menial forms of employment.

The way that global economic restructuring affects gender practices in Italy cannot be understood without considering the recent international migration of women and men during the past two decades. More Italian women have entered the labor market and engage in professional forms of work; there are growing numbers of migrant women working as live-in and part-time domestic workers for these Italian women and their families. Demand for these domestic workers to take care of children, clean homes, and care for a growing elderly population has increased over the past decade.

From the beginning of the twentieth century until the 1970s, domestic work was the principal employment category for Italian women, while in other European countries there were alternative labor opportunities for women after the Second World War (Andall 2000). In the 1970s the demographic profile of the country began to change, with a growing elderly population and the gradual substitution of an Italian labor force by an immigrant labor force. This can be explained in part by the higher numbers of Italian women employed outside of the home and by the increasingly low status of the domestic work sector, particularly among Italian youth (Mingione 1993). The process may also be explained by concerns on the part of the Italian government to reduce welfare expenditures at a moment when the changing Italian family structure has called for increasing welfare provision.

Although the structure of the Italian domestic sector has conditioned migrant women's experiences, there is not enough attention to the problems experienced by migrant women in these categories of work (with notable exceptions). The fact that there are virtually no alternative legal job opportunities in Italy available to migrant women, including those with university educations, was mentioned on many occasions during the Genoa conference. Numerous migrant women at the conference urged Italian women to take note of the problematic relationship between migrant and Italian women, as privileged employers and citizens on the one hand, and as employees without many legal or social privileges on the other.

Andall has argued that the conceptualization of care that in Italy continues to be linked with a feminine figure and the unpaid labor of the housewife is currently being transformed into the paid labor of the domestic worker—a cheap female migrant labor force (2000). Crucial to understanding this process is the way that racial and ethnic classifications are incorporated into existing gender and class structures in Italy, where, for example, the ability to hire domestic labor is associated with a historically high-ranking nobility. These shifts give Italian and Euro-American feminists the opportunity to form alliances between women of different social and economic rank. This sort of inquiry and consciousness has the potential to profoundly affect power relations by addressing the ways in which differences between women, as well as between women and men, nourish the uneven relationships between places and people.

Biology or physiognomy does not naturally determine gender and race as much as cultural meanings and power relations mediated by capitalist economic and political relationships construct these classifications. In most societies, women are not yet able to set the standards for how they are to be defined as women. It is this absence of freedom to choose one's identity and life path that makes it so important for women, and men, to confront the power hierarchies based on gender as well as race and class that divide us and keep us from realizing our humanity. Gender, under conditions of contemporary global capitalism and the attendant migrations, can be reconsidered, reevaluated, and redefined as a complex, shifting identity cross-cut by all sorts of power relationships and identities, most significantly, even in the early twenty-first-century world, by race.

It is fair to suggest that neoliberal capitalism promotes the reworking of modern identities and the social categories through which they have been culturally defined. Modernist oppositions between, for example, domestic and international and local and global, are no longer as transparent as they once appeared to be. The local workings of capitalist processes and the social values with which they are compelled are, in Italy and in Turin, commensurate with a sense of difference from non-Italians, particularly nonmembers of the European Union from economically impoverished parts of the world. The contemporary blurring of boundaries between various scales, and most dramatically between local and global places, encourages one to reflect on connections with peoples, places, and social processes outside the circumference of one's immediate surroundings. In Italy, national and urban politics are currently tied to anti-immigration and exclusionary regional or nationalist ideologies. There are considerable risks that protection of the Italian citizen-self, by creating barriers between the Italian "haves" and the extracomunitari "have-nots," will polarize the playing field even further, and expand have-not or have-little sectors among all national and ethnic populations, including "Italians."

NOTES

Introduction

1. A central component in the history of capitalism is the social classification of ethnically and racially distinct groups with specified cultural attributes, used to justify their restriction to hierarchically ranked social and occupational roles. This cultural racism has created a built-in method of self-suppression, fashioning expectations and limits and subduing resistance. The weight of ascribed negative cultural and racial attributes may serve as a conceptual barrier for both dominant and subjugated populations.

2. Different from postwar labor migration, the contemporary one is marked by the arrival of postcolonial and Eastern European migrants in a Europe officially closed to their presence and frequently denying the need for their labor. In the postwar period, predominantly male migrants eventually found secure and stable manufacturing employment in a context of rapid—and, in Italy, optimistic—movement from a struggling agricultural to a leading international industrial economy (Castles and Kosak 1973). Southern Italian migrants faced considerable hostility in northern cities like Turin, but were gradually able to integrate, albeit in a relatively unequal manner, into the local world of work and society (Fofi 1964).

3. With the removal of internal borders in the early 1990s, the European Union was concerned with strengthening external boundaries and immigration became a high-level political priority. There has been a convergence of immigration policies in European countries, as entry and residence have become more difficult for non-EU nationals. The current policies have often been described as creating a "Fortress Europe," a legal and cultural-psychological wall that defines by nationality, ethnicity, religious affiliation, and skin color those who are "inside" and "outside." One might argue that policies designed to keep people from working and settling in Europe only make it more likely that any settlement of foreigners will take place under unsatisfactory and discriminatory conditions.

4. Arguably eager to regain the influence they'd lost after the fall of Italian fascism (Harris 1994).

5. The Casa delle Donne was established by Turin feminists in the early 1980s as a nongovernmental location for feminist discussion and initiative.

203

1. The Spatial Politics of Race and Gender

1. The social category of "mediator" is widely employed in Italy and parts of Africa. In Italy, it is difficult to approach a stranger without a recommendation, and a personal introduction is generally required (Schneider and Schneider 1976). This form of mediation applies to many everyday practices, from entering a school to acquiring jobs, obtaining documents to open a business, receiving credit, and finding housing. The mediator is also an established figure in Africa, where he (rarely a woman) acts as a representative on behalf of a person, family, or village. Elderly men and men educated in European schools are frequently designated as mediators.

2. In 1990, the Italian Communist Party had not yet altered its name and splintered.

3. One of these centers is Trama di Terre, in Bologna. Bolognese feminists have had a great deal of contact with members of Alma Mater and have used the organization as a model for their own, much smaller interethnic feminist group.

4. The term *stranieri,* as it is used in Italian, does not really translate into the English term "stranger." The word for "stranger" in Italian is *sconosciuto,* which in English might be translated as "unknown." *Stranieri* means "foreign," but can also mean "alien," a term that indicates an unwanted outsider, rather than merely foreign. The consequence of employing a term that connotes strangeness in both English and French, languages that many migrants speak, may have a practical effect on the positioning of migrants.

5. This may soon change, with construction taking place in Turin in anticipation of the 2006 Winter Olympics in Turin.

6. Migration can inspire innovative thought, particularly during the early years. When migrants are living in an unfamiliar environment, they may experience a sense of distance from the cultural practices and ideologies that helped form many of their thoughts and behaviors. These experiences may lead them to reconsider taken-for-granted forms of knowledge and to apply a greater degree of critical analysis in their daily lives.

7. Enzo Mingione, personal communication, Milan, 1995.

8. The Nigerian Ethnic Association formed a committee to assess the origins and conditions of Nigerian prostitutes. Many feared that African women's passports were being seized at the Questura, and the women forced into the sex trade. In 1995, the former director of the Foreign Office (Ufficio Stranieri), Fredo Olivero, a Catholic priest who became director of Caritas in Turin, helped hundreds of prostitutes obtain work permits and leave prostitution. In 1996, a new law promised residence documents to prostitutes who divulged the names of those who managed their finances.

9. By 1994, there were three or four African hairstyling salons in the neighborhood of San Salvario.

10. Before immigration increased in the late 1980s, there were already several ethnic associations—for example, Nigerian, Somali, Filipino, and Senegalese. Immigrant ethnic associations proliferated after 1989, and the existing associations expanded. In 1994, the municipal government formalized the role of association leaders acting as informal representatives of particular national groups. The local government established what was called an Immigrant Consulta, comprised of representatives elected by migrants in Turin who would in principle play a formal role as representatives of certain national groups, or ethnoregional populations.

11. The theory that female migrants are discriminated against in multiple ways has been posited by scholars to explain their marginalization along several axes of power, including gender, race, and ethnic origin and migrant status (Brettel and Simon 1986; Phizacklea 1983; Morokvasic 1991).

12. "Soldate Ignorate," from "Progetto per un Centro di Donne Immigrate e Non," presented to the Commissione Pari Opportunita Uomo-Donna della Regione Piemonte," July 7, 1990.

13. The Italian Communist Party split into two groups and changed its name. The larger splinter was renamed the PDS, or the Democratic Party of the Left, and the smaller group the Rifondazione Communista, or the Communist Refoundation. The PDS took the lion's share of the membership and has been working to broaden its social base. The Rifondazione has enough of a following to exert influence in parliamentary debates.

2. Alma Mater

1. The handicapped entrance was constructed with one of the original migrant leaders in mind. After playing a pivotal role in the Alma Mater proposal, this Moroccan woman, who is disabled, distanced herself from the organization by the mid-1990s, becoming a prominent leader of Moroccan migrants.

2. After numerous failed attempts to establish a successful cleaning business, the facilities were removed.

3. In 1999, the Ministry of Social Affairs, directed by Livia Turco, a longtime friend of Turin feminists and member of the PDS, awarded Alma Mater a sum of two million lira. The money was intended to help keep Alma Mater in operation and to support what Turco considered a "shining example of migrant and Italian cooperation." For three years, the center was aided by this governmental support, but in the spring of 2002, the new government, led by Silvio Berlusconi, removed the award. For its survival Alma Mater is again forced to apply for various local and European grants, and to depend on its own income-generating activities.

4. For example, Trame di Terre, a migrant women's association located near Bologna, has taken Alma Mater as its model.

5. This seems to be changing as Italy is integrated into the European Union and the products sold in local stores are more frequently imported.

3. Limiting the Laboring

1. Richard Locke writes that Agnelli began constructing the basis for mass production techniques in Turin by the 1920s, but that the full realization of his goals for an automobile industry servicing a mass market were not fully realized until the late 1950s. The Lingotto factory opened in 1921 and Mirafiori in 1939 (Locke 1995).

2. David Harvey provides an excellent summary of the problems created by sustained use of the Fordist regime of accumulation. See chapters eight and nine of *The Condition of Postmodernity* (1989).

3. Richard Locke asserts that in 1969 alone, Fiat lost nineteen million work hours to strikes. In 1971 more than three million hours were lost, and more than four and a half million in 1972. Absenteeism was also rife among Fiat workers. For example, in that same year, an average of 16,800 were absent on any given day, from a total of 186,501 people employed in the company's automobile production (Locke 1995, 107).

4. Capitalist accumulation continually feeds itself by creating new needs.

5. Mirafiori is one of Fiat's largest mass-production sites, constructed in 1939.

6. Since the late 1980s, Fiat has begun to integrate a system of "total quality" derived from a Japanese industrial model of the value of living labor. The idea is to encourage worker participation in the decision-making process within "quality circles" (Volpato 1996). But, Hobson argues, instead of truly creating greater worker control over the labor process, the collective bargaining process is further eroded because rewards are based on management's judgment of worker performance, with little worker control over performance definition. Within the total quality system, the worker is increasingly isolated and disaggregated (Hobson 1992, 32).

7. This strike signals the symbolic end of the Italian labor movement.

8. Much of the Italian south is extremely impoverished, with unemployment rates in some areas at around 40 percent. Per capita income is far below the national average.

9. As the 1970s progressed, many professional workers were unhappy with the *scala mobile* agreement between the unions and Confindustria, Italy's private, big-business association. The scala mobile formula calculated wages in a manner that reduced the wage differentials based on different skill levels. Many skilled workers mobilized against the unions or established their own associations.

10. This is a term created by Arnaldo Bagnasco to describe the industrial districts of central and northeastern Italy, which he referred to as the *Terza Italia*, or the "Third Italy."

11. Ciafaloni interview, 1996.

12. Gianpiero Carpo interview at CGIL, 1996.

13. Cresto-Dino and Fornaris, 1993, 17–18.

14. This statement must be qualified, for the idea of a culturally homogenous Turin never corresponded to the city's actual cultural diversity, which became even more acute following the massive migration of southern Italians during the postwar period. Dominant ideologies portray many geographies with singular or monolithic cultural identities. Even after the postwar migration, there has been a persistent idea of Turin as a space with a distinctive cultural identity.

15. We are likely to see the further expansion of low-wage service jobs in Turin through increasing gentrification as more and more middle-class workers and professionals purchase property in the urban center (A. Segre 1994).

4. Extracomunitari in Post-Fordist Turin

1. For more elaboration on this type of argument, see Harvey 1989, 1995; and Pred 1996.

2. By this I don't wish to suggest that Turin's cultural-historical development can be entirely reduced to the movement of the economy. Social actors make economic decisions that are not always in their own best interests and usually not out of economic motives alone. What prompted Gramsci to develop a theory of hegemony was his analysis of the failures of the Italian political left to capture the imagination of the masses by appealing to the fact that they were economically exploited. See Kertzer 1984 for an excellent story about political practice and local culture in central Italy.

3. Some commentators have argued that the models of center and periphery once employed to describe the regional inequities between the industrially advanced and developing parts of the world are no longer useful when there is so much segmentation and impoverishment in the core countries as well (Nash 1984).

4. Elements of globalization include the decreasing costs of moving people and commodities; the removal of locational constraints on production and consumption activities consequent to the reconfiguration of transnational production and distribution systems; deregulation of financial markets that permitted the creation of more fluid conditions of movement of finance and money capital on the world stage; the growth of supranational political and economic forms such as the European Union and NAFTA; massive worldwide proletarianization and the generation of enormous migration streams; increasing commodification and the furious introduction of new goods and services; the linking of mass culture and personal consumption through satellite television; and deindustrialization in the traditional heartlands of advanced capitalism (Pred 1995; Harvey 1995).

5. See Storper and Walker's (1989) discussion of the analytical significance of the division of labor: "The Division of Labor is not an inert set of slots into which

pegs [people] fit—it's an active force in economic development, and the lived experience of the participants."

6. Data was obtained from the Ufficio Stranieri in Turin, figures from October 1, 1995, "Conteggio per nazione cittadini stranieri residenti."

7. Census figures are notoriously unreliable in Italy.

8. Many other migrant women, legally resident in Turin, worked as domestics on an informal basis and learned that they could acquire access to health care and other privileges if their employers declared their services.

9. Campani writes that 60 to 70 percent of Filipino and 90 percent of Cape Verdean migrants are women, the majority employed as domestics (Campani 1990).

10. Church representatives mediate relationships between Italians and foreigners, for both women and men. Muslim migrants may go to Catholic organizations for help with job location, housing, language, or health care.

11. Another explanation for the increasing demand for COLF is the expansion of households with two working parents in contemporary Italy. Greater numbers of women are unable to stay at home to care for children or aged parents, nor to accomplish all of the daily tasks necessary to run a household alone.

12. Ciafaloni, interview, IRES CGIL, 1996.

13. This discussion is focused on migrants in Turin; there are considerable regional differences in Italy that reflect the manner in which migrants are inserted into the labor market. In the Italian mezzogiorno, or south, the center, and parts of the rural northeast, many migrants work as seasonal agricultural workers. This is very precarious work, primarily in the informal economic sector or *economia sommersa*. However, some migrants are registered workers with fixed salaries. This is a highly unstable category of work, with low pay, even for Italian workers. Migrants are generally paid less than Italians (Pugliese and Macioti 1992).

14. *La Stampa*, June 24, 1995.

15. The *anagrafe* is the city's statistical documentation office for registering and obtaining documentation of births, marriages, deaths, work, and residence.

5. Race, Politics, and Protest in the Casbah, or San Salvario, Africa

1. This excerpt from the *Quaderni Storici* is taken from David Forgacs, ed., *A Gramsci Reader: Selected Writings, 1916–1935* (London: Lawrence and Wishart, 1988), 195.

2. The article about this event was posted on the Alma Mater bulletin board, printed in *La Repubblica*, without a date. Informants told me about two similar incidents, one involving two Alma Mater women returning from an international women's conference on women when they were stopped on the train by police and asked to show their documents. As the story was told, the women were taken

off the train by the police, held for several hours, and repeatedly accused of being prostitutes.

3. In the early 1990s, the term *neri* included North and sub-Saharan Africans.

4. *L'Espresso,* October 1, 1995.

5. *La Stampa,* September 18, 1995, 1.

6. *La Stampa,* November 10, 1995.

7. *La Repubblica,* April 23, 1995.

8. *La Repubblica,* April 20, 1995.

9. *La Stampa,* April 23, 1995.

10. *Il Manifesto,* June 18, 1995, 15.

11. Ibid., 1, 15.

12. I'm employing the term "community" very loosely to refer to ethnic populations in Turin who I realize do not behave as a community according to the most commonly understood meaning of the term. Here, the community of Moroccans is highly fragmented and dispersed throughout the city, composed of young, unmarried Moroccans, some religious and some not, some who seem to reject all the behavioral norms of their conationals, and others whose primary concern in Turin is to earn money to send back to Morocco, to earn a substantial enough income to bring family members to Turin, or to return to Morocco to marry. Some are highly educated; others have only secondary educational training. They follow different versions of Islam.

13. *La Stampa,* June 24, 1995, 1, 13.

14. *La Stampa,* September 23, 1995, 32.

15. *La Stampa,* September 30, 1995, 31.

16. *La Stampa,* September 23, 1995, 1.

17. "Bravo, don Piero! 'Resista!'" *La Stampa,* September 19, 1995, 34.

18. San Salvario, the Murazzi, the Borgo Dora or Porta Palazzo, and finally the Pellerina, where the majority of actual sex trading takes place (Carter, 1997).

19. For a few years beginning in 1995 immigrants with a large proportion of residents in Turin were permitted to elect one to three migrants to represent them in government offices, trade unions, and political parties. Migrants were not permitted to hold public office, and the Immigrant Consulta was established to create an official form of government representation for them in Turin.

20. Valentino Park is situated along the eastern axis of Turin, with the river Po. It is the premium site for Sunday afternoon walks taken by Italian families, a widely practiced ritual called the *passeggiata.* Families gather in their Sunday best, strolling along the park's narrow walkways, eating gelato, gazing at others while chatting. Sunday is a family day in Italy. In Turin as in much of Italy, the only commercial enterprises open on Sunday are some newsstands that rotate on a weekly basis and the bakeries where pastries are purchased for traditional family meals. Even these enterprises are open for only a few hours.

21. In the summer of 2001, when the parking garage was completed, merchants were finally able to return to their location along Via Madama Cristina.

22. This is a somewhat new type of organization, focused around a set of local issues. It is outside the traditional framework of power in parties, unions, and the church.

23. Muslims in Turin had some difficulty locating spaces where they might practice their religious rituals.

24. *La Stampa,* June 24, 1995.

25. Ibid., 13.

26. Cultural racism is deeply rooted in European intellectual history, including the history of social science. The idea of essential cultural differences is linked to the Romantic criticism of modern mechanization and nostalgia for a life more closely rooted in the earth. Cultural racism is also tied to the Enlightenment idea that there are hierarchical stages in the development of civilizations. Finally, cultural racism is reflected in the modern notion of culture as embedded in the land, and as an instance of human, evolutionary progress and development. European theories of cultural difference fuse ideas about race and biological difference with notions of cultural difference (Young 1995). Culture has always been racially constructed (Young 1995, 54). This is the manner in which Robert Young discusses the fundamentally cultural nature of what is commonly viewed as biological racism. The idea of culture was developed in relation to the construction of racial systems of classification, which linked culture and race, because both were defined through the hierarchical lens of civilization. What follows is my summary reading of a more complex argument presented by Robert Young, and my application of his discussion to contemporary cultural racism.

The "new cultural racism" is derived from eighteenth-century "polygenist" theories that the immense differences between territorial groups of human beings can be accounted for only by treating the different races of mankind as distinct species. Polygenist arguments assume that cultural differences cannot be unified. The idea of progress and social evolution informed a later version of the polygenist argument, in which cultural differences were interpreted in relation to a linear idea of evolutionary development along a scale from a lower form of culture to a higher stage, including reason. Differences were viewed as differences of kind, not of degree. The polygenists (whose arguments were developed in opposition to the Bible), apologists for slavery in the American South, wished to uphold the most extreme forms of racial differentiation.

Herder introduced what is frequently referred to as the first modernist notion of culture, which links nation with location. According to this theory, culture is derived from the soil from which it springs. Herder's idea of culture also incorporated a notion of the hierarchical ordering of civilizations. In the nineteenth century, Tyler equated civilization with culture as part of a linear, hierarchical progression from savage to civilized cultures. This was in part the foundation upon which the idea of permanent racial types was constructed.

Racism was implicit in the idea of discrete cultures, and "race" was a summation of hierarchically accumulated moral differences transmitted through the blood. In Young's words: "Race became the fundamental determinant of human culture and history" (1995, 93). European aristocracies were partially reproduced through an idea of the transmission of aristocratic blood. In modernity, this idea was translated into the notion of racial blood, which was synonymous with culture. The body and nation were viewed as the same: "Thus the distinction between race as physical difference and race as cultural difference has been fused back together to make a potent metaphor that bonds the literal and the figurative, the physical and the cultural, the sanguine and the sexual" (Young 1995, 105). In the mid-nineteenth-century writings of Gobineau, for example, racial differences were defined in cultural and sexual terms, corresponding to degrees of civilization. The qualities of culture and civilization were employed to establish a racial typology. The weaker or primitive races were feminized, with the white male always on top.

Thus, racism has always been an integral part of the modern idea of cultural differences and the construction of alterity. Statements about race are statements about culture and vice versa.

27. This argument about cultural racism originated in a discussion by Pierre Taguieff, in reference to changes he observed within forms of French racism. The concept has subsequently been widely adopted to describe the contemporary outbreak of racist violence and subtle forms of exclusion throughout much of contemporary Europe (Barker 1981; Solomos and Wrench 1993; Stolcke 1995; Pred 2000). I see a strong parallel between the argument that current European expressions of racism derive from ideas of cultural rather than biological difference and American discussions of "cultures of poverty." The notion of cultures of poverty was used by Oscar Lewis to describe the manner in which the cultures of the American poor were blamed for their own demise, instead of, for example, schools or governmental policies.

28. Henceforward, I will use the term PDS.

29. An annual festival that was, until recently, designed to celebrate the Italian Communist Party.

30. *L'Espresso,* October 15, 1995, 40.

31. *La Stampa,* September 17, 1995, 35.

32. *La Stampa,* September 16, 1995, 35.

33. *La Repubblica,* October 8, 1995.

34. Tabet, 1997, vi.

35. Diego Novelli, *La Repubblica,* October 15, 1995.

36. The exceptions were usually found among youth that frequented the same

schools, nightclubs, sports teams, and coffee shops, and were more likely to discover common cultural ground.

37. This experience is embedded in the structure of power relations between poor and wealthy nations. The cultural manners of the wealthy nations, in this instance, tend to be understood as superior to those of the poorer ones, evaluated as less "successful" and therefore not as worthwhile. The complaint that northern Italian cultural norms had to be understood by southerners, but that there was little reciprocal effort on the part of northern Italians, is paralleled by the comments made by many African migrants, both abroad and in their own countries. Postcolonial Africans who have not migrated to Europe complain that Europeans or Americans who travel to visit or work in Africa make little effort to grasp the cultural logic of various African ethnic groups, but that Africans have considerable knowledge of European and American culture, politics, and society (see the film by Jean Marie Teno, *Afrique, je te Plumerai* [Africa, I Will Fleece You]). The effects of a psychocultural predisposition to value and undervalue various societies is examined in some of the literature now called postcolonial, originally inspired by Franz Fanon and developed in the work of Edward Said, Stuart Hall, Catherine Hall, Gayatri Spivak, Paul Gilroy, and others.

38. Much has been written about Italian colonialism, especially in recent years. See, for example, Del Bocca 1992, 1993; Labanca 1992; Pankhurst 1964; Iyob 1995; Negash 1987; Ben-Ghiat and Fuller 2005; and Fuller 1988, 2004.

39. There is evidence to support the contention that Italian troops used lethal chemical weapons in East Africa. They also operated concentration camps in Libya and East Africa, and allegedly massacred thousands of Africans (Tabet 1997; Del Boca 1992).

40. *La Repubblica,* September 22, 1995.

41. *La Repubblica,* October 23, 1995.

42. *La Stampa,* October 13, 1995, 1, 11.

43. The policing of Italian prostitutes was instituted by the Italian state in an effort to control venereal diseases among poor women from the rural hinterlands. Young, unwed women could be taken into police custody and subjected to rigorous medical examination to determine their health and fitness.

44. *La Stampa,* October 14, 1995, 32.

45. *La Stampa,* October 10, 1995, 37.

46. *La Stampa,* November 18, 1995.

47. *L'Espresso,* October 1, 1995.

48. The Alliance Nazionale is the ex-MSI (Movimento Sociale Italiana), the fascist party derived from the ranks of Mussolini's Republic of Salo. The Lega Nord is also referred to as the Lega Lumbard.

49. The Schengan Treaty was initiated by the French, German, and Dutch governments to permit the unrestricted movement of citizens of EU member states

across national borders. To become a signatory of the Schengan Treaty in 1990, the Italian government needed a stricter migration policy. The history of the Trevi Group dates back to 1976, when it was constituted to combat terrorism in European countries. The group sought to control terrorist violence by facilitating the coordination of the policies of EU interior ministers. In 1987 and again in 1989, the Trevi Group expanded its focus to embrace policing and security aspects of free movement between countries. The Trevi Group is concerned with police cooperation between member states, crime, drug trafficking, and the security implications of the Single European Market (Bourdouvalis 1997).

50. There were initially several different Leagues that subsequently consolidated into a federation, the Northern League, or Lega Nord. The Leagues' central campaign themes were against state centralism, for federalism, and against the corruption of political parties. The League is localist and populist, and some of its followers have advocated the formation of a northern republic called Padania, separate from southern Italy, which is perceived as a parasite of the north. This party is also generally against immigration (see Cento Bull 1996).

51. According to Melotti, the number of undocumented immigrants is so high that if these people are taken into account, the number of foreigners in Italy would be multiplied by three (1997).

52. *La Repubblica,* September 22, 1995.

53. *La Stampa,* September 18, 1995, 1.

54. Zincone discusses the manner in which weak Italian governments try to reach consensus by appealing to as many individuals as possible. One way to accomplish this is to keep the laws vague, so that they will be left to the interpretive powers of individuals on the local level, and some cities have administrations more friendly to immigrants than others (Zincone 1994).

55. *L'Espresso,* October 1, 1995.

56. Sniderman notes that the cluster of authority values, including the importance of guaranteeing order, securing respect for authority, and maintaining discipline, has nearly as powerful an appeal to those on the political left as to those on the political right, their natural constituency (Sniderman et al. 2000).

57. I will refer to this party as the Rifondazione.

58. *L'Espresso,* October 1, 1995.

59. *La Repubblica,* October 16, 1995.

60. *La Stampa,* November 7, 1995.

61. *La Stampa,* November 9, 1995, 14.

62. *La Stampa,* November 11, 1998.

63. *La Stampa,* November 18, 1995, 2.

64. *Fortress Europe* (Canada, 2001) includes the titles *Dying to Get In: Illegal Immigration to the EU, Escape to the EU? Human Rights and Immigration Policy in Conflict,* and *One-Way Ticket to Ghana: Forced Deportation from the EU.*

65. INPS is Italy's largest social service organization. All other Italian service bodies that handle pensions, unemployment compensation, health benefits, and family allowances are being merged into INPS (Spotts and Weiser 1986).

66. This amount varied according to the length of contract.

67. *L'Espresso,* October 15, 1995, 43.

68. *L'Espresso,* October 1, 1995.

69. *La Stampa,* November 18, 1995.

70. *La Stampa,* November 4, 1995.

71. *La Stampa,* November 8, 1995.

72. Ibid.

73. Ibid.

74. A southern Italian anti-Mafia group.

75. *La Stampa,* November 20, 1995.

76. Ibid.

77. I am not suggesting that the demonstration is uniquely responsible for the suppression of tension and conflict surrounding immigration in 1995. But it is clear that the demonstration of forty thousand in Turin had a significant, if only temporary, impact on local sentiment about immigration.

78. Mayor Castellani sponsored several events to promote the idea of a multicultural Turin, under the title of "Identity and Difference." The municipal government established an Inter-cultural Center in 1996.

6. Turin Feminism

1. By the late 1960s, the labor movement had reached its peak. In 1969, more than 520 million worker hours went to strikes. The working class served as an activist forum in the workplace and beyond. During the Hot Autumn of 1969, when almost every major category of worker was struggling for a new contract, shop floor conflicts spilled into urban piazzas.

2. At the end of the 1950s, the Italian economy turned rather unexpectedly toward a period of rapid modernization, called the "Italian Economic Miracle." By the early 1960s, Italy was no longer a predominantly agrarian country; it had become one of the leading industrial nations on the globe. The 1960s were marked by growth in manufacturing, national integration into the international economy, rapid urbanization, and the massive development of private forms of consumption (Sassoon 1986).

3. For this section and my general understanding of Turin feminism, I am deeply grateful to Vanessa Maher, Rina Constantino, and Elisabetta Donini for hours of generous discussion. Although I could not in this discussion capture all of their knowledge, they helped me to develop an orientation that I found indispensable in seeking to gain insight into a complex set of social interactions and historical processes.

4. Tina Fronte, in 1987, quoted in Zumaglino 1996.

5. A member of CR and the Collettivo delle Campagne, Gianna Faccioli had studied in New Hampshire, where she came into contact with American women involved in the antiwar and women's liberation movements. When she returned to Turin, she told her friends about American feminism and helped to create the MPL, Movimento Politico Lavoratori, a kind of cultural movement that brought together the left of the Christian Democrats and socialists. Many women participated in MPL, but the group doesn't seem to have left much of a trace on Turin feminism (Zumaglino 1996, 72–73).

6. The feminists struggled to force regional governments throughout the country to establish public clinics (Consultori pubblici). New legislation was approved in 1975, and eleven publicly funded clinics opened in Turin. Though an initial victory for feminists, the "people's clinics" were replaced by government-run official establishments. Feminists found their role diminished and ultimately eclipsed by a formal institutional structure (J. Hellman 1987b).

7. The 150-hours scheme won by the trade unions and created in 1973 facilitated paid leave for workers to pursue basic educational qualifications. The program promised to provide education outside the domain of the public school institutions to supply an alternative and to make up for the inadequacies of the schooling system.

8. The following discussion of Intercategoriale Donne was gathered from two publications (La Spina All'Occhiello 1979; and Il Sindacato di Eva 1981). Additional insight came from the book *Femminismi a Torino* (Zumaglino 1996). I am extremely grateful to Patricia Celotto for giving me these much-needed documents and helping to guide me through a vast source of unorganized information on the history of Turin feminism.

9. Although increasing numbers of women obtained factory jobs during the course of the 1960s, the majority of these jobs were clerical and secretarial. Heavy forms of assembly-line work were viewed as inappropriate for women, but this was contested by union women.

10. For this section I am very grateful for discussions with Laura Scagliotti, Marite Calloni, Jessica Ferraro, Patricia Celotto, and Elisabetta Donini.

11. The distinction between domestic and public domains, spheres of reproduction and production, does not hold up under close analytical scrutiny. There is a popular notion in many societies that naturalizes women in the domain of reproduction, but class and cultural differences have considerable bearing on which women (and under what circumstances) actually do "work" in the household on a daily basis. There is so much interplay between production and reproduction that the analytical distinction is questionable (see Collier and Yanagisako 1987).

12. Shabel and AIDA were formed respectively in 1985 and 1990. Shabel was an association of Somali and Italo-Somali women, including six women and three men who wished to help develop cultural and economic relationships between

Italy and Somalia and between Somalians and other Africans in Italy. Five years later, some of the founders, including Giovanna Zaldini and Starlin Abdi Arush, created AIDA (Associazione Italiana Donne d'Africa). Among the goals of AIDA was to help women in need as a consequence of civil war in Somalia or other natural disasters, to encourage and support the creation of a cooperative and women's business, to try to get the international political classes interested in the role of women in social and economic development, to support programs and governmental development plans, to gather data and to research the participation of women in national development, to defend women when they were confronted by justice and legal institutions, and to mobilize women and the constitution in civil and penal processes (Zumaglino and Garelli 1995, 119–20).

13. Women in Black is an international peace network begun in Israel in 1988 by women protesting Israel's occupation of the West Bank and Gaza and demanding peace between Israel and Palestine. All over the world, women stand in silent vigil to protest war, rape as a tool of war, ethnic cleansing, and human rights abuses.

14. Although I cannot go into this here, Marvi Maggio has described new urban Italian social movements as "Social Centers," an outgrowth of feminist and youth movements of the 1960s and 1970s, and an indirect effect of economic restructuring (1997).

7. Making Alma Mater

1. Two divergent political and humanist philosophies are represented in the concept of civil society: the liberal philosophy of individual freedom and responsibility to help oneself, and the Marxist-Hegelian idea of historical production of the authentic social individual. These two traditions are in tension with one another and conflict may erupt, for example, between the contemporary neoliberal philosophy of deregulated, free trade between nation-states, including decreasing state welfare subsidies, and the Marxist philosophy that human freedom is possible only when states intervene to check individual excesses that are the inevitable consequences of unregulated capitalist growth. The notions of self-help and of freedom also converge with a certain strain in Marxist philosophy—the idea that the intrinsic creativity of human practice is fractured, alienated through modern forms of capitalist production, and that a more likely outlet for creative self and social production will occur through forms of artisanship, craft work—in sum, small-scale entrepreneurship.

2. Massey lecture, April 15, 1999, sponsored by the Department of Women's Studies, University of California, Berkeley.

3. A Catholic organization, SERMIG (Servizio Missionario Giovanni, Youth Missionary Service), operates out of what was once a military arsenal, or, as Maria

Viarengo put it, from an *arsenale della guerra* (place of war) to an *arsenale della pace* (place of peace).

4. These categories are often lumped together in Italian popular and sociological discourse.

5. Although there have been some objections voiced by male activists against the exclusive female-centeredness of Alma Mater, participants generally agree that many Muslim and other women would not visit the place if men were invited to participate freely in daily activities.

6. Small-scale entrepreneurial practices in which women operate businesses in such areas as retail or food trade, hairstyling, craft production, and trade, or participate in agricultural cooperatives.

7. During the fall of 1996, when I interviewed feminists connected with Alma Mater, the term "empowerment" was employed to describe the feminist philosophy of constructing a world in which women are seen and heard and can move without discrimination.

8. Some of the Turin feminists and migrant members of Alma Mater are lesbian, but their sexual preferences remain covert.

9. Retired feminists range in age from forty-five to approximately sixty, having retired because of a disability or at a time when fifty was a legal retirement age.

10. Apart from the particular national associations, any organization initiated by migrants must include an Italian board member. It is impossible to attend a meeting about migrant or migration issues that is not dominated by Italians, and it is extremely rare for migrants to be included as discussants.

11. Giovanna is Somali but she is married to an Italian named Zaldini. She was raised in Somalia but received her advanced schooling in Italy.

12. The departure of Giovanna Zaldini from the director position was far more involved than I can explain here. Giovanna has remained active in Alma Mater and has since held several other administrative positions in the organization.

13. In the early 1990s Turin was the center of the Red Cross for the Somalia relief effort, in connection with Somali migrants in Turin, most of them women. These women maintain powerful transnational networks with political figures and institutions in Somalia, but in Italy their role can be delegitimized and they are regularly denied access to resources and privileges.

14. De Lauretis suggests that Italian feminists emphasize the historical practice of becoming a woman, not the biological essence.

15. Zaire is now called the Democratic Republic of Congo.

16. Anthropologists have frequently described Italian culture as "familist." See, for example, Belmonte 1989; Banfield 1958; Kertzer 1980; Schneider and Schneider 1976. The history of Italian familism and its links with clientelism and Italian regionalism have been discussed widely by scholars; see, for example, Putnam 1993; Sniderman et al. 2000; Dickie 1999; Schneider 1998; Levy 1996; Agnew 2002.

17. This is against American and British feminist traditions of egalitarianism, which suggest that women have to be equal to men. According to Milan and other Italian feminists, the notion of equality is an ideological attempt to subject women even more by preventing the expression of their own existence (de Lauretis 1989, 1990).

BIBLIOGRAPHY

Adinolfi, Francesco. 1994. "Autoproduzione: Punto a capo." In *Communita Virtuali, I Centri Sociali in Italia,* Adinolfi et al. Rome: Manifestolibri.

Agnew, A. John. 2002. *Place and Politics in Modern Italy.* Chicago: University of Chicago Press.

Alvarez, Sonia E. 1996. "Concluding Reflections: 'Redrawing' the Parameters of Gender Struggle." In *Emergences: Women's Struggles for Livelihood in Latin America,* ed. John Friedman, Rebecca Abers, and Lillian Autler. Los Angeles: UCLA Latin American Center.

———. 1997. "Reweaving the Fabric of Collective Action: Social Movements and Challenges to Actually Existing Democracy in Brazil." In *Between Resistance and Revolution: Cultural Politics and Social Protest,* ed. Richard G. Fox and Orin Starn. New Brunswick, NJ: Rutgers University Press.

Alvarez, Sonia E., and Arturo Escobar. 1992. "Introduction: Theory and Protest in Latin America Today." In *The Making of Social Movements in Latin America: Identity, Strategy, and Democracy,* ed. Sonia E. Alvarez and Arturo Escobar. Boulder, CO: Westview Press.

Ambrosini, Maurizio. 2001. *La Fatica di Integrarsi: Immigrati e Lavoro in Italia.* Bologna: Il Mulino.

Andall, Jacqueline. 2000. *Gender, Migration, and Domestic Service: The Politics of Black Women in Italy.* Aldershot, England: Ashgate.

Appadurai, Arjun. 1990. "Disjunction and Difference in the Global Cultural Economy." *Public Culture* 2, no. 2.

Ascoli, Ugo. 1992. "L'azione volontaria nei sistemi di welfare." *Polis* 6, no. 3.

Bagnasco, Arnaldo. 1986. *Torino: Un profilo sociologico.* Turin: Giulio Einaudi.

———. 1990. "La cultura come risorsa." In *La citta dopo Ford,* ed. Arnaldo Bagnasco. Turin: Bollati Boringhieri.

Balbo, Laura, and Luigi Manconi. 1992. *I razzismi reali.* Milan: Feltrinelli.

Balbo, Laura, and Marie P. May. 1975. "Woman's Condition: The Case of Postwar Italy." *International Journal of Sociology* 5: 79–102.

Balibar, Étienne, and Immanuel Wallerstein. 1991. *Race, Nation, Class: Ambiguous Identities.* London: Verso.

Banfield, Edward C. 1958. *The Moral Basis of a Backward Society.* Glencoe, IL: Free Press.

Barkan, Joanne. 1984. *Visions of Emancipation: The Italian Workers' Movement since 1945*. New York: Praeger.

Barker, Martin. 1981. *The New Racism*. London: Junction Books.

Bascetta, Marco. 1994. "La Gabbia Delle due Societa." In *Communita virtuali: I centri sociali in Italia*, Francesco Adinolfi et al. Rome: Manifestolibri.

Battaglino, Maria Teresa. 1993. "La Formazione delle mediatrici a Torino, un'esperienza peculiare all'interno dei percorsi delle donne, Alma Mater." Unpublished.

Baumgardner, Jennifer, and Amy Richards. 2000. *Manifesta: Young Women, Feminism, and the Future*. New York: Farrar, Straus, and Giroux.

Beccalli, Bianca. 1985. "Le politiche del lavoro femminile in Italia: Donne, sindacati, e stato tra il 1974 e il 1984." *Stato e Mercato*, no. 15 (December).

Belforte, Silvia, Adriana Garizio, Emanuele Levi Montalcini, Danilo Riva, Maurizio Vogilazzo, Alberico Zeppetella. 1978. *L'occupazione nella crisi, materiali di ricerca su ristrutturazione produttiva, mercato del lavoro, e assetti territoriali in un'area industriale*. Turin: Tommaso Musolini.

Belmonte, Thomas. 1989. *The Broken Fountain*. New York: Columbia University Press.

Belpiede, Anna. 1995. "Le politiche locali sulla mediazione interculturale: Il caso Torino." Seminaire sur la mediazione interculturelle, Marseille. Unpublished.

———. 1996. "Dal mediatore ai luoghi di mediazione nel sociale." Animazione Sociale, Gruppo Abele, March 5.

Belpiede, Anna, Vanessa Maher, Palaja Sabrina, Sacchi Paola, and Giovanna Zaldini. 1997. "La professione di mediatrice/mediatore culturale," Piedmont, Italy, Associazione AlmaTerra. Unpublished.

Berman, Marshall. 1988. *All That Is Solid Melts into Air: The Experience of Modernity*. New York: Penguin Books.

Birnbaum, Lucia Chiavola. 1986. *Liberazione della Donna: Feminism in Italy*. Middletown, CT: Wesleyan University Press.

Björgo, Tore, and Rob Witte. 1993. *Racist Violence in Europe*. New York: St. Martin's Press.

Blunt, Alison, and Gillian Rose, eds. 1994. *Writing, Women, and Space: Colonial and Postcolonial Geographies*. New York: Guilford Press.

Bocca, Giorgio. 1988. *Gli Italiani sono razzisti?* Milan: Garzanti.

Bono, Paola, and Sandra Kemp, eds. 1991. *Italian Feminist Thought: A Reader*. Oxford, England: Basil Blackwell.

Bourdieu, Pierre. 1977. *Outline of a Theory of Practice*. Cambridge, MA: Cambridge University Press.

———. 1984. *Distinctions: A Social Critique of the Judgment of Taste*, trans. Richard Nice. Cambridge: Harvard University Press.

Bourdouvalis, Chris. 1997. "The European Union and the Immigration Problem: Small Steps and Possible Solutions." In *Immigration into Western Societies:*

Problems and Policies, ed. Emek M. Ucarer and Donald J. Puchala. London: Pinter.

Bravo, Anna, and Anna Maria Bruzzone. 1995. *In Guerra senza armi: Storie de donne, 1940–1945.* Rome: Laterza.

Brettel, Caroline, and Rita James Simon, eds. 1986. *International Migration: The Female Experience.* Totowa, NJ: Rowman & Littlefield.

Bryant, Raymond L. 2002. "Non-governmental Organizations and Governmentality: 'Consuming' Biodiversity and Indigenous People in the Philippines." *Political Studies* 50: 268–92.

Burawoy, Michael, ed. 2001. *Global Ethnography: Forces, Connections, and Imaginations in a Postmodern World.* Berkeley: University of California Press.

Burgio, Alberto. 2001. *La guerra delle razze.* Rome: Manifestolibri.

Butler, Judith. 1993. "Endangered/Endangering: Schematic Racism and White Paranoia." In *Reading Rodney King, Reading Urban Uprising,* ed. Robert Gooding-Williams. New York: Routledge.

Buttafuoco, Annarita. 1980. "Italy: The Feminist Challenge." In *The Politics of Eurocommunism: Socialism in Transition,* ed. Carl Boggs and David Plotke. Boston: South End Press.

Caldwell, Lesley. 1983. "Courses for Women: The Example of the 150 Hours in Italy." *Feminist Review* 14: 71–83.

———. 1991. "Italian Feminism: Some Considerations." In *Women and Italy: Essays on Gender, Culture, and History,* ed. Zygmunt G. Baranski and Shirley W. Vinall. New York: St. Martin's Press.

Campani, Giovanna. 1993. "Immigration and Racism in Southern Europe: The Italian Case." *Ethnic and Racial Studies* 16, no. 3.

Campani, Giovanna, and Salvatore Palidda. 1990. "Italie: Racisme et tiersmondisme." *Peuples Mediterraneens,* no. 51: 145–69.

Canevacci, Massimo, Roberto De Angelis, and Francesca Mazzi, eds. 1995. *Culture del conflitto giovani metropoli comunicazione.* Rome: Costa & Nolan.

Capecchi, Vittorio. 1989. "The Informal Economy and the Development of Flexible Specialization in Emilia-Romagna." In *The Informal Economy: Studies in Advanced and Less Developed Countries,* ed. Alejandro Portes, Manuel Castells, and Lauren A. Benton. Baltimore, MD: Johns Hopkins University Press.

Caponio, Tiziana. 2003. "Politics, Policy, and Immigration in Italy: The Cases of Milan, Bologna, and Naples." Unpublished paper, University of Bologna, presented at the "Comparing U.S. and European Approaches to Issues of Immigration" conference, University of Bologna, June 20–21.

Carter, Donald Martin. 1997. *States of Grace: Senegalese in Italy and the New European Immigration.* Minneapolis: University of Minnesota Press.

———. 2003. Preface to *New African Diasporas,* ed. Khalid Koser. London: Routledge.

———. Forthcoming. *Navigating Diaspora.*

Castells, Manuel, and Alejandro Portes. 1991. "The Informal Economy and the Development of Flexible Specialization in Emilia-Romagna." In *The Informal Economy: Studies in Advanced and Less Developed Countries,* ed. Alejandro Portes, Manuel Castells, and Lauren A. Benton. Baltimore, MD: Johns Hopkins University Press.

Castles, Stephen. 1993. "Migrations and Minorities in Europe: Perspectives for the 1990s; Eleven Hypotheses." In *Racism and Migration in Western Europe,* ed. John Wrench and John Solomos. Oxford: Berg.

——. 2000. *Ethnicity and Globalization.* London: Sage.

Castles, Stephen, and Godula Kosak. 1973. *Immigrant Workers and Class Structure in Western Europe.* Oxford: Berg.

Castles, Stephen, and Mark. J. Miller. 2003. *The Age of Migration: International Population Movements in the Modern World.* 3rd ed. New York: Guilford Press.

Castronovo, Valerio. 1987. *Turin.* Bari: Editori Laterza.

Cavarero, Adriana. 1987. "L'elaborazione Filosofica della Differenza Sessuale." In *La ricerca delle donne: Studi femministi in Italia,* ed. Maria Cristina Marcuzzo and Anna Rossi-Doria. Turin: Rosenberg & Sellier.

Cento Bull, Anna. 1996. "Ethnicity, Racism, and the Northern League." In *Italian Regionalism: History, Identity, and Politics,* ed. Carl Levy. Oxford: Berg.

Chalmers, Douglas, Judy Gearhart, Andrea Hetling, Adam Jagelski, Kerianne Piester, and Caroline Tsilikounas. 1995. "Mexico NGO Networks and Popular Participation." Papers on Latin America no. 39.

Cheles, Luciano, Ronnie Ferguson, and Michalina Vaughan, eds. 1995. *The Far Right in Western and Eastern Europe.* New York: Longman.

Ciafaloni, Francesco, Mariella Console, Abdelsamad El Gazzar, Laura Maritano, Roberta Ricucci, and Elena Rozzi. 1999. *Antiracist Emergency Network September 1, 1998–October 1, 1999: Final Report.* Turin: Comitato oltre il Razzismo.

CICSENE. 1996. *Problematiche di un "Quartiere Latin," San Salvario—Turin.* Turin: CICSENE.

Cole, Jeffrey. 1997. *The New Racism in Europe: A Sicilian Ethnography.* Cambridge: Cambridge University Press.

Collier, Jane, and Sylvia Yanagisako, eds. 1987. *Gender and Kinship: Essays toward a Unified Analysis.* Stanford, CA: Stanford University Press.

Colombo, Asher, and Giuseppe Sciortino, eds. 2003. *Stranieri in Italia: Assimilati ed esclusi.* Bologna: Il Mulino.

Comito, Vincenzo. 1982. *La Fiat: Tra Crisi e Ristrutturazione.* Rome: Riuniti Editori.

Conroy, Pauline. 1995. "The Voluntary Sector Challenge to Fortress Europe." In *Community Empowerment: A Reader in Participation and Development,* ed. Gary Craig and Marjorie Mayo. London: Zed Books.

Contini, Bruno, and Riccardo Revelli. 1992. *Imprese, occupazione, e retribuzioni al microscopio: Studi sull'economiea Italiana alla luce delle fonti statistiche inps.* Bologna: Il Mulino.

Corsico, Franco. 1987. "Torino, Città della Fiat." *Archivo di Studi Urbani e Regionale,* no. 29.

Cotesta, Vittorio. 1999. *Sociologia dei conflitti etnici: Razzismo, immigrazione, e societa multiculturale.* Rome-Bari: Laterza.

———. 2002. *Lo straniero, pluralismo culturale, e immagini dell'altro nella società globale.* Rome: Editori Laterza.

Craig, Gary, and Marjorie Mayo, eds. 1995. *Community Empowerment: A Reader in Participation and Development.* Atlantic Highlands, NJ: Zed Books.

Crehan, Kate. 2002. *Gramsci, Culture, and Anthropology.* Berkeley: University of California Press.

Cresto-Dino, Carlo, and Franco Fornaris. 1993. *Sapevate che le citta possono anche morire?* Documentary. Turin: Pluriverso.

Cristaldi, Flavia. 2002. "Multiethnic Rome: Toward Residential Segregation?" *Geojournal* 2–3.

Cross, Malcolm. 1994. "Economic Change, Ethnic Minority Formation, and New Identities in Europe." Paper presented at the "Transnationalism, Nation-State Building, and Culture" symposium, Wenner-Gren Foundation.

Cross, Malcolm, and Michael Keith, eds. 1993. *Racism, the City, and the State.* London: Routledge.

CSOA Auro e Marco. 1995. "Metropoli: Conflitto Continuo." In *Culture del conflitto: Giovani metropoli comunicazione,* ed. Massimo Canevacci, Roberto De Angelis, and Francesca Mazzi. Rome: Costa & Nolan.

Dal Lago, Alessandro. 1999. *NON-PERSONE, l'esclusione dei migranti in una società globale.* Milan: Interzone.

Daly, Faïçal, and Rohit Barot. 1999. "Economic Migration and Social Exclusion: The Case of Tunisians in Italy in the 1980s and 1990s." In *Into the Margins: Migration and Exclusion in Southern Europe,* ed. Floya Anthias and Gabriella Lazaridis. Aldershot, England: Ashgate.

Damilano, Ines. 1996. "Introduzione." In *Piera Zumaglino: Femminismi a Torino.* Turin: Franco Angeli.

Da Pra Pocchiesa, Mirta. 1996. *Ragazze di vita: Viaggio nel mondo della prostituzione.* Turin: Riuniti.

De Certeau, Michel. 1998. *The Practice of Everyday Life.* Minneapolis: University of Minnesota Press.

De Lauretis, Teresa. 1986. "Feminist Studies/Critical Studies: Issues, Terms, and Contexts." In *Feminist Studies/Critical Studies,* ed. Teresa de Lauretis. Bloomington: Indiana University Press.

———. 1989. "The Essence of the Triangle, or Taking the Risk of Essentialism Seriously: Feminist Theory in Italy, the U.S., and Britain." *Differences* 2: 1–37.

———. 1990. Introduction to *Sexual Difference: A Theory of Social-Symbolic Practice*, Milan Women's Bookstore Collective. Bloomington: Indiana University Press.

Del Boca, Angelo. 1992. *L'Africa nella coscienza degli Italiani, miti, memorie, errori, sconfitte*. Rome: Laterza.

Dell'Aringa, Carlo, and Fabio Neri. 1989. "Illegal Immigrants and the Informal Economy in Italy." In *European Factor Mobility: Trends and Consequences*, ed. Ian Gordon and A. P. Thirlwall. London: Macmillan.

Delle Donne, Marcella. 1993. "Razzismo, pregiudizi, e conflitti." In *Immigrazione in Europea: Solidarieta e conflitto*, ed. Marcella Delle Donne, Umberto Melotti, and Stefano Petilli. Rome: Centro Europeo di Scienze Sociali.

Dematteis, Giuseppe, and Anna Segre. 1988. "Da città-fabbrica a città-infrastruttura." *Spazio e società*.

Di Carmine, Roberta. 2004. "Cinematic Images, Literary Spaces: The Presence of Africa in Italian and Italophone Literature." Ph.D. diss., University of Oregon, Portland.

Dicken, Peter. 2002. *Global Shift: Transforming the World Economy*. New York: Guilford Press.

Dickie, John. 1999. *Darkest Italy: The Nation and Stereotypes of the Mezzogiorno, 1860–1900*. New York: St. Martin's Press.

Donini, Elisabetta. 1996. "Donne, uomini, economia sociale." *Il Manifesto* (February 15).

Douglas, Mary. 1966. *Purity and Danger: An Analysis of the Concepts of Pollution and Taboo*. London: Routledge.

Edwards, Richard. 1979. *Contested Terrain: The Transformation of the Workplace in the Twentieth Century*. New York: Basic Books.

Fanon, Frantz. 1967. *Black Skin, White Masks*. New York: Grove Press.

———. 1968. *The Wretched of the Earth*. New York: Grove Press.

Fazel, Shirin Ramzanali. 1999. *Lontana da Mogadiscio*. Rome: Datanews.

Fedeli, Leone Iraci. 1990. *Razzismo e immigrazione: Il caso italiano*. Rome: Acropoli.

Fernandez-Kelly, Maria Patricia. 1983. *For We Are Sold, I and My People: Women and Industry in Mexico's Frontier*. New York: SUNY Press.

Ferrarotti, Franco. 1988. *Oltre il razzismo: Verso la società multirazziale e multiculturale*. Rome: Armando.

Fisher, William F. 1997. "Doing Good? The Politics and Antipolitics of NGO Practices." *Annual Review of Anthropology* 26: 439–64.

Fofi, Goffredo. 1964. *L'immigrazione meridionale a Torino*. Milan: Feltrinelli.

Form, William. 1995. *Segmented Labor, Fractured Politics: Labor Politics in American Life*. New York: Plenum Press.

Fortunato, Mario, and Salah Methnani. 1997. *Immigrato*. Rome: Theoria.

Foucault, Michel. 1978. *The History of Sexuality*. New York: Vintage Books.

―――. 1980. *Power/Knowledge: Selected Interviews and Other Writings, 1972–1977.* Trans. Colin Gordon. New York: Pantheon.

Frogett, Lynn, and Antonia Torchi. 1981. "Feminism and the Italian Trade Unions." *Feminist Review* 8: 35–42.

Fuller, Mia. 1988. "Building Power: Italy's Colonial Architecture and Urbanism, 1923–1940." *Cultural Anthropology* 3, no. 4.

―――. 2005. *Moderns Abroad: Italian Colonial Architecture and Urbanism.* New York: Routledge.

Gabaccia, Donna R. 2000. *Italy's Many Diasporas.* Seattle: University of Washington Press.

Gabaccia, Donna, and Franca Iacovetta, eds. 2002. *Women, Gender, and Transnational Lives: Italian Workers of the World.* Toronto: University of Toronto Press.

Galjart, Benno. 1995. "Counter-development: Possibilities and Constraints." In *Community Empowerment: A Reader in Participation and Development,* ed. Gary Craig and Marjorie Mayo. London: Zed Books.

Gall, Gregor. 1995. "The Emergence of a Rank and File Movement: The Comitati di Base in the Italian Worker's Movement." *Capital and Class* (journal).

Gallini, Clara. 1992. "Scenari del razzismo in Italia." In *Il razzismo e le sue storie,* ed. Girolamo Imbruglia. Naples: Edizioni Scientifiche Italiane.

―――. 1996. *Giochi Pericolosi: Frammento di un immaginario alquanto razzista.* Rome: Manifestolibri.

Gallino, Luciano. 1990. "'Policy Making' in Condizioni Avverse." In *La città dopo Ford: Il caso di Torino,* ed. Arnaldo Bagnasco. Turin: Bollati Boringhieri.

Gamble, Sarah. 2001. "Post-Feminism." In *Feminism and Postfeminism,* ed. Sarah Gamble. London: Routledge.

Gill, Lesley. 1995. "Power Lines: Nongovernmental Organizations (NGOs), the State, and Popular Organizations in an Urban Bolivian Slum." American University, Department of Anthropology, unpublished.

Gilman, Sander. 1985. *Difference and Pathology: Stereotypes and Sexuality, Race and Madness.* Ithaca, NY: Cornell University Press.

―――. 1986. "Black Bodies, White Bodies: Toward an Iconography of Female Sexuality in Late-Nineteenth-Century Art, Medicine, and Literature. In *"Race," Writing, and Difference,* ed. Henry Louis Gates Jr. Chicago: University of Chicago Press.

Gilmore, Ruth Wilson. 2002. "Race and Globalization." In *Geographies of Global Change: Remapping the World in the Late Twentieth Century,* ed. R. J. Johnston, Peter J. Taylor, and Michael J. Watts. Oxford, England: Blackwell.

Gilroy, Paul. 1991. *"There Ain't No Black in the Union Jack": The Cultural Politics of Race and Nation.* Chicago: University of Chicago Press.

―――. 2000. *Against Race: Imagining Political Culture beyond the Color Line.* Cambridge, MA: Harvard University Press.

Ginsborg, Paul. 1990. *A History of Contemporary Italy, Society, and Politics, 1943–1988*. London: Penguin Books.

———. 2003. *Italy and Its Discontents: Family, Civil Society, State, 1980–2001*. New York: Palgrave Macmillan.

Goddard, Victoria. 1987. "Honour and Shame: The Control of Women's Sexuality and Group Identity in Naples." In *The Cultural Construction of Sexuality*, ed. Pat Caplan. London: Routledge.

Goffman, Erving. 1963. *Stigma: Notes on the Management of Spoiled Identity*. New York: Touchstone.

Goldberg, David Theo. 1993. *Racist Culture: Philosophy and the Politics of Meaning*. Oxford, England: Blackwell.

Gramsci, Antonio. 1989. *Selections from the Prison Notebooks*. Ed. and trans. Derek Boothman. New York: International Publishers.

———. 1995. *Further Selections from the Prison Notebooks*. Ed. Derek Boothman. Minneapolis: University of Minnesota Press.

Guillaumin, Colette. 1995. *Racism, Sexism, Power, and Ideology*. London: Routledge.

Gupta, Akhil, and James Ferguson. 1992. "Beyond 'Culture': Space, Identity, and the Politics of Difference." *Cultural Anthropology* 7, no. 1.

Hajimichalis, Costis, and Dina Vaiou. 1990. "Whose Flexibility? The Politics of Informalization in Southern Europe." *Capital and Class* (journal) 42.

Hall, Stuart. 1982. In *The Empire Strikes Back: Race and Racism in 70s Britain*, Centre for Contemporary Cultural Studies. Birmingham: University of Birmingham.

———. 1988. "Minimal Selves." In *Identity: The Real Me*, ICA Document 6. London: Institute of Contemporary Arts.

———. 1991a. "The Local and Global: Globalization and Ethnicity." In *Culture, Globalization, and the World System*, ed. Anthony D. King. Binghamton: State University of New York.

———. 1991b. "Old and New Identities, Old and New Ethnicities." In *Culture, Globalization, and the World-System*, ed. Anthony D. King. Binghamton: State University of New York.

———. 1996a. "Gramsci's Relevance for the Study of Race and Ethnicity." In *Stuart Hall: Critical Dialogues in Cultural Studies*, ed. David Morley and Kuan-Hsing Chen. London: Routledge.

———. 1996b. "New Ethnicities." In *Stuart Hall: Critical Dialogues in Cultural Studies*, ed. David Morley and Kuan-Hsing Chen. London: Routledge.

Hanson, Susan, and Geraldine Pratt. 1994. "Geography and the Construction of Difference." *Gender, Place, and Culture* 1, no. 1.

———. 1995. *Gender, Work, and Space*. London: Routledge.

Haraway, Donna J. 1991. *Simians, Cyborgs, and Women: The Reinvention of Nature*. New York: Routledge.

Hargreaves, Alec G., and Jeremy Leaman. 1995. "Racism in Contemporary Western Europe: An Overview." In *Racism, Ethnicity, and Politics in Contemporary Europe*, ed. Alec G. Hargreaves and Jeremy Leaman. Aldershot, England: Edward Elgar.

Harris, Geoffrey. 1994. *The Dark Side of Europe: The Extreme Right Today*. Edinburgh: Edinburgh University Press.

Harrison, Bennett. 1997. *Lean and Mean: The Changing Landscape of Corporate Power in the Age of Flexibility*. New York: Guilford Press.

Harstock, Nancy C. M. 1998. "Moments, Margins, and Agency." *Annals of the Association of American Geographers* 88, no. 4.

Harvey, David. 1989. *The Condition of Postmodernity: An Enquiry into the Origins of Cultural Change*. Cambridge, England: Blackwell.

———. 1993. "Class Relations, Social Justice, and the Politics of Difference." In *Place and the Politics of Identity*, ed. Michael Keith and Steven Pile. New York: Routledge.

———. 1996. *Justice, Nature, and the Geography of Difference*. London: Blackwell.

———. 1997. "The Work of Postmodernity: The Laboring Body in Global Space." Unpublished.

———. 2000. *Spaces of Hope*. Berkeley: University of California Press.

Haycroft, John. 1987. *The Italian Labryinth: Italy in the 1980s*. London: Secker and Warburg.

Hellman, Judith Adler. 1984. "The Italian Communists, the Women's Question, and the Challenge of Feminism." *Studies in Political Economy* 13 (Winter): 57–82.

———. 1987a. "Turin: Women's Struggles in a Worker's City." In *Journeys among Women: Feminism in Five Italian Cities*. New York: Oxford University Press.

———. 1987b. "Women's Struggle in a Worker's City: Feminist Movements in Turin." In *The Women's Movement of the United States and Western Europe: Consciousness, Political Opportunity, and Public Policy*, ed. Mary Fainsod Katzenstein and Carol McClurg Mueller. Philadelphia: Temple University Press.

Hellman, Stephen. 1976. "The 'New Left' in Italy." In *Social and Political Movements in Western Europe*, ed. Martin Kolinsky and William E. Paterson. London: Croom Helm.

———. 1988. *Italian Communism in Transition: The Rise and Fall of the Historic Compromise in Turin, 1975–1980*. New York: Oxford University Press.

Hess, Robert L. 1966. *Italian Colonialism in Somalia*. Chicago: University of Chicago Press.

Hesse, Barnor. 1993. "Black to Front and Back Again: Racialization through Contested Times and Spaces." In *Place and the Politics of Identity*, ed. Michael Keith and Steve Pile. London: Routledge.

Hobsbawm, Eric. 1994. *Nations and Nationalism since 1780: Programme, Myth, Reality*. Cambridge: Cambridge University Press.

Hobson, Sherran. 1992. "Fiat's Cultural Revolution, TQM as Functional Integration." *Science as Culture* 3, part 1, no. 14.

Holmström, Mark. 1989. *Industrial Democracy in Italy: Workers' Co-ops and the Self-Management Debate.* Aldershot, England: Avebury.

hooks, bell. 1990. *Yearning, Race, Gender, and Cultural Politics.* Boston: South End Press.

Hornblower, Margot. 1993. "The Skin Trade." *Time* magazine, June 21.

Il Sindacato di Eva. 1981. *L'attivita dell'intercategoriale donne CGIL-CISL-UIL e dei coordinament: Donne di diverse categorie documenti, 1978–1981.* Turin: CGIL-CISL-UIL Piedmont, Italy.

Imbruglia, Girolamo, ed. 1992. *Il razzismo e le sue storie.* Napoli: Edizioni Scientifiche Italiane.

IRES. 1992. *Uguali e diversi, il mondo culturale, le reti di rapporti: I lavori degli immigrati non Europei a Torino.* Piedmont, Italy: Rosenberg & Sellier.

———. 1995. *Relazione sulla situazione economica sociale e territoriale del Piemonte 1995.* Piedmont, Italy: Rosenberg & Sellier.

———. 1996. *Lavoro, Genere, Etnia.* Turin: IRES.

———. 2000. *Piemonte economico sociale.* Turin: IRES.

Iyob, Ruth. 1995. *The Eritrean Struggle for Independence: Domination, Resistance, Nationalism, 1941–1993.* New York: Cambridge University Press.

Jackson, Peter. 1987. "The Idea of 'Race' and the Geography of Racism." In *Race and Racism: Essays in Social Geography,* ed. Peter Jackson. London: Allen and Unwin.

Jackson, Peter, and Jan Penrose. 1993. Introduction: "Placing 'Race' and Nation." In *Constructions of Race, Place, and Nation,* ed. Peter Jackson and Jan Penrose. Minneapolis: University of Minnesota Press.

Jones, John Paul, and Wolfgang Natter. 1997. "Identity, Space, and Other Uncertainties." In *Space and Social Theory: Interpreting Modernity and Postmodernity,* ed. Georges Benko and Ulf Strohmayer. Cambridge, MA: Blackwell.

Keith, Michael. 1993. "From Punishment to Discipline? Racism, Racialization, and the Policing of Social Control." In *Racism, the City, and the State,* ed. Malcolm Cross and Michael Keith. London: Routledge.

Keith, Michael, and Steve Pile, eds. 1993. *Place and the Politics of Identity.* London: Routledge.

Kertzer, David L. 1980. *Comrades and Christians: Religion and Political Struggle in Communist Italy.* New York: Cambridge University Press.

Knox, Paul, John Agnew, and Linda McCarthy. 2003. *The Geography of the World Economy.* New York: Arnold.

Kopkind, Andrew. 1991. "Communism Bolognese: In Italy Red Is Dead." *Nation,* October 21.

Korten, David C. 1990. *Getting to the Twenty-first Century: Voluntary Action and the Global Agenda.* West Hartford, CT: Kumarian Press.

Kramer, Ralph M. 1992. "Il ruolo delle organizzazioni voluntarie in quattro welfare state: Uno studio comparato." *Polis* 6, no. 3.

Labanca, Nicola, ed. 1992. *L'Africa in Vetrina: Storie di musei e di esposizioni coloniali in Italia.* Treviso: Pagvs Edizioni.

La Spina All'Ochiello. 1979. *L'esperienza dell'intercategoriale donne CGIL-CISL-UIL Attraverso, I Documenti, 1975–78.* Turin, Italy: Musolini Editore.

Levy, Carl, ed. 1996. *Italian Regionalism: History, Identity, and Politics.* Oxford, England: Berg.

Liu, Laura. 2000. "The Place of Immigration in Studies of Geography and Race." *Social and Cultural Geography* 1, no. 2.

Locke, Richard M. 1995. *Remaking the Italian Economy.* Ithaca, NY: Cornell University Press.

Lombroso, Cesare. 1923. *La donna delinquente, la prostituta, e la donna normale.* Milan, Italy: Fratelli Bocca.

Lumley, Robert. 1990. *States of Emergency: Cultures of Revolt in Italy from 1968 to 1978.* London: Verso.

MacGaffey, Janet. 1987. *Entrepreneurs and Parasites: The Struggle for Indigenous Capitalism in Zaire.* Cambridge, England: Cambridge University Press.

Macioti, Maria Immacolata, and Enrico Pugliese. 1991. *Gli immigrati in Italia.* Rome: Laterza.

Maggio, Marvi. 1997. "The Fight for Sociality and Communication: Production of Meanings and Identities. Urban Movements in Italy (1970–1977) Facing the Issue of Public Space: Towards a Conflict on Reproduction of Capital." Unpublished.

Maggiorotti, Piergiorgio. 1993. "La mediazione culturale." Giornata di Studio sul Tema, 17 Dicembre, Centro Interculturale delle Donne, Alma Mater.

Magni, Roberto. 1995. *Gli immigrati in Italia.* Rome: Edizioni Lavoro.

Maher, Vanessa. 1996. "Immigration and Social Identities." In *Italian Cultural Studies: An Introduction,* ed. David Forgacs and Robert Lumley. Oxford: Oxford University Press, 1996.

Maneri, Marcello. 1998. "Immigrati e classi pericolose: Lo statuto dell' 'extracomunitario' nella stampa quotidiana." In *Relazioni etniche stereotipi e pregiudizi: Fenomeno immigratorio ed esclusione sociale,* ed. M. Delle Donne. Rome: Edizione dell'Università Popolare.

———. 2001. "Lo straniero consensuale." In *Da lagoed, lo straniero, e il nemico: Materiali per l'etnografia contemporanea.* Genoa: Costa and Nolan.

Marazziti, Mario, ed. 1993. *L'ospite inatteso: Razzismo e antisemitismo in Italia.* Brescia, Italy: Morcelliana.

Marcellino, Nella. 1975. "La partecipazione femminile e il movimento sindacale." In *Quaderni, Rassegna Sindacale.* Rome: Editrice Sindacale Italiana.

Marcus, George E. 1998. *Ethnography through Thick and Thin.* Princeton, NJ: Princeton University Press.

Marcus, George E., and Michael M. J. Fisher. 1986. *Anthropology as Cultural Critique: An Experimental Moment in the Human Sciences.* Chicago: University of Chicago Press.

Marini, Rolando. 1996. "L'immigrazione e la prospettiva di una societa multiculturale." In *Multiculturalism e democrazia,* ed. Franco Crespi and Robert Segatori. Rome: Donzelli.

Marx, Karl. 1987. *Economic and Philosophical Manuscripts of 1844, and The Communist Manifesto.* Buffalo, NY: Prometheus Books.

Massey, Doreen. 1993. "Power-Geometry and a Progressive Sense of Place." In *Mapping the Futures: Local Cultures, Global Change,* ed. John Bird, Barry Curtis, Tim Putnam, George Robertson, and Lisa Tickner. New York: Routledge.

———. 1994. *Space, Place, and Gender.* Minneapolis: University of Minnesota Press.

Matteo, Sante, ed. 2001. *ItaliAfrica: Bridging Continents and Cultures.* Stony Brook, NY: Forum Italicum.

Mayo, Marjorie, and Gary Craig. 1995. "Community Participation and Empowerment: The Human Face of Structural Adjustment or Tools for Democratic Transformation?" In *Community Empowerment: A Reader in Participation and Development,* ed. Gary Craig and Marjorie Mayo. London: Zed Books.

McDowell, Linda. 1999. *Gender, Identity, and Place: Understanding Feminist Geographies.* Minneapolis: University of Minnesota Press.

McDowell, Linda, and Joanne P. Sharp, eds. 1997. *Space, Gender, Knowledge: Feminist Readings.* London: Arnold.

Melossi, Dario. 2000. "The Other in the New Europe: Migrations, Deviance, Social Control." In *Criminal Policy in Transition,* ed. Andrew Rutherford and Penny Green. Oxford, England: Hart.

———. 2003. "'In a Peaceful Life': Migration and the Crime of Modernity in Europe/Italy." *Punishment and Society,* May 4.

Melotti, Umberto. 1997. "International Migration in Europe: Social Projects and Political Cultures." In *The Politics of Multiculturalism in the New Europe,* ed. Tariq Modood and Pnina Werbner. London: Zed Books.

Melucci, Alberto. 1981. "New Movements, Terrorism, and the Political System: Reflections on the Italian Case." *Socialist Review* 56: 97–136.

Merrill, Heather. 1994. "Gender, Vision, and Image in Manet's *Olympia* and the Contemporary African Migration to Italy." MA thesis, University of California, Berkeley.

———. 2001. "Feminism and Antiracism: International Struggles for Justice." In *Feminism and Antiracism: International Struggles for Justice,* ed. France Winddance Twine and Kathleen Blee. New York: New York University Press.

———. 2004. "Space Agents: Anti-Racist Feminism and the Politics of Scale in Turin, Italy." *Gender, Place, and Culture,* no. 2.

Merrill, Heather, and Donald Carter. 2002. "Inside and Outside Italian Political Culture: Immigrants and Diasporic Politics in Turin." *GeoJournal* 58.

Michelsons, Angelo. 1989. "Local Strategies of Industrial Restructuring and the Changing Relations between Large and Small Firms in Contemporary Italy: The Case of Fiat Auto and Olivetti." *Economy and Society* 18, no. 4.

Migliasso, Angela. 1993. "La mediazione culturale." Unpublished.

Milan Women's Bookstore Collective. 1990. *Sexual Difference: A Theory of Social-Symbolic Practice.* Bloomington: Indiana University Press.

Miles, Robert. 1993. *Racism after "Race Relations."* London: Routledge.

Miles, Robert, and Victor Satzewich. 1990. "Migration, Racism, and 'Postmodern' Capitalism." *Economy and Society* 19, no. 3.

Mingione, Enzo. 1993. "New Urban Poverty and the Crisis in the Citizenship/Welfare System: The Italian Experience." *Antipode* 25, no. 3.

Mohan, Giles. 2002. "The Disappointments of Civil Society: The Politics of NGO Intervention in Northern Ghana." *Political Geography* 21: 125–54.

Mohanty, Chandra. 1991. "Cartographies of Struggle: Third World Women and the Politics of Feminism." In *Third World Women and the Politics of Feminism,* ed. Chandra Talpade Mohanty, Ann Russo, and Lourdes Torres. Bloomington: Indiana University Press.

Moore, Henrietta. 1996. *Space, Text, and Gender: An Anthropological Study of the Marakwet of Kenya.* New York: Guilford Press.

Morokvasic, Mirjana. 1991. "Fortress Europe and Migrant Women." *Feminist Review* 39: 69–84.

Mottura, Giovani ed. 1992. *L'arcipelago immigrazione: Caratteristiche e modelli migratori dei lavoratori stranieri in Italia.* Rome: Ediesse.

Mouffe, Chantal. 1992. "Feminism, Citizenship, and Radical Democratic Politics." In *Feminists Theorize the Political,* ed. Judith Butler and Joan W. Scotts. New York: Routledge.

Mudu, Pierpaolo. 2002. "The Transformation of Rome: An Exploration of New Trends in the Social Geography of the City." IGU "Rights to the City" conference, Rome.

Nash, June. 1984. "The Impact of the Changing International Division of Labor on Different Sectors of the Labor Force." In *Women, Men, and the International Division of Labor,* ed. June Nash and Maria Patricia Fernandez-Kelly. Albany: State University of New York Press.

Negash, Tekeste. 1987. *Italian Colonialism in Eritrea, 1882–1941: Policies, Praxis, and Impact.* Uppsala, Sweden: Almqvist and Wiksell International.

Negri, Antonio. 1996. "Twenty Theses on Marx: Interpretation of the Class Situation Today." In *Marxism beyond Marxism,* ed. Saree Makdisi, Cesare Casarino, and Rebecca E. Karl. New York: Routledge.

Negri, Nicola. 1982. "I nuovi torinesi: Immigrazione, mobilità, e struttura sociale."

In *La città difficile: Equilibri e disugualglianze nel mercato urbano*, ed. Guido Martinotti. Milan, Italy: Franco Angeli.

Niceforo, Alfredo. 1898. *L'Italia barbara contemporanea. Studi e appunti.* Milan, Italy.

Nielsen, Waldemar A. 1979. *The Endangered Sector.* New York: Columbia University Press.

Ong, Aihwa. 1987. *Spirits of Resistance and Capitalist Discipline: Factory Women in Malaysia.* Albany: State University of New York Press.

———. 1990. "Industrialization and Prostitution in Southeast Asia." *Southeast Asia Chronicle,* no. 96.

Paci, Massimo. 1992. *Il mutamento della struttura sociale in Italia.* Bologna, Italy: Il Mulino.

Pankhurst, Richard. 1964. "Italian Settlement Policies in Eritrea and Its Repercussions, 1889–1896." In *Boston University Papers on African History,* vol. 1, ed. Jeffrey Butler. Boston: Boston University Press.

———. 1969. "Fascist Racial Policies in Ethiopia, 1922–1941." *Ethiopia Observer* 10, no. 4.

———. 1998. *The Ethiopians: A History.* Oxford, England: Blackwell.

Parati, Graziella, and Rebecca West, eds. 2002. *Italian Feminist Theory and Practice: Equality and Sexual Difference.* Madison, NJ: Fairleigh Dickinson University Press.

Pasquinelli, Carla. 1984. "Beyond the Longest Revolutions: The Impact of the Italian Women's Movement on Social and Cultural Change." *Praxis International* 4, no. 2 (July).

Passerini, Luisa. 1984. *Torino operaia e fascismo una storia orale.* Rome: Laterza.

Phizacklea, Annie, ed. 1983. *One Way Ticket: Migration and Female Labour.* Boston: Routledge and Kegan Paul.

Pitch, Tamar. 1979. "Notes from within the Italian Women's Movement: How We Talk of Marxism and Feminism." *Contemporary Crises* 3: 1–16.

Pred, Allan. 1990. "In Other Wor(l)ds: Fragmented and Integrated Observations on Gendered Languages, Gendered Spaces, and Local Transformation." *Antipode* 22, no. 1.

———. 1995a. "Out of Bounds and Undisciplined: Social Inquiry and the Current Moment of Danger." *Social Research* 62, no. 4.

———. 1995b. *Recognizing European Modernities: A Montage of the Present.* London: Routledge.

———. 1998. "Memory and the Cultural Reworking of Crisis: Racisms and the Current Moment of Danger in Sweden, or Wanting It like Before." *Society and Space* 16.

———. 2000. *Even in Sweden: Racisms, Racialized Spaces, and the Popular Geographical Imagination.* Berkeley: University of California Press.

Pred, Allan, and Michael Watts. 1992. *Reworking Modernity, Capitalisms and Symbolic Discontent.* New Brunswick, NJ: Rutgers University Press.

Produrre e riproddurre (P&R). 1984. Cambiamenti nel rapporto tra donne e lavoro, 1st convegno internazionale delle donne dei paesi industrializzati promosso dal movimento delle donne di Torino, Turin, Palazzo del Lavoro, April 23–25, 1983. Milan, Italy: Cooperativo Manifesto.

Pugliese, Enrico, ed. 1993. *Razzisti e solidali: L'immigrazione e le radici sociali dell'intolleranza.* Rome: Ediesse.

Putnam, Robert D. 1993. *Making Democracy Work: Civic Traditions in Modern Italy.* Princeton, NJ: Princeton University Press.

Raffy, Serge. 1993. "Prostitution, les nouvelle fililere de l'esclavage." *Le Nouvel Observateur* 25.

Ranci, Costanzo. 1992. "La mobilitazione dell'altruismo: Condizioni e processi di diffusione dell'azione volontariata in Italia." *Polis* 6, no. 3 (December).

Rattansi, Ali, and Sallie Westwood, eds. 1994. *Racism, Modernity, and Identity: On the Western Front.* Cambridge, England: Polity Press.

Reyneri, Emilio. 1998. "The Role of the Underground Economy in Irregular Migration to Italy: Cause or Effect?" *Journal of Ethnic and Migration Studies* 24, no. 2: 313–31.

Riccio, Bruno. 2003. "The Ambivalent Politics of Difference and Equality: The Experiences of Foreign Delegates and Practitioners within a Local Union." Presented at the conference "Comparing U.S. and European Approaches to Issues of Immigration," June 20–21, 2003, University of Bologna, Italy.

Rifkin, Jeremy. 1995. *The End of Work: The Decline of the Global Labor Force and the Dawn of the Post-Market Era.* New York: G. P. Putnam's Sons.

Sabel, Charles F. 1985. *Work and Politics: The Division of Labor in Industry.* Cambridge: Cambridge University Press.

———. 1989. "Flexible Specialization and the Re-emergence of Regional Economies." In *Reversing Industrial Decline: Industrial Structure and Policy in Britain and Her Competitors,* ed. Paul Hirst and Jonathan Zeitlin. New York: St. Martin's Press.

Said, Edward W. 1978. *Orientalism.* New York: Pantheon.

Sandoval, Chela. 1991. "U.S. Third World Feminism: The Theory and Method of Oppositional Consciousness in the Postmodern World." *Genders* 10.

Sassen, Saskia. 1994. "Rethinking Immigration: A Transnational Perspective." Presented at Wenner Gren Foundation conference.

———. 2001. *The Global City: New York, London, Tokyo.* Princeton, NJ: Princeton University Press, 2001.

Sassen-Koob, Saskia. 1984. "Notes on the Incorporation of Third World Women into Wage-Labor through Immigration and Off-Shore Production." *International Migration Review* 18, no. 4.

Sassoon, Donald. 1986. *Contemporary Italy: Politics, Economy, and Society since 1945.* London: Longman.

Sayer, Andrew, and Richard Walker. 1992. *The New Social Economy: Reworking the Division of Labor.* London: Blackwell.

Sbacchi, Alberto. 1985. *Ethiopia under Mussolini: Fascism and the Colonial Experience.* London: Zed Books.

Scagliotti, Laura. N.d. "Corso di Formazione alla Funzione di Mediatrici Culturale, Alma Mater." Unpublished.

Schneider, Jane, ed. 1998. *Italy's "Southern Question": Orientalism in One Country.* Oxford, England: Berg.

Schneider, Jane, and Peter Schneider. 1976. *Cultural and Political Economy in Sicily.* New York: Academic Press.

Sciarrone, Rocco. 1996. "Il lavoro degli altri e gli altri lavori." *Quaderni di Sociologia* 40, no. 11.

Scobie, H. M., S. Mortali, S. Persaud, and P. Docile. 1996. *The Italian Economy in the 1990s.* London: Routledge, European Economics and Financial Centre.

Segre, Anna. 1994. "Turin in the 1980s." In *Europe's Cities in the Late Twentieth Century,* ed. Hugh Clout. Amsterdam: Royal Dutch Geographical Society.

Segre, Claudio G. 1974. *Fourth Shore: The Italian Colonization of Libya.* Chicago: University of Chicago Press.

Simmel, George. 1971. "The Metropolis and Mental Life." In *On Individuality and Social Forms: Selected Writings,* ed. D. Levine. Chicago: University of Chicago Press.

Simon, Rita James, and Caroline B. Brettell, eds. 1986. *International Migration: The Female Experience.* Totowa, NJ: Rowman and Allanheld.

Skrobanek, Siriporn. 1990. "In Pursuit of an Illusion: Thai Women in Europe." *Southeast Asia Chronicle* 96.

Smith, Anna Marie. 1994. *New Right Discourse on Race and Sexuality: Britain, 1968–1990.* Cambridge: Cambridge University Press.

Smith, Neil. 1992. "Contours of a Spatialized Politics: Homeless Vehicles and the Production of Geographical Scale." *Social Text* 33.

Smith, Susan J. 1993. "Residential Segregation and the Politics of Racialization." In *Racism, the City and the State,* ed. Malcolm Cross and Michael Keith. London: Routledge.

Sniderman, Paul, Pierangelo Peri, Rui J. P. de Figueiredo Jr., and Thomas Piazza, eds. 2000. *The Outsider: Prejudice and Politics in Italy.* Princeton, NJ: Princeton University Press.

Solomos, John, and John Wrench. 1993. *Racism and Migration in Western Europe.* Oxford, England: Berg.

Spivak, Gayatri Chakravorty. 1987. *In Other Worlds: Essays in Cultural Politics.* New York: Methuen.

———. 1999. *A Critique of Postcolonial Reason: Toward a History of the Vanishing Present.* Cambridge, MA: Harvard University Press.

Spotts, Frederic, and Theodor Wieser. 1986. *Italy, a Difficult Democracy: A Survey of Italian Politics.* Cambridge: Cambridge University Press.

Stolcke, Verena. 1995. "Talking Culture: New Boundaries, New Rhetorics of Exclusion in Europe." *Current Anthropology.*

Storper, Michael, and Richard Walker. 1989. *The Capitalist Imperative: Territory, Technology, and Industrial Growth.* New York: Blackwell.

Tabet, Paola. 1997. *La Pelle Giusta.* Turin, Italy: Einaudi.

Taguieff, Pierre-André. 1990. "The New Cultural Racism in France." *Telos,* no. 83.

Torti, Maria Teresa. 1995. "Identità e passione, la bussola interiore e la tempesta del 'magnetismo.'" In *Culture del conflitto giovani metropoli comunicazione,* ed. Massimo Canevacci, Roberto De Angelis, and Francesca Mazzi. Rome: Costa and Nolan.

Trouillot, Michel-Rolph. 1994. "Culture, Color, and Politics in Haiti." In *Race,* ed. Steven Gregory and Roger Sanjek. New Brunswick, NJ: Rutgers University Press.

———. 2003. *Global Transformations: Anthropology and the Modern World.* New York: Palgrave Macmillan.

Twine, France Winddance, and Kathleen Blee, eds. 2001. *Feminism and Antiracism: International Struggles for Justice.* New York: New York University Press.

Varagliotti, Giuseppe. 1993. "La mediazione culturale." Giornata di Studio sul Tema, Centro Interculturale delle Donne, Alma Mater.

Vasta, Ellie. 1993. "Rights and Racism in a New Country of Immigration: The Italian Case." In *Racism and Migration in Western Europe,* ed. John Wrench and John Solomos. Oxford, England: Berg.

Vecchi, Benedetto. 1994. "Frammenti di una diversa sfera pubblica." In *Comunita virtuali: I centri sociali in Italia,* Francesco Adinolfi et al. Rome: Manifestolibri.

Viarengo, Maria Abbebu. 1990. "Scirscir 'n Demma: Autobiography of Maria Abbebu Viarengo." Unpublished.

Vinay, Paul. 1993. "Family Life Cycle and the Informal Economy in Central Italy." In *Work beyond Employment in Advanced Capitalist Countries: Classic and Contemporary Perspectives on the Informal Economy,* vol. 1, ed. Louis Ferman, Louise Berndt, and Stuart Henry. Lewiston: Edwin Mellen Press.

Volpato, Giuseppe. 1996. *Il caso fiat: Una strategia di riorganizzazione e di rilancio.* Turin, Italy: ISEDI.

Ward, David. 1997. "'Italy' in Italy: Old Metaphors and New Racisms in the 1990s." In *Revisioning Italy: National Identity and Global Culture,* ed. Beverly Allen and Mary Russo. Minneapolis: University of Minnesota Press.

Waterman, Peter. 1998. *Globalization, Social Movements, and the New Internationalisms.* London: Mansell.

Wieviorka, Michel. 1993. *Lo spazio del razzismo.* Milan, Italy: Il Saggiatore.

Wolch, Jennifer. 1989. "The Shadow State: Transformations in the Voluntary Sector." In *The Power of Geography: How Territory Shapes Social Life,* ed. Jennifer Wolch and Michael Dear. Boston: Unwin Hyman.

Young, Robert. 1995. *Colonial Desire: Hybridity in Theory, Culture, and Race.* London: Routledge.

Zaldini, Giovanna. 1992. "Il centro interculturale delle donne di Torino." Unpublished.

Zincone, Giovanna. 1994. *Uno schermo contro il razzismo: Per una politica dei diritti utili.* Rome: Donzelli Editore.

Zumaglino, Piera. 1996. *Femminismi a Torino: Pari e dispari,* with contributions by A. Miglietti and A. Piccirillo, introduction by I. Damilano. Milan, Italy: FrancoAngeli.

Zumaglino, Piera, and Annamaria Garelli. 1995. *La nuova Africa: Un laboratorio di solidarietà femminili.* Turin, Italy: Casa delle Donne, Edizione Realizzata con il Contributo del Researu a 1841.

for, 20, 21–22, 26, 205n.4; gender identity binding participants in, 170, 179; hegemony and difference in, 170–81; hierarchy within, 171, 173–78; initiatives for empowering migrant women, 25–26; intercultural mediation and, 17; Italian customers of, 26, 165; laundromat, 23, 40, 165, 172; location of, 20, 22; making common place at, 181–87; as mediator for jobs for migrants, 38, 178; membership of, 26, 167–70; migrant women who initiated, 167–68; neoliberal-Marxist tension reflected in, 156; NGOs and, 157–60, 177; objective of, 21, 22; operation within Italian and Turinese institutional practice, 189–90; organizational structure of, 160–61; original conception of, 16–17; as place of convergence, 161; political and social activities of members, 26–27; politics of space and scale, 160–64; proposal for, 18, 20; role as help organization, debate over, 177–78; seizure of space facilitated by, 7–8, 189–90; seminars and meetings organized by, 23–24; small-scale entrepreneurial activities at, 16–17, 34, 39; as social politics in process, 192; tension about commonsense identification of participants as feminists, 178–80; tensions based on asymmetry in material conditions, 162, 180–81; theater group (Almateatro), 23, 25, 37, 121, 183–87; training courses at, 21–22, 31–34; Turin feminists and, 20–22, 34, 123–24, 148–54, 164, 167, 174–80; Turkish bath in, 23, 24, 25, 26, 40, 121, 165, 172; uniqueness in

encouraging interethnic bonds, 171–72; work as central theme in, 119–22; work cooperatives, 24–25, 40, 119, 120, 158, 160, 172–73, 175
Almateatro, 23, 25, 37, 121, 183–87
alterity, codes of, 100–101
Alternative Femministe (AF), 132–33
"altero-referentiality," system of, 77
Alvarez, Sonia, 159
American feminism, 215n.5; egalitarian tradition, 218n.17; influence of literature of, 132
amnesty for illegal immigrants, 110; in 1990, 61; in 1995, 70, 71
AN (Alliance Nazionale), xxii, 107, 109, 112, 114, 212n.48
anagrafe (registry office), 14, 71, 208n.15
Andall, Jacqueline, 200
anthropological vs. geographical research, xv–xvi
anti-immigrant demonstrations, xxii, 114; in San Salvario (1995), 84, 109
anti-immigrant organizations, 90–91
anti-immigrant violence, xxi–xxiii, 105
antiracist politics, emergence of feminist, 8–17
antiracist protest, xxi, 84; of November 19, 1995, 111–15
AO (Avanguardia Operaia), 130–31, 151
apprenticeships, 3, 4, 15, 32–33
Arabs, North Africans described as, 174
Arendt, Hannah, 130
aristocracy, 42, 211n.26
Artisanal Association, 3, 4
Arush, Starlin Abdi, 216n.12
Assistance organizations, Italian, 177–78. *See also* Catholic organizations
Associazione Italiana Donne Africane. *See* AIDA (Associazione Italiana Donne Africane)

authoritarianism and patriarchy, 130
automobile industry. See Fiat in Turin
autonomy, drive for women's, 136
Avanguardia Operaia (AO), 130–31, 151

Bagnasco, Arnaldo, 42, 51, 206n.10
Battaglino, Maria Teresa, 129–30, 151–52
Belpiede, Anna, 27, 30, 33–34
Berlusconi, Silvio, 205n.4
Berman, Marshall, 56
biological racism, 210n.26
birthing practices: migrant vs. Italian, 26
birth rate in Italy, 62
black bodies: perceived threat of, 98
Blunt, Alison, xix
bodily concepts of immigrant women, 25–26
Borghezio, Mario, 109
Boso, Ermino, 109–10
Bossi, Umberto, xxii
Bossi-Fini legislation, 65
bourgeoisie, 50; CLD and feminist attack on hegemony of, 133; demand for domestic servants by, 60–62; petty, 50. See also middle class
Boutallaka, Abdella, 114
Bread and Chocolate (film), 97
bureaucratic system, Italian, 29, 30; civil servants, 29–30, 34, 71, 208n.15; incorporation of NGOs into, 159–60
Bureau of Women of the EEC, 142
business: social and legal requirements to establish, 15. See also self-employment
Butler, Judith, 97–98

CAD (computer-assisted design), 44
Caldwell, Lesley, 134–35

Calloni, Marite, 152–53, 215n.10
capital: internationalization of, 57
capitalism: disintegration as integrative force in modern, 56; feminist collectives' critique of, 132; neoliberal, 195–96, 198, 200–201; recent changes in global, 156. See also globalization
capital mobility: indirect consequences of global, xxiii
carabinieri (military police), 105
Cariplo (Italian bank): employment initiative involving, 118
Caritas, xxvi, 11, 158
Carpo, Gianpiero, 114
Carter, Donald, 42, 50
Casa delle Donne (Women's House), xxviii, 11, 19, 20, 133, 142, 148, 149, 150, 179, 203n.5
Casbah. See San Salvario, neighborhood of
cassa integrazione: Fiat workers forced into, 45, 46
Castellani, Mayor, 214n.78
Castronovo, Valerio, 42
Catholic Church: central role of women in family in, 134–35; crisis in San Salvario and, 83–84; illegal immigrants and, 108; support for migrant cultural traditions, 113, 114
Catholic organizations, 11; Alma Mater's use of voluntary networks, 38; as employment agencies for domestic workers, xx, 61, 208n.10; missionary work in Africa, xxv–xxvi; privileged relationship to funding sources, 158; SERMIG, 156, 216n.3
Celotto, Patricia, 133–34, 215n.8, 215n.10
center and periphery: models of, 207n.3
Center for Information on the Health

communication, intercultural, 32–33: *See also* cultural mediation

Communist Refoundation (Rifondazione Comunista), 109, 111, 112, 114, 168, 205n.13

competition: for mediator positions, 35; among women, 197

comportment, different models of, 100

computer-assisted design (CAD), 44

Comunicazioni Rivoluzionarie (CR), 132

Confederazione Generale Italiana del Lavoro. See CGIL (Confederazione Generale Italiana del Lavoro) trade union

Confederazione Italiana Sindacati Lavoratori (CISL), 11, 114

Confindustria, 206n.9

consciousness-raising, 134

Constantino, Rina, 214n.3

construction: migrant men in, 70

Consultori (health clinics), 135, 140, 151, 215n.6

contraception, 135

cooperatives, work, xxi, 6, 158, 160, 172–73; initiated by women in Africa, 146–48; La Talea, 24–25, 40, 119, 120, 165, 172, 175, 182–83; Mediazione, 24, 40, 172–73, 175; as model for dealing with economic crisis, 144–45

Coordination against Racism (Coordinamento Control il Razzismo), 91

counterpolitics, 190

countries of origin, xii; Alma Mater members involved in political and social activities in, 26; migrants organized according to, 172

CR (Comunicazioni Rivoluzionarie), 132

crime, organized, 68, 105

crime in San Salvario, 88, 91; crisis and, 79–85

crime rates, 53

criminalization of migrants: political consciousness among migrants awakened by, 112–13; in San Salvario, 103–6

Croce, 76

Crocetta market, 10

cultural alienation, 27

cultural differences: cultural defensiveness among migrants and, 113; in definition of "noise," 96–97; intolerance of, 93–94; logic of, in racialist discourse, xviii; mutually incomprehensible, notion of, 93; as part of war of position, 192; tolerance for, trade union defense of, 113–14

cultural-ideological forms of power, 76

cultural meanings, gender and race classification constructed by, 200

cultural mediation, 94; as experimental category of work, 29; precariousness of, 35; problems with, 34–35; purposes of, 29–30

cultural mediators, 17; competition for positions, 35; example of, 122–23; qualifications for, 172; training course for, 21–22, 31–34; women's critical role as, 32

cultural norms, 212n.37

cultural racism, xviii–xix, 191, 203n.1, 211n.27; new, 93–94, 210n.26; roots of, 210n.26

cultural social-spatial processes, racialization through, xvii–xviii

culture: beliefs and practices as medium for defense of migrant dignity, 163–64; as integral to modern European forms of politics and state power, 76; modernist notion

of, 210n.26; produced and reproduced in negotiations of everyday
life, 191; reification of, 94
cultures of poverty, 211n.27

day care at Alma Mater, 140, 161, 165
decentralization of production and
decision making, 47; at Fiat, 45
De Certeau, Michel, 85
decolonization, xxv
de Lauretis, Teresa, xi, 135, 189, 190–91,
217n.14
Del Boca, Angelo, 101–2
Demau (Demistificazione Autoritarismo, or Demystification of
Authoritarianism), 130, 151
Democratic Left (DS), 168
Democratic Party of the Left. See PDS
(Partito Democratico della Sinistra)
demographic shift in Italy in 1970s,
199
dependency of migrant women on
feminist Italians, 176
deportation, 65, 83; legal facilitation
of process of, 110, 111
developing countries: growing pressure to migrate from, 156
development, economic, xxiv; uneven
distribution of development sites,
xxiii; women speaking out against,
194–95
developmental model of gender relations within families, 145
Dickie, John, 99
difesa della razza (defense of the race):
Fascist norms of, 130
difference(s): color as axis of, 172–74;
global capitalism and production
and reproduction of, 7; hegemony
and difference in Alma Mater,
170–81; language of, 191; within
multiscaled power relations, racial

and gender classifications based on,
7–8; politics of, xiii, xiv, xix, xxvi.
See also cultural differences
differentialism, 93
differentialist racism. *See* cultural
racism
discrimination: double or triple forms
of, 123; gender, 123; legal system of,
in African colonies, 102–3; against
migrant women, 123, 205n.11;
against southern migrants, 100;
against the young, 51
disintegration: as integrative force in
modern capitalism, 56
dispossessed sectors: labor force of,
xxiv
division of labor, 207n.5; international, xxiii–xxvi, 55–57, 156;
sexual, 14–15, 57, 133, 136, 137
domestic service, 6, 13–15; Alma
Mater and work in, 178; association
with servitude and exploitation,
39; care linked with housewife
labor transformed into paid, 200;
class structures and ability to hire,
60–62, 200; contracts for, 62; costs
of social contributions for, 61;
demand for domestic servants, 41,
60–62, 199, 208n.11; elder care, 41,
62, 178; inferiority derived from,
145; migrant women in, 13–14,
60–63, 122; P&R's view of, 145–46;
varying experiences in, 63
Donini, Elisabetta, 194, 214n.3,
215n.10
Donne in Nero (Women in Black), 149,
195, 216n.13
Donne in Sviluppo (Women in Development), 19, 20, 21, 32, 146, 147–48,
160, 176, 177
doppio lavoro ("double work"), 68–69
"double militancy," model of, 133

downsizing: at Fiat, 43–47; reduction in manufacturing labor force, 56
DS (Democratic Left), 168

Eastern European migrants, 171
economia sommersa. See informal economy
economic determinism, 76
economic development: contemporary, xxiii, xxiv, 194–95
economic miracle, Italian, 43, 214n.2
economy. See informal economy; restructuring, industrial
education: Alma Mater training courses, 21–22, 31–34; formally educated migrants, 71, 167–68; lack of fit between labor market demands and, 50–51, 150-hours courses, 31, 136, 140–41, 215n.7
egalitarianism, American and British feminist traditions of, 218n.17
elder care, 41, 62, 178
employee insurance coverage, 61, 70, 110–11, 214n.65
empowerment: Alma Mater initiatives for, 25–26; of civil society, globalization and, 155–56; different meaning for Italians and migrants, 178; notion of female, 164; Turin feminists and, 179; use of term, 217n.7
entrepreneurship: in Africa, promotion of women's, 147–48; Alma Mater and small-scale, 16–17, 34, 39; research and development, 48–49. See also self-employment
equality: American and British feminist tradition of egalitarianism, 218n.17; cultural mediation to promote, 33–34; Italian feminist argument against struggles for, 134
equal opportunity: cultural mediation to promote access to, 33–34

Eritrea: Italian colonialism in, 101, 102
Escobar, Arturo, 159
Espresso, L' (magazine), 79, 97, 107, 108
Ethiopia, Italian campaign against, 101–3
ethnic associations, 6, 172, 205n.10; See also Alma Mater
ethnic goods: expanding taste for, 64
Europe: history of ties of postcolonial migrants with, xxiii, xxv–xxvi, 101–3, 212n.39. See also colonialism
European Economic Union, 21–22
European Union: concern over Italy becoming third world entryway to, 107–8; immigration as high-level political priority in, 203n.3
Europol, 110
exchange rates, global, xxv
exploitation: of domestic workers, 39, 63; in informal economy, 69, 70; of prostitutes, 68
exploration in Africa, 101
expulsion: immigration debates about, 107. See also deportation
extracomunitari: as metaphor for crime, 92–93
extracomunitari in post-Fordist Turin, 55–73; areas of employment of, 60–66; connections to Italy, 58; female, 60–65; globalization and international division of labor, 55–57; informal economy and, 60, 61, 66–71, 208n.8; job vulnerability of, 59–60; male, 58–59, 65–66; perception and classification of, 71–73

Faccioli, Gianna, 215n.5
factories: disappearance of, 52–53; gender relations within family mirrored in hierarchies of, 138–39; migrant men working in, 65–66;

women working in, 126–27, 152–53,
215n.9. *See also* Fiat in Turin
familial knowledge of women: expansion into public sphere of, 32
familism: Italian, 217n.16
family: central role of Italian, income
reduction effects cushioned by,
46–47; developmental model of
gender relations within, 145; gender relations within, mirrored in
factory hierarchies, 138–39
family labor: Italian practice of using,
69
Fanon, Frantz, xi, 98, 212n.37
Fascist Italy: colonial empire of, 101–3;
defense of the race, norms of, 130;
Italian Fascist Party (MSI), xxii,
107, 212n.48
female migrants. *See* migrant women
female subjectivity, 186
"female work." *See* "women's work"
feminism: Alma Mater and, 18,
178–80; American, 132, 215n.5,
218n.17; criticism of, by migrant
women, 123; egalitarian tradition, 218n.17; feminist collectives,
131–32, 135, 137; Milan, 124, 134;
mistrust of, 131; self-consciousness
as "critical method" of, 190–91.
See also feminists, Turin
feminist collectives, 131–32, 135, 137
feminist geographers, xvi–xvii, xix
feminists, Turin, xxvii, 117–54; absence of young Italians among,
148, 150, 153–54; acute sense of
workerism among, 178; Alma
Mater and, 20–22, 34, 123–24,
148–54, 164, 167, 174–80; comfortable living conditions of, 167; distance from state institutions and
political parties, 34, 137; extensive
experience and knowledge of,

150–53; feminist antiracist politics, emergence of, 8–17; feminist
as activist, 134; influences on, 124;
Intercategoriale Delegati Donne
CGIL-CSIL-UIL and, 135–42, 143,
151; New Left extraparliamentary
groups and, 128–35; Produrre e
Riprodurre and, 19, 20–21, 31, 32,
142–48, 150, 175; Unione Donne
Italiane (UDI) and, 124–28; work
as central theme of, 160
feminization of women, mother's role
in, 184–85
Ferraro, Jessica, 215n.10
Fiat in Turin, xxv, 41–49; domination
over Turin society and culture, 42;
expansion to urban peripheries,
43; Fordist strategies of 1950s and
1960s, 43–44, 206n.1; increased
productivity and profits for, 47; indirect influences of, 42; industrial
restructuring and downsizing of,
43–47; joint venture with General
Motors Company, 45; layoff process at, 45–46; product strategy at,
44–45; southern Italians migrating to work for, 99; strikes and absenteeism at, 206n.3; total quality
system adopted by, 206n.6
first-generation migrants, 12–13, 30
flea market *(balon),* 10
Fofi, Goffredo, 100
Fordist organizational style and production strategy, 43–44, 206n.1;
disappearance of, 49
Fortress Europe (film series), 110,
213n.64
funding for Alma Mater, 20, 21–22,
26, 205n.4

Gallino, Luciano, 42
Gallo, Don Piero, 82–84, 103, 108, 113

of, xvii; ordering of civilizations, 210n.26; of power and meaning, xviii
high-tech labor market: preparing workers for current, 51
hiring and firing system, "flexible," 52
historical geographies, constellations of ongoing, xiii
Hobsbawm, Eric, 77
Hobson, Sherran, 206n.6
Hot Autumn of 1969, 127, 214n.1
housing: landlord abuses, 82, 83, 89, 108; in San Salvario, 89; for southern Italians in Turin, lack of, 99

identity: within different power relations, shifting, xvii, xviii; gender identity binding Alma Mater members, 170, 179; of Italians, transformed by presence of migrants, 112; mother-daughter bond as integral to woman's, 185; multiple and overlapping, 191–92; political, of *immigrati/immigrazione*, xiii; racialized national identities, xvii
ideology: ideological misconceptions of migrants, xiv; as integral to modern European forms of politics and state power, 76; right-wing and anti-immigrant, xxii
illegal immigrants, 58, 83; amnesty (regularization) for, 61, 70, 71, 110; legislation against, xxi, 108; media portrayal of, 84; number in Italy, 213n.51; political debates about, 107–11; prostitutes, 80
Il Manifesto (newspaper), 81
Immigrant Consulta, 84, 114, 205n.10, 209n.19
immigrant rights, 11
immigrants. *See* illegal immigrants; migrants

immigration, large-scale, xx
immigration legislation, xx–xxi: effect on Italian citizens' rights, 111; Law 943, xxi; Martelli Law, xxi, xxvii, 30, 84, 107–8; reawakening of political debate about, 106–11; San Salvario of Turin as centerpiece in debates about, 79–80, 84; Trevi and Schengan agreements and, xxi, 107, 212n.49, 213n.49
immigration policies, xx–xxi, 203n.3
income reduction, 46–47
industrial belts in Turin, 43
industrial relations and wages, new agreement on, 47
industrial restructuring. See restructuring, industrial
industrial robotics, 44
industrial workers, percentage of, 49
informal economy, 60, 61, 66–71, 208n.8; *doppio lavoro* ("double work"), 68–69; expansion of, 52, 68, 69; familial labor used in, 69; gender and, 69–70; labor costs in, 69; in social services, 69–70; street sellers, 65; undocumented work in, 38
informants, xxviii–xxix
Informazioni Salute per Immigrati (Center for Information on the Health of Immigrants), 32
injury on job, 68
INPS (Istituto Nazionale della Previdenza Sociale), 110–11, 214n.65
Institute for Social and Economic Research (IRES), xxix, 12–14, 41, 94; studies, 47, 61, 63, 69–70, 89
Intercategoriale Delegati Donne CGIL-CISL-UIL, 135–42, 143, 151, 153, 215n.8; goals of, 137–40; leadership, 136; 150-hours courses operated by, 140–41; parameters of

union structure limiting, 141–42; women drawn to, 136

intercultural communication, 32–33

intercultural mediation, practice of, 17. *See also* cultural mediation; cultural mediators

interdependencies, global economic, 156

interethnic associations, 6, 12. *See also* Alma Mater

international division of labor, xxiii–xxvi, 156; globalization and, 55–57

international feminism of Produrre e Riprodurre, 142–48, 150

internationalization: of capital, 57; of national economies, xx. *See also* globalization

International Labor Organization, 172

International Monetary Fund, xxv

interunion organization, 135–42

intolerance, xxi–xxiii, 93–94

IRES. *See* Institute for Social and Economic Research (IRES)

Irigaray, Luce, 134

Islamic migrants, 11

Israel: international peace network begun in, 216n.13

ISTAT (Istituto Nazionale de Statistica), 58

Italian Communist Party (PCI), 3, 4, 13, 168, 204n.2, 205n.13; New Left extraparliamentary groups emerging from, 128–35; Unione Donne Italiane (UDI) as flanking organization of, 125–28

Italian Confederation of Workers' Unions (CISL), 11, 114

Italian economic miracle (1958–1963), 43, 214n.2

Italian Fascist Party (MSI), xxii, 107, 212n.48

Italian General Federation of Labor. *See* CGIL (Confederazione Generale Italiana del Lavoro) trade union

Italian Leagues, xxii

Italian Social Movement (MSI), xxii, 107, 212n.48

Italian women: employed outside of home, 199; problematic relationship between migrant and, 200; use of Turkish bath in Alma Mater, 26, 165. *See also* feminists, Turin

Italy: aging population of, 41, 62, 178; attraction of West African and postcolonial migrants to, xxiii; birth rates in, 62; demographic shift in 1970s, 199; immigration policy, xx–xxi; international migration to, xx; links between Africa and, xxv–xxvi, 101–3, 212n.39; racial system in, 98; as third world entryway to European Union, concern over, 107–8; transformation from country of emigration to country of immigration, xii, xx

job polarization: increasing degree of, 52

job vulnerability, 59–60, 138–39

John Paul II, Pope, xxv

Kafila, 80–81

Keith, Michael, 104

kinship, doppio lavoro embedded in Italian forms of, 69

Kurdish festival in San Salvario, 113

labor market: global, 196–97; lack of fit between education and demands of, 50–51; polarization in highly differentiated, 198–99; post-Fordism and insecurity in,

189; women's fit in, 143; women's job vulnerability in, 138–39. *See also* division of labor; informal economy

labor migration: postwar vs. contemporary, 203n.2

labor movement: "150 hours" of courses program for workers, 31, 136, 140–41, 215n.7; peak in late 1960s, 214n.1; symbolic end of Italian, 45–46, 206n.7; Unione Donne Italiane (UDI) and, 124–28. *See also* trade unions

landlord abuses, 82, 83, 89, 108

La Talea, 24–25, 40, 119, 120, 165, 172, 175; ethnic fundraising dinner for Zairean woman (1996), 182–83

Latin American migrants: ambiguous category of, 171

laundromat, Alma Mater, 23, 40, 165, 172

lavoro autonomo. See self-employment

lavoro nero. See informal economy

Law 943, xxi

Law 39 (Martelli Law), xxi, xxvii, 30, 84, 107–8

layoffs at Fiat, 45–46

left political culture: cooperatives of Italian left, 158; Turin feminism embedded in, 128–35

Lega Nord (Lega Lumbard, Northern League), xxii, 107, 109–10, 111, 112, 114, 212n.48, 213n.50

legislation. *See* immigration legislation

Lewis, Oscar, 211n.27

liberalization of trade restrictions, xxiii

liberal philosophy of individual freedom and self-help, 216n.1

library, Alma Mater, 165

Libya: Italian colonialism in, 101

license: for hairstylists, 15; for street sellers, 65

lighter-skinned migrants: belief about preferential treatment given to, 162

Lingotto, 9, 206n.1

Locke, Richard, 206n.1, 206n.3

Lombroso, Cesare, 101

Lotta Continua, 130, 151

Lotta Femminista, 132

lowest earning sectors: demand for laborers in, xxiv, xxv. *See also* domestic service; service sector

Luna Nera (play), 183–87

Maastricht Treaty (1993), 110

MacKinnon, Catharine, 190

Madama Cristina Market, 90

madame system *(madamism)*, 102–3

Mafioso, 68

Maggio, Marvi, 216n.14

Maggiorotti, Piergiorgio, 29–30

Maher, Vanessa, 12, 214n.3

male migrants, 58–59; temporary contract jobs of, 65–66

Manconi, Luigi, 109

manufacturing: side effects of radical dispersal of, 56–57. *See also* Fiat in Turin

markets, open, 9–10

marocchino (southern Italians), 100

marriage to Italian men, 122–23, 167

Martelli, Claudio, xxi

Martelli Law (Law 39), xxi, xxvii, 30, 84, 107–8

Marx, Karl, 125, 144

Marxism: tension between neoliberal self-help philosophy and, 155–56, 216n.1; women's movement and first major break with, 129

Massey, Doreen, xv, xvi, 7

Masslo, Jerry, xxi

mass production: Fordist strategies of, 43, 206n.1

maternity leave, 140

Mazzacurati, Carlo, 67
media: attention to crisis in San Salvario, 79–85, 103; portrayal of clandestine migrants, 84
mediator: social category of, 204n.1. *See also* cultural mediation; cultural mediators
Mediazione, 24, 40, 172–73, 175
medical model of health and deterioration, 100–101
medium-sized firms, increase in, 47–48
Melotti, Umberto, 213n.51
memory: colonial imaginary in familial and collective, 103
meridionali (southern migrants), 99–101
Methnani, Salah, 9
methodology, xxvii–xxix
middle class: broadening, increasingly female, 60–61, 197, 198; demand for domestic servants by, 60–62; percentage of white-collar workers in Turin, 49–50; polarization between working-class women and, 198; women in feminist collectives, 131–32
migrant networks, 64
migrants: as alien intruders, xviii; classified as uneducated and unskilled, 71; classified in relation to assumed spatial origins, 71–73; countries of origin, xii, 172; first-generation, 12–13, 30; government representation for, 209n.19; as inheritors of activist Italian tradition, 153–54; mixed Italian reactions to, xxii–xxiii; pervasive ideological misconceptions of, xiv; political consciousness among, 112–13; political identity as *immigrati/immigrazione* claimed by, xiii; role in Italy's shifting political

culture, xiv; from same nations, differences between, 10–11; as scapegoats, 53; selective perception of, 97; viewed as devoid of political significance, xiv
migrant women, xiii–xiv; categories of Alma Mater participants, 167–70; cultural classification of, 5–6; daily life in Turin experienced by, 1–5, 167–70; dependence on feminist Italians within Alma Mater, 176; discrimination and marginalization of, 123, 205n.11; domestic service employment of, 6, 13–15, 39, 41, 60–63, 122, 145–46, 178, 199, 200, 208n.11; first generation of, 12–13, 30; formally educated, 71, 167–68; marriage to Italian men, 122–23, 167; newcomers to Turin, 168–69; as self-described political soldiers, 18; shifting identities within different power relations, xvii, xviii; stereotypes of, 66–67, 78, 169, 208n.2; work world of, 13–15, 63–64
migration: innovative thought inspired by, 204n.6
Milan: women's collectives of, 133
Milan feminism, 124, 134
military aid from superpowers, xxv
Ministry of Social Affairs, 205n.4
Mirafiori, 44, 53, 206n.1, 206n.5
missionary work: Catholic, xxv–xxvi
mixed economy of welfare, 157–58
mobility: social groups' distinct relationships to, xvi
modular system of interchangeable components: automobile as, 44
Mohanty, Chandra, xii
monocultura, Italian, 27–28
Moore, Henrietta, xv

political consciousness among migrants, 112–13

politics: of difference, xiii, xiv, xix, xxvi; feminist antiracist, emergence of, 8–17; racial, 106–11; of space and scale, 160–64; spatial politics of gender, xiv, xvii, 1–22

polygenist arguments, 210n.26

Po River, 10

Porta Palazzo market, 10

postcolonial migrants, xiii; Alma Mater as alliance between Italian women and, 6–7; history of ties with Europe, xxiii, xxv–xxvi, 101–3, 212n.39; marked as physically and culturally distinct, 71; relationship with Europeans, 164; subjectivities, 190. *See also* migrant women

poverty, cultures of, 211n.27

power relations: appropriation of women's bodies by medical profession and familial institutions, 141; cultural-ideological forms of power, 76; entwined at different scales, xvi–xviii; in everyday world of civil society, 75–76; gender and race classification constructed by, 199, 200; identities of women migrants shifting within different, xvii, xviii; between poor and wealthy nations, 212n.37; recognizing broad matrix of, 164

P&R. *See* Produrre e Riprodurre (P&R, Production and Reproduction)

practices: based on respective positions in European society, 5; birthing, migrant vs. Italian, 26; criminalization of migrants in San Salvario, 103–6; daily, mediated by local and broader Western assumptions about differences, 170; madame system in African colonies, 102–3

praxis, ethico-political dimension of human, 76

Pred, Allan, xv, 75

prejudice toward migrants, 15

process technologies: Fiat's investment in new, 44, 46

production and reproduction: interplay between, 143–44, 215n.11

Produrre e Riprodurre (P&R, Production and Reproduction), 19, 20–21; courses training cultural mediators, 31, 32; international feminism of, 142–48, 150; right and obligation to direct Alma Mater, 175

prostitution, 6, 15, 63; alternatives to, 39; Catholic aid to former prostitutes, 38; conditions of, 67–68; judicial actions against criminal exploitation, 68; organized crime and, 68; policing of Italian, 212n.43; in San Salvario, 80–81, 104; stereotypes of migrant women as prostitutes, 66–67, 78, 208n.2

protest, social: anti-immigrant demonstrations, xxii, 84, 109, 114; antiracist, xxi, 84, 111–15; social cooperatives and voluntary associations equated with, 158–59

psychological internalization of oppression, 130

public clinics (Consultori pubblici), 215n.6

Pugliese, Enrico, 61–62, 93

race: classifications constructed with elastic boundaries, 170–71; crisis in San Salvario and, 79–85; differential location within multiscaled relations of power, xvi; historical construction of, xvii, 98–99; power relations based on racial classifica-

tions, 199; southern Italians classified as separate, 101; spatialization
of, 85, 104; spatial politics of, xiv,
1–22

racialization: through cultural social-
spatial processes, xvii–xviii; modernist project of, xvii; of people
and places in Italy, xvii–xix; racialized stereotypes, 71–73; of space,
75–79, 84–85, 104

racial politics, 106–11

racial system in Italy, 98

racism: within Alma Mater, 173–74;
Alma Mater and challenge to
Italian, 21; biological, 210n.26;
colonialism and, 101–3, 212n.39;
cultural, xviii–xix, 93–94, 191,
203n.1, 210n.26, 211n.27; denial of,
92–93, 98, 103; among foreigners,
174; grassroots politics of difference in response to, xiii; intensity
of, in Turin, 49, 53; migrants perceived as threat, 97–98; in new and
reinvigorated forms of right-wing
and mainstream political discourse, 77; racialized accretions of
the past, 98–103; reincarnated in
language of "cultural difference,"
93, 94; in San Salvario, fighting
against, 91

rationalization of supplier network of
Fiat, 44–45

real wages, reduction in, 46–47, 53

recession of mid-1970s, 56

Red Cross, Somalia relief effort of,
217n.13

Reggio Parco, 20, 164

regionalism, traditional Italian, xxii

registry office *(anagrafe)*, 71, 208n.15

regularization of illegal workers (amnesty), 61, 70, 71, 110

religious beliefs: as medium for defense of migrant dignity, 163–64;
range of migrant religious affiliations, 11; religious institutions in
San Salvario, 86

remittance money, 58–59

Reprendiamoci la Vita (Let's Take
Back Our Lives), 141

reproduction: interplay between
production and, 143–44, 215n.11;
P&R and issues of, 145

research: anthropological vs. geographical, xv

research and development entrepreneurship, 48–49

residence and work permits: for employed illegal immigrants, 110;
expiration of, 70–71; Martelli bill
and, 108; permission of stay, 38,
70–71, 81

reskilling of workers, 51

resources, economic and political:
Italians in control of, 176; tension
and struggles over access to, 162,
174, 183

restructuring, industrial, xix–xx,
37–54: at Fiat, 43–47; global
economic restructuring, xiii, xv,
xxiii–xxvi, 199; new "social contract" and, 47; P&R conference to
address contraction of jobs due
to, 144; shifting world of Turin's
workers, 49–54; small- and
medium-sized firm proliferation,
47–48; Turin as company town in
transition, 41–49; vulnerability of
women to effects of, 137–38

Rete, 114

Reyneri, Emilio, 66, 111

Rifkin, Jeremy, 157–58

Rifondazione Comunista (Communist
Refoundation), 109, 111, 112, 114,
168, 205n.13

rights: immigrant, 11; women's, 179–80; worker, 68
Robotgate, 44
robotics, industrial, 44
"Rom," category of, 171
Rome, women's collectives of, 133
Rose, Gillian, xix

Said, Edward, 212n.37
San Salvario, neighborhood of, 78–115: anti-immigrant demonstration in, 84, 109; criminalization and policing in, 103–6; crisis in, 79–85; cultural festivals in, 113; demographic shifts during past twenty-five years, 87–88; as economically dynamic commercial zone, 85–86, 89–90; eight streets of, 85–91; "ethnic shops" in, 90; example of social conflict in, 96; growing multiethnic composition of, 91; housing in, 82, 83, 89; landlord abuses in, 82, 83; migrants restricted to, 104; nostalgia for supposed "Italian" past of, 94–96; opposition to intercultural center proposed in, 96; religious institutions in, 86; shopowners' behavior in, 85–86; social-economic composition of, 86–88; as symbol for crime, racial conflict, and immigration, 84, 86; "turf war" in, 91
San Salvario Decree, 106–11
Sant'Anna Maternity Hospital, 32, 33
Scagliotti, Laura, 27, 147, 150–51, 152, 175, 215n.10
scala mobile (wage-indexing system), 46, 206n.9
scale: Alma Mater's politics of, 160–64; spatial, concept of, xvi; spatial politics of, 7–8
scapegoats, migrants as, 53

Schengan Treaty, xxi, 107, 212n.49
sconosciuto, 204n.4. *See also straniere, stranieri*
Segre, Claudio, 102
self-consciousness, practice of, 190–91
self-employment, xxi, 16–17, 39; *doppio lavoro* ("double work"), 68–69; migrant traders, 64–65; for women, 144–45, 160
self-suppression, 203n.1
Semi di Zucco (Pumpkin Seeds), 25
Senghor, Leopold, 16
SERMIG (Servizio Missionario Giovanni, Youth Missionary Service), 156, 216n.1
servants, domestic. *See* domestic service
service sector: employment demand in growing, xxiv–xxv; in Turin, 48–49; women working in, 57, 197. *See also* domestic service
servitude, association of domestic work with, 39
sexual abuse, 63
sexual difference: theory of, 135, 186; women united by, 184
sexual division of labor, 14–15, 57, 133, 136, 137
sexual harassment, 139
Shabel, 147, 215n.12
Simmel, George, 8, 9
small industry, rebirth of, 47–48
Smith, Neil, 161
Smith, S., 75
Sniderman, Paul, 77, 93, 213n.56
"social contract," new, 47
social control, in San Salvario, 103–6
social relations, as power relations entwined at different scales, xvi–xviii
social security contributions, 61, 70, 110–11, 214n.65
social services: informal economy in,

69–70. *See also* domestic service; service sector
social transformations through practices of speaking and hearing, 191
social welfare: shifting responsibility for, 157–59, 199. *See also* nongovernmental organizations (NGOs), "third sector" of
Société Géografique, Le, 101
solidarity between women, P&R's goal of international, 146–48
Somalia: Italian colonialism in, 101, 102; woman's position in, 179
southern Italians: institutionalized racialization and sexual discrimination of, 60; postwar internal migration of, 99–101
space: Alma Mater and seizure of, 7–8, 189–90; Alma Mater's politics of, 160–64; racialization of, 75–79, 84–85, 104
spatial boundaries, expanding, 17–22, 191
spatialization of race, 85, 104
spatial politics of race and gender, xiv, xvii, 1–22; emergence of feminist antiracist politics in Turin, 8–17; expanding boundaries, 17–22; experience of migrant women in Turin, 1–5; spatial politics of scale, 7–8
spatial scale: concept of, xvi
speaking subjects, 189–92
specialization of production at Fiat, 45
Spivak, Gayatri, xiv, 212n.37
Spontaneous Anti-Crime Committee, 90–91
Spontaneous Committee of Foreigners, 82
Stampa, La (newspaper), 79, 82, 103
stereotypes: of Africans, 93; asserting cultural practices to transform, 192;

of Italian south, 99; of migrants as criminals, 104; of migrant women, 66–67, 78, 169, 208n.2; racialized, 71–73; of southern Italian migrants, 100–101
stigma, racial, 75–79, 85; elastic boundaries, 170–71
strangers: urban dwellers as, 8, 9. *See also straniere, stranieri*
straniere, stranieri, xiii; colonization of mind of, 176; meaning of, xiv, 9, 204n.4. *See also* extracomunitari in post-Fordist Turin
street sellers: migrants working as, 65
Structural Adjustment Programs of World Bank, 195
subjectivity: female, 186; postcolonial migrant, 190; speaking subjects, 189–92
Sub-Saharan Africa: intercontinental migrants generated by, xxv–xxvi; North African divide from, 174; obstacles to economic development of, xxv
superpowers: military aid from, xxv
supplier network of Fiat: rationalization of, 44–45
symbolic mother: in Italian feminist philosophy of sexual difference, 186; role of, 134–35

Tabet, Paola, 98, 103
Taguieff, Pierre, 211n.27
Tamtamtavola, 147
technical assistance from superpowers, xxv
technology(ies): Fiat's investment in new process, 44, 46; high-tech labor market, preparing workers for, 51; technological development in Turin, 48–49
temporary contract basis: hiring on, 52

Teno, Jean Marie, 212n.37
terminal contracts, use of, 52
terms of trade, xxv
terrorism, 189
tertiary-sector growth in Turin, 48–49.
See also service sector
Texas Oil, 194
"third sector." *See* nongovernmental
organizations (NGOs), "third sector" of
threat, migrants perceived as, 97–98
"Together We Construct Our City"
(antiracist demonstration), 111–15
Togliatti, Palmiro, 125
tolerance thresholds, xviii
toll-free phone number for reporting
crime, 106
trade, migrants working in forms of,
64–65
trade restrictions, liberalization of,
xxiii
trade unions: antiracist protest in San
Salvario and, 114–15; CGIL, 11,
13, 24, 41, 111, 112, 114, 152; CISL,
11, 114; defense of tolerance for
cultural differences, 113–14; factory work and, 66; Intercategoriale
Delegate Donne CGIL-CISL-UIL,
135–42, 143, 151, 153, 215n.8; "150
hours" of courses program for
workers, 31, 136, 140–41, 215n.7;
weakening of, 45–46, 47
training courses, Alma Mater, 21–22;
in cultural mediation, 31–34
Trama di Terre (Bologna), 204n.3,
205n.5
Trevi Group agreement, 107, 213n.49
Tschotscha, Jean Marie, 12, 14
Turco, Livia, 205n.4
Turin: activist culture of, xx, 11; as
center of Red Cross for Somalia
relief effort, 217n.13; common

political identity of migrants as
immigrati, xiii; as company town
in transition, 41–49; declining
population of Turin proper, 58;
educational institutions and labor
market demands, lack of fit between, 50–51; emergence of feminist antiracist politics in, 11–17;
experience of migrant women in,
1–5, 167–70; extracomunitari in
post-Fordist, 55–73; historic center
of, contradictory social interests
representing, 88–89; historic
cultural diversity of, 29, 207n.14;
as home of former Italian monarchy, 42; image as one remaining
"real" Italian city, 79; increasing
gentrification of, 207n.15; intensity of racism and intolerance in,
49, 53; international migration
to, xx; labor demand in, 49; local
"identity," uncertainty of, 53;
open markets as central feature of
everyday practices in, 9–10; people
considered strangers in, 8–9;
physical geography of, 9; political administrative system in, 42;
population growth (1951–1971),
43; population growth (late
1990s), 49; postwar bread riots
in, 125; racial incidents in 1990s,
78, 79–85; restructuring in, effect
of, xix–xx, 41–54; shifting world
of workers in, 49–54; social and
economic transformation of, 8–9;
social classes in, 42–43, 49–50,
73; southern Italians in, 99–101;
tertiary-sector growth in, 48–49;
unemployment rates (1980s and
1990s), 50, 52; workerist culture
of, 28
Turin character, 8

women's rights: identification as feminists to fight for, 179–80

"women's work": hidden, 15, 63–64; labor market identified with, 57; migrant women positioned on margins of, 6; undervaluation of, 145. *See also* domestic service; prostitution

work: as central theme in Alma Mater, 119–22; as central theme of Turin feminism, 160; redefinition of, by P&R, 144–45; work sites in Alma Mater, 16–17, 34, 39. *See also* cooperatives, work; Turkish bath (hammam)

workerism: acute sense of, among Turin feminists, 178; feminism conditioned by, 125–28; Intercategoriale Delegate Donne CGIL-CISL-UIL and, 135–42; workerist culture of Turin, 28

worker rights, lack of awareness of, 68

working conditions, 50–51, 60

work permits for employed illegal immigrants, 110. *See also* amnesty for illegal immigrants

World Bank, xxv, 196; Structural Adjustment Programs, 195

world economy, unequal structure of, xxiv. *See also* restructuring, industrial

World Trade Organization, 198

xenophobia, 77

Young, Robert, 210n.26, 211n.26

young, the: children of migrants, 102–3, 140, 168, 169; discrimination against, 51; work expectations of, 51–52

Youth Missionary Service (SERMIG), 156, 216n.1

Zaldini, Giovanna, 17, 19, 27, 37, 175, 216n.12, 217n.11, 217n.12

Zincone, Giovanna, 213n.54

Zumaglino, Piera, 147

Heather Merrill is assistant professor of geography and anthropology at Dickinson College in Carlisle, Pennsylvania.